The Inner Principal

Student Outcomes and the Reform of Education

General Editor: Brian J. Caldwell, Professor of Education, Head, Department of Education Policy and Management, University of Melbourne, Australia

Student Outcomes and the Reform of Education is concerned with the reform of public education and its impact on outcomes for students. The reform agenda has gripped the attention of policy-makers, practitioners, researchers and scholars for much of the 1990s, with every indication of more to come with the approach of the new millennium. This series reports research and describes strategies that deal with the outcomes of reform. Without sacrificing a critical perspective the intention is to provide a guide to good practice and strong scholarship within the new arrangements that are likely to provide the framework for public education in the foreseeable future.

The Inner Principal

David Norman Loader

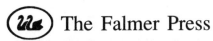 The Falmer Press

(A member of the Taylor & Francis Group)
London • Washington, D.C.

UK   Falmer Press, 1 Gunpowder Square, London, EC4A 3DE
USA   Falmer Press, Taylor & Francis Inc., 1900 Frost Road, Suite 101,
          Bristol, PA 19007

First published in 1997

A catalogue record for this book is available from the British Library

ISBN 0 7507 0679 1 cased
ISBN 0 7507 0680 5 paper

**Library of Congress Cataloging-in-Publication Data are available on
request** ·

Jacket design by Caroline Archer

Typeset in 10/12 pt Times by
Graphicraft Typesetters Ltd., Hong Kong.

*Printed in Great Britain by Biddles Ltd., Guildford and King's Lynn on
paper which has a specified pH value on final paper manufacture of not
less than 7.5 and is therefore 'acid free'.*

Contents

Dedication

This book is dedicated to my immediate
family, Roslyn, Andrew, Celeste, Campbell,
Jackie, Stafford and David.

Prologue: The External Principal

Brian J. Caldwell
Professor of Education
University of Melbourne

David Loader is in the front rank of school leaders in his generation. In 1997 he became Principal of Wesley College, Australia's largest school, an independent co-educational institution that enrols 3400 primary and secondary students on three campuses in Melbourne. When his appointment was announced in 1996, a spokesperson for Wesley College reported that its worldwide search for an outstanding leader brought it to a school just a few kilometres away, for David Loader was then Principal of Methodist Ladies College, also in Melbourne.

By any criteria, Methodist Ladies College is an exceptional school. It offers a rich curriculum for 2200 primary and secondary students located on a single campus in the Eastern suburb of Kew. Its national and international reputation derives from a decision in 1989 for students to learn with the aid of a laptop computer. Now, all girls and all staff use a laptop in what is more, much more, than a change in technology. Virtually every aspect of the school has changed, whether it be the role of teachers, the design of buildings, the shape of rooms, or the style of furniture. More significantly, students are engaged in 'excited live exploration' in the manner envisaged by Seymour Papert in *The Children's Machine* (Papert, 1992), with utilization of these 'mobile work stations' across all areas of the curriculum.

David Loader was Principal of MLC for eighteen years, being only the fifth Principal since the school was established in 1882. His key role in the adoption of the laptop and in other respects, including the establishment of Marshmead, a remote residential community on Mallacoota Inlet where year 9 students spend eight weeks, has led to the view of many that he is an exceptional strategic leader. An orientation to the future is reflected in his statement that MLC is 'four walls around a future', the future of its students. He is a much sought after speaker at conferences and seminars on the themes of strategic leadership and strategic thinking, as well as technology in school education. Deep empowerment of other leaders and all staff is a characteristic of MLC. Many former senior staff now hold appointment as Principal of other leading independent schools.

This is the external evidence of the leadership of David Loader. The student of theory in leadership will readily match this evidence to what may be found in the literature. David Loader is surely a transformational leader, given the extent of change that has been wrought, though not a transformational leader in the heroic sense, a subject of criticism by scholars such as Peter Gronn (1995), for there has been much empowerment of others in achieving the outcomes. He has the characteristics of the leader in a learning organization, in the deeper sense of individual and organizational growth and development. Indeed, MLC aspires to be a learning organization in the style proposed by Peter Senge (1992) in *The Fifth Discipline*. He is surely a strategic leader along the lines described in *Leading the Self-Managing School*, the book I co-authored with Jim Spinks (Caldwell and Spinks, 1992).

These theories and perspectives on leadership describe the actions and outcomes of leaders and leadership. They are a helpful guide to good practice, and a biographical or autobiographical account of the work of David Loader along these lines would surely enrich the literature. Such an account would, be incomplete, both as an explanation for what has been achieved and as a guide to others. More recently scholarly work has turned to the values and ethics of leadership, with writers such as Robert J. Starratt (1996) and Thomas Sergiovanni (1992) making important contributions in the search for a more complete theory of leadership. The work of Robert Greenleaf on servant leadership has also deepened the concept (Spears, 1995).

Very little has been written about the feelings and emotions of leaders, especially of leaders in schools. We know much about the 'external principal' but little of the 'internal Principal'. Patrick Duignan (1996) has made a start with his reflections on authentic leadership, but no extended work has been done that draws on the experiences of school leaders. Filling this space is surely a priority, given the extraordinarily demanding role of the Principal at the dawn of the third millennium. There are outstanding school leaders such as David Loader and, to those who observe or aspire, there is a sense of wonder about their achievement. What does such a leader feel in the day-to-day events and decisions that may lead to a landmark success or catastrophic failure? How does such a leader cope with the white heat of public scrutiny when a strong public stand is taken? This book by David Loader offers some answers to these questions and more in an astonishingly frank and honest account of his personal journey as a leader.

Like many others, I know the 'external principal' that is David Loader, especially in his role as strategic leader. It was appropriate then to invite him to conduct seminars for postgraduate students at the University of Melbourne on the topic of strategic leadership. The outcome was as powerful as it was engaging, for the focus throughout was on the 'inner principal'. Consistency with the extant literature was readily established, but imagine the surprise and delight of participants who learned that many of his high profile achievements were the result of stumbles, with formulation of rules for 'The Stumble Principal'.

What was especially evident in these seminars was how the appeal of the approach transcended boundaries that have frequently constrained a discourse on the topic of leadership, whether they be those that separate schools, public or private, or communities, advantaged or disadvantaged. That the approach should be shared with a much wider audience was readily apparent, hence the invitation for David Loader to write this book.

An explanation of this capacity to cross boundaries is evident in David Loader's background. He is Principal of Australia's largest independent school and former Principal of a school that has an international reputation as leader in technology, but he has taught in both public and private sectors. His own school education was at North Sydney Technical High. Further evidence may be found in his recent statement on 'This I Believe' in a book with that title edited by John Marsden (1996), a collection from 100 eminent Australians. He describes his early years, first of loneliness in a new suburb, then of acceptance into the wider community of the Church. His early university work in mathematics and science ('my academic record was dismal') was followed by his discovery of psychology and philosophy ('my love of learning did begin at this time') and the work of Martin Buber and 'I-Thou' relationships.

This is but the start of a journey that is shared in the pages that follow. *The Inner Principal* is an important contribution to a more complete theory of leadership, and a guide and a reassurance to all who lead or aspire to lead in schools in times of dramatic change. In a series on *Student Outcomes and the Reform of Education*, this book makes clear that success in the leadership of reform is as much a matter of discovering self as discovering strategy.

References

CALDWELL, B.J. and SPINKS, J.M. (1992) *Leading the Self-Managing School*, London, Falmer Press.

DUIGNAN, P.A. (1996) '"Get real": Some reflections on authentic leadership', keynote address to the annual conference of the Australian Council for Educational Administration, Victoria, Caulfield, May.

GRONN, P. (1995) 'Greatness re-visited: The current obsession with transformational leadership', *Leading and Managing*, **1**, 1.

MARSDEN, J. (Ed) (1996) *This I Believe*, Sydney, Random House.

PAPERT, S. (1992) *The Children's Machine*, New York, Basic Books.

SENGE, P.M. (1992) *The Fifth Discipline: The Art and Practice of the Learning Organisation*, Sydney, Random House.

SERGIOVANNI, T.J. (1992) *Moral Leadership: Getting to the Heart of School Improvement*, San Francisco, CA, Jossey-Bass.

SPEARS, L.C. (Ed) (1995) *Reflections on Leadership*, New York, John Wiley & Sons.

STARRATT, R.J. (1996) *Transforming Educational Administration*, New York, McGraw-Hill.

Acknowledgments

I would like to acknowledge the help of many in my journey, of which this book records only a part.

With respect to this book, I acknowledge the encouragement and inspiration of Professor Brian Caldwell. I thank my friends who have assisted with comments, questions and editing, Irene, Ailsa, Roger, Gillian, Jackie and Andrew. I am particularly indebted to Margaret, Roslyn and Mary who have assisted me to think through and articulate some of the ideas presented.

The author and publisher would like to thank Faber and Faber Ltd for permission to reproduce excerpts from *The Collected Poems of Wallace Stevens* by Wallace Stevens.

Introduction: The Transparent Principal

Invited

Although various people had at one time or another suggested that I should write a book, I had not really contemplated this seriously. Certainly I had not expected to be commissioned to write a book. While I have had twenty-six years experience as a Principal and have always enjoyed a very active dialogue within the school, I had not recognized the broader importance of what was happening to me as I grappled with leadership and educational issues. In these tussles, it became evident that my experience was not an isolated one and that what I did had implications for others. When Methodist Ladies' College adopted successfully the philosophy of personal computing, insisting that all students and teachers have personal mobile computers, other schools could not ignore this. Conversely the limitations that external exams imposed on curriculum meant that to achieve some freeing of the internal school curriculum, I had to try to influence the external educational decision makers. In raising my voice on themes of importance to our school, I became acutely aware of the risks and the loneliness of leadership. So in the midst of this I was encouraged that others were prepared to listen to my voice and thus dialogue began at another level. I wrote about the issues that I was facing, initially to clear my thinking, and then to influence others. As a maths graduate, whose education gave scant attention to writing, this activity was something new to me. I was surprised that I was increasingly being asked to speak at conferences, national and international, and that people who stayed after these talks were excited by some of the ideas. Then I was invited to talk to doctoral students in education and from them I realized the power of the personal voice. It was in the narrative rather than in the abstractions that their learning and ability to integrate came alive.

Looking Through

As I sat contemplating this my mind went back to a hymn whose meaning I grappled with in church one Sunday. The author was George Herbert (1593–1633). Despite his lack of inclusive language, one verse really appealed to me. It read as follows:

> *A man that looks on glass*
> *On it may stay his eye*
> *Or if he pleaseth, through it pass,*
> *And then the heaven espy.*

This seemed to me a remarkably succinct and poignant statement. In some ways my experience as a school principal can be seen as the glass. We can focus on the events, the relationships and even the reflected image that we see in the glass. Alternatively, we can look through the glass and see more. I hope that the following narratives will give the reader a vista beyond the glass. From the school experience of one person who attempts to be honest about his inner life as a principal, I hope that you may be able to explore your inner life and outer behaviour as a leader and create your own alchemy.

Psychoanalytic Perspective

This book is written from a psychoanalytical perspective. It is concerned with exploring leadership by looking at the inner person, considering the personal qualities of a school leader, her/his vision, beliefs and ways of acting and thinking. In this, *The Inner Principal* is a book perhaps unlike any others that you have read before.

John Keats has talked about the mystery of life; he said 'I mean **negative capability**, that is when man is capable of being in uncertainties, Mysteries, doubts without any irritable reaching after fact and reason' (Perkins, 1967, p. 1209). In a similar way this book hints at the mystery of leadership. It does not seek to cement ideas and theories in dot points, or to provide certainties.

Barth (1991) argues that what is 'equally difficult to overcome is the belief harboured by some principals that the knowledge base for improving schools lies more in universities than in themselves' (p. 78). I would argue that we cannot look to others for solutions. Worse we should not blame others if things do not go right. The future is in our hands and we need to actively shape that future. We can do this by looking to ourselves, feeling, thinking, reading, meeting, conferencing, journeying and then daring to carry through with what we believe. So it is that the person of the leader, in all her/his complexity and contradictions, is the focus of this book.

Foolhardiness?

Amongst my friends there have been those who have counselled me against going ahead with the publication of this book, arguing: 'It could do you professional harm because it is so personal.'; 'You may limit your future options by setting down the sort of person you now see yourself to be.'; 'Why wear your heart on your sleeve?'; 'People will be able to take advantage of you because you have revealed so much of your self.' I will have to wait and see if these are the outcomes.

I have a different point of view. I think that it is important that books like this are written so that we, the readers, obtain a more balanced view of leadership. Leadership has its highs and lows, its successes and failures. Principals cry, laugh, dream and become suspicious. There are times when principals do want the fairy godmother to come and save them. While leadership is about courage, about creating the tomorrow of our choice, heroism does not come easily and this book is a case in point. My hope is that this is the first of a series of books that will come from many authors and that these books will inform and sustain those of us who attempt leadership. We are not looking for war stories but personal tales of everyday events. Their publication will make accessible craft knowledge, will facilitate personal insight, stimulate good discussion and lead to the establishment of better schools.

I am not alone in wanting to read the personal stories of others. Those who have researched the current educational writing have identified a gap in what has been published. Little seems to have been written about the person of the leader and the emotions that person experiences while leading. Yet it is argued by Leithwood *et al.* (1992) that future school leaders, and those responsible for their development, need

> ... a better understanding of principals' internal mental processes and states: the rational aspects of these processes, such as the content and organization of knowledge structures, as well as such non-rational elements as beliefs, attitudes and values. (p. 27)

About this Book

'The journeying principal' chapter explores the journey metaphor, which is integral to the book. In terms of development of ideas it would normally have come first. However in this hypertext milieu, it comes later in the book, as a summary. I have preferred to commence with a significant event in this journey, my departure from a work of eighteen years. 'The journeying principal' chapter first moves from fear of self disclosure to 'coming out'. I talk about my feelings while undertaking leadership. In this way I explore leadership from within the psychoanalytic perspective. I see this as a chapter about personal growth where the walls, whether in the mind of the principal or physically within the school, are broken down. Could there be such a person as a no-walls-principal?

The opening chapter is called 'The alchemist principal'. It begins at a deeply emotional period in my life and explores this event in the context of *The Alchemist*, a book written by Paulo Coelho. *The Alchemist* is a magical story about a shepherd boy who sets out on a purposeful journey following his dreams, listening to his heart and reading the omens while he travels. I was impressed by this story and found myself intuitively and intellectually reaching out to Santiago as a role model for an effective leader. Why not in 1997 follow my heart rather than my head, consider omens as well as empirical evidence and see the world as having a spiritual foundation as opposed to an objective scientific bedrock. In the context of this story — the experiences of the shepherd boy — I look at my role as principal of a large city school and my attempts at alchemy in such a school.

'The paranoid principal' had its genesis in an early morning beach walk. While I can confidently assert that neither I nor my fellow principals are paranoid, feelings of anxiety sometimes come close to being dysfunctional for many of us. This confession may be a little disconcerting to those who hope for great things from schools, their staff and specifically from principals. This chapter explores ideas such as authority; principals as vulnerable professionals; insecure employment for principals; perfection; competition; confidence; attentive listening; peer support and institutional paranoia.

The previous chapter needed a conclusion and I have turned to Cinderella for help. In 'The Cinderella principal' I ask whether principals should emulate Cinderella? Should we wait, hope and pray for someone to come and save us? Or are there some initiatives that we should be taking? Cinderella allows me to explore such important themes as the status of principals and the way in which their relationship to their organizations appears to be moving from a hierarchical model to a new model where leaders work more collaboratively with those in their learning communities; a new definition of leadership which has courage as the essential element; strategic thinking; backcasting and gender.

The emptiness that I have known leads me to ask if there are any school principals who have not felt at some stage, and maybe many times, that they have so depleted their energy sources that there is nothing left, that they are running on empty? In 'The empty principal' I explore the experiences of one principal who spent a week as a sojourner in a Quaker retreat for educationalists. This sojourn gave me a new sensitivity to myself, a new awareness of others and a better understanding of the educational task. A significant part of this experience was silence, something that people of action have trouble coping with. The experience opened up a new and exciting world where people were attentive listeners, where honesty and openness were the norm and where reflection followed naturally. In such a setting it was interesting to ask again what is the nature of the principal's work. It was also a time when the idea of a 'living community' could be explored.

Once emptiness had been acknowledged, learning can follow. In 'The learning principal', a theoretical base for this learning is provided from readings and experiences including those from the Tavistock Institute of Human Relations in London and the Australian Institute of Social Analysis. The potential of peer-assisted learning also is considered. This chapter attempts to answer a fundamental question: How can a principal continue learning so that s/he may survive the stress of the role? My experience had been that as the professional demands increased, I gave more time to my principal role working hard to train himself to focus on the task and ignore some of the personal consequences. I needed to find a new and more satisfying way. There are many ways of learning and the one you choose will relate to your style of learning. In this chapter, one person's learning style is explored and his learning quilt is depicted.

'The transformed principal' moves from the personal to the generic. This chapter records how those principals whose experiences are similar to the author's, would have emerged from the classroom and proved themselves in administration through managing a timetable; running a boarding house; directing a curriculum area; managing pastoral and discipline issues for a segment of a school; and then become a principal. The change from teacher into principal is not one of continuous growth but of transformation. The focus of this chapter is on transformation then growth and the implications for pre-service and post-service education for principals. The chapter considers both the personal and professional growth of principals. A principal needs a different set of skills, works with different priorities, requires less curriculum and more general knowledge and these are not derived from prior teaching experience.

Next is 'The stumble principal'. This was to have been the first chapter but it has been moved back in the book because of its less personal nature. This chapter is where the honesty began. But the self-revelation has increased and this has left this important chapter as a more academic statement of theory, grounded as it is in experience. In a time when we practise strategic thinking, it is important to recognize that many of the best ideas and policies had their origin in a stumble. This chapter looks at stumbling theory; the three Rs that become four; the constraints; the regrets; the rules and then puts all this theory together as the 'stumble principal'. By stumbling it is meant that in the course of venturing forth, one chances upon something unexpected, maybe even falls over it. This stumble becomes the basis of a new educational practice. A case study of stumbling is taken of the introduction of mobile computing to a large city school of 2200 students; 1800 of these students, all grade 5 or above, have their own mobile computer and all teachers in that school have personal mobile computers.

In 'The reculturing principal' I explore the unhappy culture in which principals and teachers both work. The chapter is about developing a new culture for schools. It examines such issues as conflict resolution; deep listening; the need for a quantum community (holistic rather than the isolated mechanistic units); caring; choosing leadership; the restructuring of the school; school evaluations and ceremonies.

While dreams have been part of everyday personal experience, they have not been part of institutional thinking and planning. In 'The dreaming principal' I take up the challenge to explore the role of dreams in the life of a school. I look first at the principal's dream of a different school, but then ask if it really was the principal's dream or whether it belonged to the community. I consider the challenge of 'dreaming together' in a dreaming matrix. A specific focus of this chapter is upon the home-school dreams.

In 'The big top principal' I explore another metaphor for a school, the circus. Much of the book has a serious flavour and this chapter attempts to step outside such normality. In offering this chapter, I want to provide the reader with the opportunity to laugh with us and at those of us who are in the school business. Also I have a serious intent of obtaining some educational insights. Using the circus metaphor, I explore older unconscious metaphors that constrain our thinking. In circuses as well as schools we ban wild animals; live in a big top; ride two horses;

entertain death defying feats; become invisible; struggle for coherence; act as clowns; experience the critics.

In the final chapter I look at the kind of school that I would like. In naming it 'The frog prince'pal', I am hoping for some future magic. Can there be a transformation, and if there were, what would it look like? The chapter spells out some of the reform agendas hinted at within the other chapters.

Chapter 1

The Alchemist Principal

... man sallies forth into nature to discover the originals of the forms presented to him in his own intellect. Over these shadows ... Narcissus-like, he hangs delighted: till ... he learns at last that what he seeks he has left behind. (S.T. Coleridge, *The Friend I*, pp. 508–9)

The Inside Story

I resigned my position as Principal of Methodist Ladies' College in order to take up the position of Principal of Wesley College, Melbourne. This resignation was not an everyday event either for the school or for me. I had been Principal for eighteen years and the school in that time had grown in enrolments, had changed significantly and become a recognized innovator in education.

I submitted my resignation to the President of the Council and she in turn submitted this resignation to the College Council. I was pleased when the President said that she would like to announce my resignation to the staff. I gathered together as many of the staff as I could for a special morning tea, without indicating the purpose of the morning tea, and more than 150 people were present. The President, Vice President and Treasurer from Council each spoke to the staff. The President announced my resignation and then described some of my achievements while I was Principal, congratulated and thanked me. It was hard to take all this in while I struggled with my emotions. The President then proceeded to talk about the new era that was beginning. She emphasized that this would be an important and exciting period in the life of the school. The other two members of Council gave the same message. I had a sense from these talks that I had been appreciated but that I was already past tense, that the school already had begun to move on beyond me. As the speeches continued I felt a freeing of responsibility for the College. It was in good hands. I was not needed. Discharged of this responsibility for the College, I looked around at the staff and wondered what they were thinking and feeling. Then I made the personal jump. I asked myself: 'What am I thinking and feeling?' I discovered just how sad I was about leaving these many friends and fellow professionals with whom I had worked long and hard over eighteen years. Some sense of the enormous loss that I was about to experience swept over me. These friends would no longer be part of my daily life and I wouldn't be part of theirs.

When the three Council speeches were finished I was invited to speak. I moved forward but only managed one or two words before I broke down in tears. I tried a couple of times to start again but it was hopeless. Suddenly I was overwhelmed by my grief. I was acutely aware of the pain of parting but also the closeness and joy of present friendships. Suddenly it was obvious to me that these friendships would not be as rich in the future as they had been in the past. As well it was clear that the College was already moving on confidently beyond me and I was left standing there.

As I reflected on this event later I thought about how I had gone to that morning tea thinking about how the staff would take the news. I knew that some staff would think that I had abandoned them and their projects, and I was doing that by leaving. Others would be critical that I would now be responsible for a competitor school. Others would think that I had sold out on single sex education because Wesley is coeducational. I also knew that a lot of staff would be pleased for me. This was the reason for scanning the faces to read their emotions. Amazingly, as considered in retrospect, I had not thought about how I was feeling about leaving my friends and the school. I know that too much of my life is lived through the eyes of others. The good news is that I was in this instance saved from myself so that I could experience the moment. I had been able to get in touch with my emotions on such an important occasion. In my professional role I spend a lot of time thinking and caring about other people and their emotions. Sometimes, maybe even often, this caring is at the expense of my own emotional life. How healthy is that either for the person cared for or for the carer?

The strong emotional experience that followed from getting in touch with my personal feelings reminded me of a book that I had read a few months earlier, *The Alchemist* by Paulo Coelho. *The Alchemist* is a magical story about a shepherd boy, Santiago, who sets out on a purposeful journey following his dreams, looking for worldly treasure. The amazing thing about Santiago was that he listened intently to his heart and he read the omens while he travelled. I was very impressed by this story but I did wonder whether I might have rejected this story had I read it ten years earlier. At that time I would not have liked it to be known that I might follow my heart rather than my head, that I might consider omens rather than evidence, that the world might have a spiritual foundation as opposed to an objective scientific bedrock. Yes, today I can accept Santiago and indeed believe that he could well be the very model of a good school principal.

Could I be Santiago?

Santiago was a poor Spanish boy whose parents had wanted him to be a priest. They had placed him in a seminary where he had studied Latin, Spanish and Theology. However, Santiago wanted to travel and his poor family decided that he couldn't be stopped. So his parents gave him his inheritance which he used to buy sheep. These sheep became his constant companions as he led them to green and safe pastures. With them he began his travels. This was Santiago's luck to be given such a start, such an opportunity.

As I reflected on this, I perceived Santiago's experience to be similar to my own. I received a university education, when very few people in Australia did. It was not that I was an outstanding student specially chosen for this. I know that there was a substantial element of luck in this wonderful opportunity that I was given.

The next part of Santiago's life is also true to my experience. In order to fulfil a dream that he had had while as a shepherd, he decided to forsake this new found stability, setting out alone on new travels to distant and unknown lands. He sold his sheep, not just any sheep but ones that he called by name, sheep with whom he had shared his life for two years, to finance a journey that he hoped would fulfil his dream. During this travel Santiago was severely tested before he could reach his goal. Again I find a lot of similarity in this story with my own. To fulfil my dreams I left the warmth of family and security of tenure within the government school system to travel overseas, to adventure, to consider alternative futures. While I was overseas my mother became ill and died suddenly and unexpectedly before I knew that she was sick. This meant that I was unable to spend time with her in her illness, nor be there when she died. This loss hastened my return to Australia where I had to find a new job and make another beginning. My experience is that no worthwhile outcome is won without losses and courage to rise above these is necessary.

Santiago had the beginner's luck that we who have managed to make it to a principalship have experienced. But then Santiago was severely tested as he pursued his dream and a school principal would agree that being tested, challenged and even threatened is part of her/his experience of leadership.

Unfortunately for Santiago he was robbed of all that he had in this strange new land. Again I could identify with this as I think about maintaining my self-esteem, my self-confidence in a new role of school principal when confronted by the conflicting demands of the many audiences that I must satisfy. Santiago worked hard and long to establish himself again while just managing to hold his dream. He travelled through a desert and avoided the local wars. All of this has a ring of truth too in terms of my principal experience. Holding onto the dream is often difficult and there are desert experiences and local wars to be avoided.

Then Santiago came to a beautiful oasis where he found love and was tempted to stay. For a principal the oasis could be the stasis of safety in the institution when you can rest and not worry about attack, safe in tradition and bolstered by full enrolments. However, it was the next event that particularly caught my attention. When I described this next event at a principals' conference, they immediately identified with it. While at the oasis Santiago interpreted an omen to mean that the oasis was going to be attacked and the people on the oasis killed. He reported this to the leaders of the oasis who initially rejected this idea asserting that there is an agreement among all the local people that the oasis cannot be attacked; it is a safe haven. However the seriousness with which Santiago brought the message to the oasis people made them go into conference and consider his assessment. After significant deliberation they came back to Santiago. They told him that if he was correct and they were attacked that night and if they were able to successfully defend themselves, then Santiago would be the richest person on the oasis. However they also told Santiago that if his prediction was wrong then tomorrow he would die.

Can't you just picture in an organization known to you what happens when a principal presents an unpopular or even revolutionary idea to the School Council that governs the school. The response of the Council is immediate and direct. The Council makes it clear that if the principal has got this wrong, then tomorrow s/he will die. People do not like to receive bad news, but even worse they do not like to receive wrong messages. Who will dare when the consequences are so exaggerated, when the choice is between being rich or dying. In the case of Santiago, he dared. Consequently he became rich because his prediction had come true and the people of the oasis were both attacked and were able to defeat their attackers. We do not all have the stamina of Santiago. Permission to take risks without the fear of death hanging over us is important. Without this permission, creative, enterprising leadership rarely emerges.

Staff too in their daily school life take risks and it is important that they can do this without fear. If this can happen then the organization will be a great deal more creative.

Now that Santiago is rich success could become a distracter. Yes I have to confess I have sometimes been distracted towards other careers which seemed easier, and more prestigious.

Unfortunately for Santiago his riches were short lived. When subsequently he travelled from the oasis with his riches he was robbed and worse, beaten. It really is hard to carry your riches with you, and in my recent case, hard to enjoy the successes of the past. While no one person or group of persons robbed me, I do allow a preoccupation with school matters and a desire to be politically correct to distract me from the deep human contacts that can sustain and enrich me personally. Unfortunately for school principals, and others who commit themselves strongly to their professional goals, relationships with family and friends and even attentiveness to that which is really us, is sometimes lost in the helter skelter of our daily activities and commitments. I was reminded of this fact recently when I read about a clear sighted young lady who was dying of cancer[1]. Being conscious of her imminent death, she was able to plan for it. The day before she died she was able to say that she was at peace. She had been able to strip herself of all the unnecessary concerns and to focus her life around that which she valued as essential, her family and her friends and their love for each other. Family and love are important because they contribute significantly, to that elusive chase for identity and purpose.

The Santiago story had a happy ending as Santiago finally discovered his treasure, albeit that it was under his feet where he began his original journey. Yet the truth was that he had to travel to find the treasure and of course the journey was part of the treasure. Our riches are already around us and beside us but we do need to travel to discover just how good these are. For me, writing this book is like travelling. As well as having a cathartic effect, more importantly, I am finding it richly satisfying because it is bringing more meaning and integration into my life.

While I would like to see a book as an outcome I imagine that in retrospect it will be the writing journey and the excitements from insights on the way which is what I will value.

Alchewmist Thoughts

The Alchemist is a wonderful fable and I recommend it to you. As I read it again and reflected on it, I found myself thinking about a number of messages. I have chosen five of these and I am calling them Alchemist thoughts.

The first one appears early in the book (Coelho, 1994, p. 11) 'It's the possibility of having the dream come true that makes life interesting.' Such a philosophy makes the world of difference as to how you go to work. Am I going to work simply to fill the day, to complete the work, to earn enough money to do . . . or am I going because I have a purpose and that purpose is an exciting one. The purpose does not have to be grand, to save the world. But it is more significant if it is personal, something to which I can commit myself. Sometimes the fear that we cannot carry through on our dream stops us from dreaming and that is to our detriment.

This takes me to the second Alchemist thought that I would like to extract. This is the message of the Alchemist to Santiago. 'Remember that wherever your heart is, there you will find your treasure' (*ibid*, p. 122). This had two messages for me. If your heart is not in something, then there is no personally satisfying outcome to be found in pursuing that goal. The other message is 'rest well tonight, as if you were a warrior preparing for combat' (*ibid*, pp. 121–2). It is a matter of focus. As the Alchemist says: (*ibid*, p. 117) 'You must love the desert, but never trust it completely. Because the desert tests all men; it challenges every step, and kills those who become distracted.'

A third Alchemist thought that I found powerful was in this statement: 'Courage is the quality most essential to understanding the Language of the World' (*ibid*, p. 117). Courage, however, can be very specific. A lot of my peers describe me as courageous with respect to some of the educational goals that I have pursued in the face of opposition. Yet when it comes to joining the students and climbing over the wall in an abseil I find myself lacking in courage. I found it very hard to step out over the edge, to trust the rope, to believe in the technique.[2] Eventually I did manage to let go the inhibitions and climb down the wall. Yes it did provide some subsequent satisfaction and confidence but I have not tried to repeat the feat! There could be some transfer of courage to other activities; however I am not a strong believer that this is the way to strengthen my resolve or my courage in my daily life as a school principal. The courage I need as principal is the specific courage that relates to having a dream and to following my heart.

The next alchemist thought that I would offer is one about suffering. We all fear suffering. My worst fear is the dentist, although I am sure there are worse things to fear. But there are the professional fears associated with task. What will people say? What will they think? How will they respond to my decisions as principal?

The alchemist says: 'Tell your heart that the fear of suffering is worse than the suffering itself. And that no heart has ever suffered when it goes in search of its dreams, because every second of the search is a second's encounter with God and with eternity' (*ibid*, p. 137). The boy's response: 'When I have been truly searching for my treasure, every day has been luminous, because I've known that every hour was a part of the dream that I would find it. When I have been truly searching for my treasure, I've discovered things along the way that I never would have seen had I not had the courage to try things that seemed impossible for a shepherd to achieve' (*ibid*, p. 137).

I also enjoyed what I would call the Zen part of the book. Santiago as a shepherd boy noticed that as soon as he awoke in the mornings, most of his sheep also awoke. It was '. . . as if some mysterious energy bound his life to that of the sheep, with whom he had spent the past two years'. (*ibid*, p. 4)

My final alchemist thought is that 'when you are loved you can do anything. When we are loved, there is no need at all to understand what is happening, because everything happens within you and even men can turn themselves into the wind (*ibid*, p. 155). We see this in our students. When the home is good, the child is a delight, free to be a person and not needing to move into attention-seeking behaviour or misbehaviour. This is also true of principals. They are more effective when they feel wanted by their governing bodies. Then they do not have to spend large amounts of their time protecting their backs. Then they can get on with the real business of education. So it is with staff. They too wish to be appreciated and respected.

Three Alchemist Rules

As I moved my reflection of Santiago from a personal to an organizational level, I found additional helpful advice. I intend to state these as rules. This is the school principal in me coming out!

The first and most important rule would be that any good alchemist needs to be working within a philosophy with articulated goals. Santiago had a special dream. He probably had others but did not allow these to distract him. In the case of Methodist Ladies' College there is a driving educational purpose that gives meaning to all that is attempted. It is to work towards a more active, self-directed student learning. This is not an original statement. It follows the work of John Dewey and Seymour Papert. It stands in marked contrast to a teaching model where the teacher is 'out the front' and students are lined up in front of the teacher following the teacher's direction. It is in even more marked contrast to the image of the teacher dragging the reluctant student along by the ear. It does not support the identification of dunces although it can accommodate a Dux. These were my experiences of school and I am pleased to note that changes are occurring under the influence of new learning theories, assisted by technology and with different outcomes being sought from the schooling experience. The educational goal for a school cannot be less than to empower all students and staff.

The second rule is about dreaming. Look inside yourself and find your dream and if there is not one there, dare to dream one now. Do more than dare to dream it. Try to make that dream come true. In the case of MLC we dared to dream that every student and teacher would have a mobile computer by 1994. It was a dream that was laughed at by fellow professionals but we clung to it, believing, and it was achieved. Currently we are daring to dream of a school day that doesn't begin at 8.30am and finish at 3.30 pm. We are daring to dream of a school without walls. A personal dream is to break out of the limitations imposed by the walls of my mind. In another chapter I will be exploring the institution that we hold in our minds and which does not necessarily exist in reality.

The third rule is to question conventional wisdom. Will the learning spaces always be classrooms and will the adults who work with students always be teachers? Will the core curriculum always be academic? It is very hard to think of tomorrow when our experiences are tied to the past. It is amazing to think that our students learned to watch TV before they began reading whereas our experience was to read and then to watch television. Does this make any difference? For us, most of our learning has come through text-based literature but that is unlikely to be the experience of our students.

Virtual Reality

As I have read and reflected on Santiago, I have become very fond of this adventurous and plucky young fellow. Even more I have found immense encouragement from his perception of reality. Unlike me, he has been able to let himself go, to feel the world and to let the world speak to him other than through science or logic or text. Because of the audacity of his story I find that I am now asking the question: can leadership, and for that matter living, only be informed by facts and objective evidence? Is leadership a brain-based activity or a creative tension between heart and brain? Another question that now comes to me is: what is real as opposed to what is imagined or dreamed or constructed? What are the 'mental constructions that we project onto an 'objective world'' (Brooks and Brooks, 1993, p. 24).

I imagine I am not different from anyone else when I assert that my personal world is real. Yet, along with the rest of my community, I am increasingly living in a virtual world. When I read newspapers, magazines and books I am entering another world, a virtual world. Then there is the time spent listening to the radio, trips to the cinema/theatre, talking about things that are not present, and plain old-fashioned daydreaming. This is virtual reality. And then there are the dream worlds of sleep. I rarely watch TV but I understand that it is not uncommon that many people spend three to four hours a day in front of a television, a quarter of their waking lives in that virtual reality. Virtual reality is not in tomorrow's land, it is a feature of today!

A lot of what has happened in classrooms in the past has been virtual-reality based. We have read poetry and novels and seen how skilfully the authors have used words to generate effectual virtual realities in the minds of their readers. We have reduced the world to abstract symbols, as in maths, in order to study the world. Foreign languages have been learnt while poring over books. It is interesting to ask how reality has been affected by the kind of virtual realities that students have experienced.

In the future, the abstracted virtual world for students, in some areas of study, might decrease. For example, in foreign language study, immersion in a actual culture by studying overseas either electronically or in person will be possible. Creating a microworld like a simulated city, while not real, is more real than abstracted ideas that do not interact as in a simulation. I vividly remember the despair and disappointment that I experienced on my first botany excursion at university. I could not identify any of the plants that we found from the printed taxonomy of plants, and nor could my friends. There were not enough teachers or tutors on the excursion to help. We floundered and I was determined not to take this subject again. In retrospect I needed an intermediary experience that might have been provided by some sort of simulation that enabled me to interpret the printed text in order that I could identify the real plants. The virtual world can help us to understand the real world.

There are other ways in which the virtual world for students could usefully increase. 'The idea of a virtual class is that everybody can talk and be heard and be identified and everybody can see the same words, diagrams and pictures, at the same time' (Tiffin and Ragasingham, 1995, p. 6). This improved classroom will be possible through the use of telecommunications and computers. There will be the possibility of a class meeting in the Amazon Forest or some other exciting venue. Using models and graphics, students will be able to witness the solar system operating like a game of marbles in front of them or to walk through the atomic structure of an element as if they were walking through a sculpture park. One view of schools of the future is provided by this graphic image: 'Shirley zips into her skin tight school uniform which on the outside looks something like a ski suit . . . She is in the virtual world of her virtual school' (*ibid*, p. 13).

As leaders we use telephones and they give us televirtual voices. We read documents and they give us virtual conversations and instructions. We go to conferences and meetings now but soon we will have teleconferencing in our office which will provide the effect of a meeting without us actually meeting. 'When the technology itself grows powerful enough to make the illusions increasingly realistic . . . the necessity for continuing to question reality grows more acute' (Rhinegold, 1994, p. 229).

Principals will continue to have meetings but let us hope that they will be around a task requiring interaction or coming together for a meal or a game of golf, the outcome of the meeting being better personal understanding and sharing. These community times will be precious, not to be wasted on listening to what is often a boring exposition received within a crowd setting, but experienced as a solitary event. Telecommunications can give us the talk and other data at our desks. When we come together it needs to be for real human interaction.

A Lost World

Is Santiago's world a lost one or can we participate in it still?

In another interesting and challenging book, *The Gutenberg Elegies*, Birkerts (1994), expresses fear that technology is taking us away from Santiago's world. His writing is so rich and metaphorical that I will quote his text rather than paraphrase it.

> Over the past few decades, in the blink of the eye of history, our culture has begun to go through what promises to be a total metamorphosis. The influx of electronic communications and information processing technologies, abetted by the steady improvement of the micro processor, has rapidly brought on a condition of critical mass. Suddenly it feels like everything is poised for change; the slower world that many of us grew up with dwindles in the rear view mirror. The stable hierarchy of the printed page — one of the defining norms of that world — has been superseded by the rush of impulses through freshly minted circuits. (p. 3)

His writing is full of strong images of a world that is disappearing for him: 'A finely filamented electronic scrim has slipped between ourselves and the so called "outside world"; The idea of spending a day, never mind a week, out of the range of all our devices sounds bold, even risky' (*ibid*, p. 5); 'The formally stable system — the axis with writer at one end, editor/publisher and bookseller in the middle, and reader at the other — is slowly being bent into a pretzel' (*ibid*).

Birkerts asks the question as to why man, and he is specifically talking about himself, feels so sad in this twentieth century. He sees this as a surprising question because it has been in this age that man has succeeded, more than in any other, in satisfying his needs and making over the world for his own use. But have we only satisfied our material needs?

Perhaps this is the reason why I had such a positive response to the story of Santiago — he was a person who wasn't cut off from those important character-istics that give meaning and purpose to our lives. He had time for beauty, for love, for true passion, and for the spiritual. Time stretched out for him. There were no million tasks that all had to be completed yesterday. My present life more closely approximates that described by Birkerts. He believes that we 'have destroyed the duration. We have created invisible elsewheres that are as immediate as our actual surroundings. We have fractured the flow of time, layering it into competing sim-ultaneities. We learn to do five things at once or pay the price' (*ibid*, p. 219). I have no problem with the 'invisible elsewheres' because I like some of these, including the one conjured up by Santiago. However I do have a problem about the lack of time but I am not sure that equates with the disappearing 'duration'.

Today we are embracing the microchip and all its magic because of the desired outcomes that it delivers. Birkerts fears the consequences of such an action, at least for himself. He fears that it will close him off

> from a great many habits and attitudes, ones that define me to myself, I would have to reposition myself on the space time axis. I would have to say goodbye to a

certain way of looking at the world because that way is bound up with a set of assumptions about history and distance, and difficulty and solitude and the slow working of self making — all of which go against the premises of instantaneousness, interactivity, sensory stimulation and ease which makes the world of Wired attractive to so many. (*ibid*, p. 213)

Those who wonder why schools in general have been slow to take up technology probably have their answer in this quotation. In order to become a teacher, one had to be a text master. To throw away one's expertise let alone one's developed love is a tall order!

Birkerts concludes his book using imagery that could have emanated from Santiago's world.

The devil no longer moves about on cloven hooves, reeking of brimstone. He is an affable, efficient fellow. He claims to want to help us all along to a brighter easier future and his sales pitch is very smooth. Otherwise, as the old song goes, almost persuaded, I saw what it could be like, our toil and misery replaced by a vivid, pleasant dream. Fingers tap keys, oceans of fact and sensation get down loaded, are dissolved through the nervous system. Bottomless worlds of data are accessed and manipulated, everything flowing at circuit speed. Gone the rock in the field, the broken hoe, the gruelling distances. 'History' , said Steven Dedalus, 'is a nightmare I am trying to awaken'. This may be the awakening, but it feels curiously like the fantasies that circulate through our sleep. From deep in the heart I hear the voice that says, refuse it. (*ibid*, p. 229)

Creative Tension

In one sense the apparent freedom of Santiago beckons and our present predicament, as described so clearly by Birkerts, frightens us so that we are inclined to escape into reverie. Do we accept one world view and reject the other? Senge (1992) would have us hold both views, see the whole. He would have us use creatively the tension between the views. He sees a 'creative tension' being generated 'by holding a vision and concurrently telling the truth about current reality relative to that vision' (p. 357). Creative tension is not about paralyzing anxiety as much as about purposeful and motivated activity. It essentially is a different view of reality in which individuals and organizations can be powerful and in control, not at the mercy of larger forces. The vision of a leader or of a community is what establishes the target. After that there needs to be a relentless commitment to finding out both what is actually happening and what are the forces underlying the current reality. This information is essential so that gaps between the reality and the vision can be highlighted. 'Leaders generate and manage this creative tension, not just in themselves but in an organization. This is how they energize an organization. That is their basic job. That is why they exist' (*ibid*).

It is interesting to speculate whether this information age in which we find ourselves demands a different type of perception of reality from the age that is passing. Have the Santiagos the potential to succeed today whereas are the Birkerts, who are clinging to the past, doomed to despair? Is it appropriate for us today to be looking back before the scientific age where there was room for fantasy and heart. The so-called scientific age may have been only one oasis on the journey and not the final resting point of our civilized march to somewhere.

Seeing the Whole

Santiago may have lived many years ago but, in another sense, his time has come again. We are once again in the mood to listen to the heart, to read the signs and to see the big picture. This change has been coming since the 1950s when we began to move away 'from the mechanical into the information age, from Newtonian to quantum physics, from a "hearing" culture into a highly networked, interactive "seeing" culture'. Neil Postman has said of this highly paced, accelerating transition that 'change changed' (*Visual Tools*, p. 13).

I am reminded of a wonderful book that I read recently, the story of Richard Feynman, a world famous physicist. Feynman was interesting because he could enjoy what many described as outrageous adventure while at the same time achieving eminence as a theoretical physicist, winning the Nobel Prize for his research.

Feynman as a top scientist was asked by a school district to help identify good science text books for schools in the district. He saw this as a worthy challenge and agreed to do so, assuming that his expenses for travel would be met.

> 'How much did (the travel) cost, Mr Feynman?'
> 'Well I flew to San Francisco, so it is the airfare plus the parking at the airport while I was away.'
> 'Do you have your ticket?'
> 'I happen to have the ticket.'
> 'Do you have a receipt for the parking?'
> 'No, but it cost $2.35 to park my car.'
> 'But we have to have a receipt.'
> 'I told you how much it cost. If you don't trust me why do you let me tell you what I think is good and bad about the school books.'
> 'So I am perfectly satisfied, but I never did get compensation for the trips'.
> (Feynman, 1986' pp. 272 and 273)

If it can be measured, then people will measure and this measurement seems more important than anything else. When it comes to multimillion dollar school buildings, the details like colours rather than the contents of the building are what will get the attention. As one principal, who does not want to be quoted by name, said: 'In a project of $2.002 million, I can spend two million dollars but the committee wants to debate how the two thousand dollars is spent.'

Unfortunately the same happens in school curriculum. Much of traditional education breaks wholes into parts, and then focuses separately on each part. Students spend so much time on the bits and pieces and are often unable to see the whole.

Alchemy

Santiago asked the alchemist to teach him about alchemy. He was told: 'It is about penetrating to the Soul of the World, and discovering the treasure that has been reserved for you.' 'No that is not what I mean. I'm talking about transforming lead into gold,' said Santiago (Coelho, 1993, p. 144).

However Santiago was to learn that gold is only the symbol and not the reality. Where your heart is, there will be the gold, the treasure that you seek. Alchemy in this sense is not about crass material wealth but spiritual wealth, finding and achieving your destiny.

Santiago had been transformed by his travels. At the end of the story we read that with pride Santiago let his heart remind him that this shepherd boy had left his flock to follow a dream. 'He thanked God for making him believe in his destiny, and for leading him to meet a king, a merchant, an Englishman, and an alchemist. And above all for his having met a woman . . . (*ibid*, p. 168). It is about destinies, meetings, journeys, discoveries, lane books and change.

Alchemy is about transforming something which is already valuable into something which is better. What a wonderful way to conceive of the role of the principal, helping to transform lives into even better lives. This is the alchemist principle.

Well

My reader, may I call you Santiago?

I suspect that your search began with beginner's luck. I suspect too that in the midst of your search you have encountered some severe testing.

The story of Rabbi Zusya offers us advice:

'In the world to come
I shall not be asked,
'Why were you not Moses?'
I should be asked,
'Why were you not Zusya?'

Postscript

I thought that I had finished this chapter. I had tried to respond in the spirit of Santiago by endeavouring to get in touch with my feelings. The chapter seemed to reflect where I was emotionally. When I was discussing it with a school principal friend, the friend asked to read it. So I faxed the chapter. Within an hour I had a response faxed back. It was a poem. There were no other comments. This was the poem.

For Santiago . . .
Your world moved on and left you
standing, weeping,

Just when you thought it was you
who would make all the moves.

But in a week when we now know-
for sure!
There is life on Mars- maybe even
Jupiter,
Perhaps there is something to be said
for being a traveller
in time, and space.

My first reaction to the poem was not too positive. What is wrong with a tear or two? One has to grieve before one can move on! To leave, after eighteen years, a task to which I have been so fully committed and a community of people of whom I am so fond, is hard. And what is this about me 'making all the moves'?

Yes I guess it is true that some of the control that I had is now passing to others and this is hard. It is also true that I am now having to confront another life. My present school has been more to me than a place of work. It has been my life. Yes, friend, I do hear what you say so eloquently in your poem. I hope my readers have friends like this.

As I reflected more on the poem I found not only insight into my personal predicament but encouragement to move forward to a new state of being. Indeed a new era has begun not just for the school but also for me. That same night I had a chance to put into action this new learning. I had to speak in reply to the toast to the school at the Annual Old Collegians' Dinner. I chose to reflect briefly on the past 115 years of school history, where there had been only five principals, and then give most of my speaking time to speculation about the future. What would the new principal be like? Will school always start at 8.30 am and finish at 3.30, or could we see the introduction of a flexible day which could start at 7.30 am and finish at 7 pm? I put many questions forward and made some guesses. What I was trying to do was rejoin the community. The community is thinking about its future, not about the present or the past.

I am indebted not only to my friend but also to the power of writing and electronic communication. To write is to put the ideas or emotions out there where they can be examined and commented upon. I invite critics of the fax and e-mail and the expectation of immediacy to contemplate whether my learning could have been so great if I had had to wait for a letter to travel out and a reply to travel back. I may have moved emotionally in that time, no longer feeling the deep sadness, holding only mild distress. The returning letter would then have been read with less insight because the emotional need was no longer great. There is no doubt in my mind that the contiguousness of modern communication enabled greater personal learning.

Yet More

Buoyed by this response and my feeling that I had moved on, I showed this chapter, complete with poem, to a member of staff. Again I was disconcerted by the analysis.

I cannot stand emotionally apart from this chapter as if I was writing about electrons or other personally remote particles or waves. This writing is about a person trying to be open and honest about his feelings in a work milieu. It is about a person who is grappling with the intrusive experiences of personal feelings, which are having the effect of metamorphosing his otherwise discrete conglomerate life and work understandings. The personal reflective comments of friends are therefore useful, although not always easy to accept as I do want to retain some professional self-respect! While I will not be able to enjoy the reader's response, I hope that this writing is eliciting reflective responses from my readers too.

Here is one of the comments:

> I found your assessment about the staff's reactions to your leaving rather simple. I think they were more complex than that. Your reaction was complex. Like Santiago you were moving on from your oasis into the unknown, and you were experiencing the sense of loss that inevitably comes when you move on. You were also experiencing a loss of power as you felt 'some of the control passing to others'. If, as you have argued in this chapter, we exist as a whole, what is the nature of your relationship to the community? There may be some of us who are glad to see you move on and grow, but will miss you as well, for all kinds of reasons. And how much was the talking by management at the staff meeting — 'the school must go on show' — due to the fear that someone of your stature was leaving? The problem for a school when its dynamic principal leaves is that it goes into shock — and then the automatic goes on for a while. Your feelings of loss perhaps came about because you had had time to get used to the news.
>
> I felt really strange, and I still do. It made me want to move on too. It seemed to pull some of the central colour, the interest, the excitement out of the school. I felt uneasy as if we had been dealt a mortal wound. I know others who were close to you felt that too. The administration went around shoring up people. I was approached by at least three people — ensuring that I had a firm sense of where I was going. I wanted to grieve though and I wonder whether not allowing that is a fault of our school. After all, we need to be able to express the feelings we have if we are to be able to operate as a body, as opposed to a mechanical system. I would love you to explore these notions in more depth, because I think it demonstrates what you talk about with Santiago — the zen bit — 'as if some mysterious energy bound his life to that of the sheep, with whom he had spent the past two years' — I'm not sure about the analogy of sheep and shepherd — a more equal relationship than that — those patriarchal cultures! — but if an institution is organic, there is bound to be a complex reaction to the departure of its principal.

This writer's assessment is that when the leader of any organization moves on, it is dealt a blow, and like anything living it defends itself as it strives to survive and come to terms with its changing reality. As I was contemplating this appraisal, another staff member with responsibility for our school publications came to speak to me. She said: 'The school prospectus has your photo on page one. Are you happy if we do a reprint of the prospectus without this photo?' Before I could recover enough to reply, she added: 'There is also the leaflet describing Marshmead. It has some quotations of yours in it. May I remove your name and attribute those comments to a student?' When I did speak I replied: 'Now I seem to have forgotten your name. What is it again please?' Not a good response but it did relate a little to how I was feeling about losing identity while I was still at the school and would be for another four months. Of course all of this has to happen and, in reality, the question was asked out of politeness. It was unfair of me to respond as I did. Yet in another sense it did introduce into the work dialogue personal feelings that also have a right to exist. If we can get in touch with our personal emotions, then collectively we may be able to get in touch with the 'mysterious energy' that binds us together in an organic work setting.

There is more gold to be mined from both *The Alchemist* and the 'exiting' principal. However it will be placed in later chapters.

Notes

1   This is from a story written by Louise Vickers-Willis in *This I Believe*, a book edited by John Marsden.
2   The students encouraged me by shouting: 'Jump Mr Loader, jump!'

Chapter 2

The Paranoid Principal

Swift as a spirit hastening to his task
Of glory and of good, the Sun sprang forth
Rejoicing in his splendour, and the mask
Of darkness fell from the awakened Earth.
(P.B. Shelley, *The Triumph of Life*)

The Morning After

Lying restless in bed, my mind full of the previous night's discussions, with the arrival of daylight I resolved to rise and walk. Instead of a radio to relax or to stimulate, I decided to take as my companion a tape recorder to try to capture some of the inner thoughts and stirrings. Here I am now walking along a beautiful Australian beach at 5.00 am, dictating what might be a chapter of a book. With a group of principals on holidays, I had shared a good meal, good wine and good fellowship until a late hour last night. As we sat and chatted, the conversation came around to a discussion about the principals that we are, have been and, of course, the principals we have known. It was fun doing this. The similarity and dissimilarity of the two words principal and principle had encouraged us to think laterally as well as personally and professionally. We had talked about the absent principal, the paranoid principal, the Humpty Dumpty principal, the moral turpitude principal, the lazy principal, the proper principal, the peremptory principal, the crowing principal, the humble principal and there were many more. We even contemplated what would be the collective name to be used for a group of principals. We decided that it might be a 'lack of principals'! For personal sanity it is important to be able to laugh at one's profession and at oneself. It is equally important to be able to undertand one's profession, to see the challenges and the risks and to be able to choose a mature path between them.

If the night before had engendered ideas for me, my present activity of walking and talking to myself is producing some funny looks from those early morning athletes who are running past and those early coffee drinkers who are sitting in their windows sipping. If they had known that this was a school principal thinking and writing, they probably would have labelled me the crazy principal. Furthermore if they had looked around they would have seen other galahs, a flock in fact, flying past out for the early air too.

Of all the options from last night I have chosen to consider the paranoid principal. To my knowledge I have not read about this in the many books on my shelves which discuss the principal's role. Instead the indexes of these books list tasks such as assemblies, communication, curriculum, decision making, finance, mail, meetings and self-development. Then there are lists of less tangible items such as accountability, authority, morale, motivation, planning, stress, style and values. In the light of this, my discussion of the paranoid principal, empty principal, alchemist principal and other principals may be a first!

It would be wrong to assume that this entire chapter is what I dictated on that fateful, early morning. Oh that I had such skills with a dictaphone! What was dictated formed the basis of this chapter. More content has been added and some of the original ideas abandoned as I have thought through the issues. However the authenticity that the morning dictation brought has inspired my other attempts at trying to combine feeling and thinking into some integrated whole.

Less Individual Authority

In this chapter on 'The Paranoid Principal', it is appropriate to begin with a little self-preoccupation, as that can be a part of paranoia. While I can confidently assert that neither I nor my fellow principals are paranoid, the feelings of anxiety sometimes come close to being dysfunctional for many of us. This confession may be a little disconcerting to those who hope for great things from schools and their staff. To those who are not members of the principal's club, the image of the principal is often a confident lion rather than a fearful cub, or a powerful monarch rather than a submissive servant. People continue to associate power and confidence rather than vulnerability and paranoia with those who are principals. In the past, principals were more powerful. Some male readers may join me in remembering their school days and their principal greeting them in his office, cane in hand, with 'bend over that desk young man' and 'this will hurt me more than you'. Fortunately that rough power base has now gone, together with some of the authority traditionally associated with sea captains and army generals.

Today in schools there are many who exercise power over decisions. There is the power asserted by governing parent and teacher councils who are making decisions about schooling, by parents who are not frightened, some of whom may even be disdainful, of teachers and principals, and by students who are speaking out for their personal rights. This inverting of the old pyramid of authority has made some principals very uncomfortable. These disorientated principals probably got to where they are by conforming to accepted rules and patterns and now people, for whom they are responsible, are not accepting the principal's rules and structures. The accepted wisdom while they were preparing for their principal role was that principals were responsible for directing and controlling schools. Their training was in pyramid organizations where the people at the top direct the people in the middle and they in turn tell the people at the bottom, usually the students, what to do. Successful principals in this model exerted power by virtue of the authority vested in them. By this means they could make things happen as they had planned. A principal could have a vision and then expect others to make it a reality. It is therefore not surprising that such principals today feel disorientated. 'How can I do my job when I no longer have the authority to do it?' some ask. Less authoritarian principals, who recognize that their professional authority now resides less in command and more in knowledge, networks and skills, also find it difficult today. These gentler principals have to deal with their constituents, many of whom have the impression that principals still have magical authority and thus (personally) should be able to make things happen. Principals, whatever their style of leadership, are under pressure as a result of the changing authority structures in their work settings.

The pressure is not just from the change in authority from one person to many. It follows from a more subtle style shift that is gender linked. Without intending such bias, I used images of lion and monarch for the principal, images normally stereotyped as male. I described my male experience of a principal who caned. In contrast to these I described today's principal as one who copes with networks and whose skills would include feeling and intuition. These more feminine characteristics are not the exclusive modes of females, males can and do network and can be personal, intuitive and sensitive! However this change from male to female stereotypes does provide another fertile ground for growth in paranoia like behaviour, particularly for males.

Some Definition

The literature makes these assessments. 'Individuals with paranoid personality disorders are more than suspicious or cautious: they are highly distrustful, always on the lookout for signs and clues of danger or deceit. Everyone is a potential threat or enemy' (Hales and Hales, 1995, p. 548). 'The paranoiac is someone who continually feels that people are persecuting him. He feels that the neighbours are talking about him or that someone is trying to poison him' (De Board, 1978, p. 33). 'The paranoiac gets rid of his unpleasant feelings and projects them (that is transfers them) on the external world' (*ibid*).

To be professionally diagnosed as paranoid, as defined above, would be to have a serious affliction that would preclude you from real leadership in today's schools. Similarly for an organization to be assessed as being paranoid would mean that it has lost control of its future because it would be in a destabilizing reactive mood. In this chapter I do not want to talk about either of these extremes. Rather I want to discuss the source and significance of paranoid analogous behaviour.

Specifically I am asserting that the principal's job has so many paradoxes, tensions and dangers and that the principal is subject to so many bosses that principals may become excessively suspicious and overcautious. Some principals become so cautious that they are paralyzed, unable to make decisions. When suspicion and caution dominate a leader's thinking, that leader can turn inwards, preferring her/his own counsel. Such a response can create a situation of isolation and alienation and this in turn deprives principals of their feed-back loops. If the principal does become isolated then that principal will be deprived of the information which facilitates true insights into the nature of problems and not able to make realistic assessments of their seriousness. This will limit the effectiveness of the principal because s/he no longer has the information on which to make appropriate informed decisions. Failure here will reinforce those feelings of isolation and aloneness. Thus a spiral begins and only ends when the principal breaks out and begins trusting and hearing again or crashes into the vortex of that spiral, a black hole if ever there was one!

Principals as Vulnerable Professionals

Today we hear derogatory statements about judges and doctors, particularly male judges and doctors. They are not the only professionals under attack. In general, attitudes to professionals including teachers and principals are changing. The historic norm of professional autonomy and practice is passing. Professionals are increasingly struggling with value weighted issues which underlie the technical expertise of the professional. Can a doctor make a decision about life and death? Do school principals determine curriculum? How accurate is that teacher's assessment? There is a demand by the community for greater participation in valuing and decision-making. Once there may have been the powerful knowing professional out there alone playing a heroic role. Now that professional is part of a team some of whose members are not professionals. With professionals knowing more and more about less and less, others have to find and hold the larger picture, the synthesis. When something like the Westgate Bridge collapses in Melbourne or the explosion of the Challenger Space Shuttle in the USA occurs, the professional's independence is again queried.

Professionals make mistakes and they have to account for them. Personally I would not dare to give career advice to students, something that would have been expected of principals in previous times. I leave that to the specialists, career teachers and counsellors, and invite parents to obtain other opinions. How careful we are becoming! Today the aggrieved consumer has lots of support by law and some of what could have been called professional behaviour before might now by called intimidatory behaviour. 'My child was left out of the football team because of favouritism', claims one parent. There is no paper and pencil test that will give conclusive evidence that the teacher is acting fairly. If all this is not bad enough for professionals, coping with greater complexity that follows from the greater involvement by many, and the increasing number of stakeholders and bosses, means that many professionals (and executives) no longer enjoy the same level of confidence or satisfaction in their role as was previously the case. How can they enjoy something that keeps slipping out of their hands? Certain basic security needs such as understanding and holding territory, which traditionally were associated with the status of professionals, have been removed. The consequent vulnerability of the professional can elicit deep primitive and painful anxieties such as paranoia and these can paralyze some professionals (Gilmore and Krantz, 1989).

Different Audiences, Different Demands

A potential source of significant anxiety to principals is the insecurity of their employment. In independent schools at least, principals have employment contracts with limited tenure. 'Will my three year contract be renewed, and if it is not, what employment will I find?' While such limited tenure contracts give confidence to employing bodies, they can unsettle principals arousing negative defensive behaviour as they perceive that their performance is continually being discussed. Unlike some business managers who can point out that their company has made a profit, principals have trouble finding those tangible measures that clearly indicate that they are doing a good job. Education is about the growth of persons and that is not easily measured. Furthermore it is best facilitated in a setting of confidence, trust and mutual support.

Another unsettling fact for principals is the large number of people to whom they are directly accountable. What makes it worse is that these accountabilities could be different and potentially conflicting for each person to whom they are responsible. The ex-students may be interested in the sporting success of the first rowing crew, the parents in academic success as measured by university entrance tests, and the students by the degree of freedom that is permitted them. Staff may be interested in workloads and timetables. The community may be interested in the behaviour of the students on public transport, or student dress or student help with public events. Then principals are accountable to their family for their lack of participation because of school commitments. It is not surprising that these accountabilities are regularly at odds with each other. The different audiences have different demands and whose voice is the more important?

But it is not just the different audiences that create problems. There are the differences within groups that have to be moderated and directed. Within the staff group, despite their common training and similar responsibilities, one finds different beliefs, values, attitudes and practices. Within the student and parent groups there are differences arising from their different socioeconomic backgrounds, culture or race. To the principal come the worst of the disagreements. If the principal cannot resolve what are in some instances unresolvable conflicts, the principal is left to bear the brunt of the dissatisfaction of one or more of the contending parties.

Then there are the specific accountabilities to a governing body. In my case I am responsible to a Council of twenty-four members. I find it very hard to know personally those twenty-four people, many of whom I meet only once a month at the Council meeting. I have heard myself asking, irrationally or not, will the majority of the twenty-four support me when they hear about this initiative or this blunder?

The lack of definition of the task, the public nature of the role about which everyone is an expert, the many audiences and the different accountabilities do not always produce the environment for good sleeping at night. What can a principal do about this? One could retreat to the hills, grow organic vegetables using permaculture, consume only renewable sources of energy such as wind and solar and enjoy a virtual world through books and the odd day dream of what it could have been like. An alternative escape path is to stay at work and retreat from the conflicts by attending only to trivial routine matters. However, while that may have worked in the past in some settings for some people, the competitive nature of the work place and the more direct accountability of the role make this withdrawal option untenable. The best hope seems to lie in what would probably be an impossible option to those who have become too distrustful. The option is for the principal to undertake a regular appraisal of some form with the people to whom s/he is accountable. It is amazing that this suggestion is only now coming to the fore in professional circles. For some years we have been reading, and in my case writing, about appraisal and evaluation of teachers. Yet I have never had a formal evaluation in my role of principal, a role that has extended over twenty-six years. Of course there have been many informal evaluations and these occur over dinner tables, on the telephone, in committee. The time has come for instruments to be developed for the purpose of the evaluation of principals. This will not be easy as the different audiences may well be asking for different qualities. As I write I know that this is being worked on in our professional association but I wonder whether principals who are feeling vulnerable will participate?

Perfection

A potential source of dysfunctional anxiety for principals is our expectations that we must get things right the first time we do it. A mistake, a near miss is not good enough. Maybe this expectation comes from our background as teachers where we commended students who did get 100 per cent in some of the tests that we set. These were our good students. They worked hard, were motivated and were intelligent. They deserved such good results. We have a measure of goodness and it is 100 per cent. A lot of our time as teachers was involved with assessment and it is natural that we would apply the same principles to ourselves. Will I get an A+ for this? If I don't then that is not good enough. Teachers too are hard on themselves. When our teaching staff go back to further study at university, they too expect good marks. If these teachers don't get High Distinction in their courses then they are very upset. A lesser mark is regarded as a failure. These high expectations are a dreadful burden that we take from our school environment and which we continue voluntarily to place upon ourselves. I should have been able to do that interview better. I am not happy with the outcome of that staff meeting; I should have handled those staff questions better. Why wasn't I better prepared for that accident in the school yard? Instead of taking the view that we can learn from our mistakes, we punish ourselves. Even worse, sometimes we project out the failure on to others by blaming them, students, staff and parents, and in so doing protect ourselves. In projecting out the blame for failure we do most harm to ourselves in that we bolster the false image that all has to be, and we can be, 100 per cent correct. It is only when we admit to failure that we are open to learning. This may seem to go against common sense and our experience of the world to this time. Yet I am convinced that living in a world where failure and learning go together, is to live in a real world where personal growth follows, dysfunctional anxiety is reduced and health in mind and in the community is the outcome.

In trying to make sense of my experiences, I have been reading widely. I was delighted to find some support for the idea that lack of perfection does not have to be a deficit in a principal. I found this succinct statement quite powerful. Imperfection is 'an important companion to reflection' (Patterson, 1993, p. 32). Our lives would be so much easier if only we could believe this. Learning is the transformation of our direct experience, including mistakes, into knowledge as meaning and this in turn is a precursor to action. Learning requires commitment to action. As such it involves us intimately with the world around us, encouraging us to feel, to sense and to value, as well as to reflect and then to act again.

Mistakes can be an important way of learning as they provide important feedback on what we are doing. This feedback is only unwelcome because of our present framework of mind. Through mistakes we can grow both personally and professionally, yet it must be acknowledged that 'openness to mistakes is a rare phenomenon in most organizations' (*ibid*). The Appleton School District has embraced and institutionalized the ideas that openness and innovation are sought-after characteristics of staff and importantly that mistakes do occur and that one can learn from these mistakes. Appleton School District gives all of the staff in the district a card each year and the card allows and encourages a discussion of the mistake(s) that they have made and promises a safe environment for this discussion. The card states:

I BLEW IT!
> I tried something new and innovative and it didn't work as well as I wanted.
> This coupon entitles me to be free of criticism for my efforts.
> I'll continue to pursue ways to help our district be successful. (*ibid*)

Can you imagine someone coming to a job interview for a principalship and confessing to mistakes? 'Well I made a mistake with the timetable, argued with a parent, . . .' It seems foolish. Maybe this is the deeper problem. We continue to use the word 'mistake'. By using this word we give tacit agreement to this notion of perfection. In conversation we explore ideas, in relationships we expect both parties to take responsibility for themselves, in planning we talk about incrementalism which allows us to make corrections all the way. Even with missiles we talk of guidance systems and we have satellites in orbit to help direct these fearful objects to their destination. An accepted scientific intervention is to interrupt, disrupt or even create a 'mistake' so that the result can be observed and from the outcome, learning can follow. Yet in our work situations we continue to talk of mistakes!

In my dealing with my staff I don't use the word 'mistake'. I want to encourage risk taking as we want change, evolution, growth and a better fit between the world of school and the world outside. You cannot have risks without mistakes. What we need urgently is a new terminology that takes us past this morass, beyond the Newtonian idea that something is right or wrong. We need to adopt quantum thinking[1] and language.

Competition

Despite the rhetoric about the value of cooperative behaviour, most successful principals are, by nature or by osmosis, competitive. Their school programs include competitive sport and this has become so important that schools are now competing for outstanding sports achievers by offering sporting scholarships to attract them to their schools. It is rumoured that one boys' school in that school's centenary year was so keen to look good in front of the Old Boys that they bought a whole rugby football team with sporting scholarships. While that school did win the premiership, competing schools were not impressed! Our school includes competitive drama, debating and music in house competitions. The outcome of schooling in Australia is a competitive examination for all students in which students compete against each other for the best marks so that they can enter the prestigious faculties of medicine and the like. The results of this final examination at the end of schooling are reported in such a way that every student is left in no doubt about their competitive ranking. This method not only adversely affects the self confidence of a lot of our students, it also fails to engender the spirit of cooperation and the bonding of peers that is a sought-after outcome of education. An English teacher told me that, with one of her classes, it is hard to facilitate the sharing of views about novels and plays as students in these classes are so preoccupied with getting high marks and that means beating others in the class by keeping one's best ideas to oneself. Similarly in schools we are obsessed with cheating. 'Is this your work? No one has helped you with this, have they?' teachers ask. Yet if we are completing a Doctor of Philosophy degree we are not put in an isolation room and told to see no one, talk to no one. The opposite happens; people are allocated to work with you in your research and writing. Competition is a major, and not always positive, part of school life and this competition carries over into the lives of principals, creating both opportunities and unnecessary difficulties.

It is therefore not surprising to find that another source of deep anxiety for some principals is the comparative and competitive relationship with one's peers and their schools. We discover that the neighbouring schools have something that we do not have. This could be a physical entity such as a playing field, a music hall or e-mail within the school. Or it could be a program; they are teaching Chinese; they train their prefects with leadership courses. Or it could be outcomes such as exam results, computer literacy, sporting results. Whatever is the perceived deficit, the principal is left feeling vulnerable. S/he may be able to explain these differences; our exam results are not as high because we do not have a selective academic entry into the school, but the principal knows that in doing that s/he will appear defensive and that is not a strong position to be in. Because the school is judged to have a deficit, does it follow automatically that the principal is judged not to be as good? For many principals the answer is yes. They feel vulnerable. They want perfection; being second is little better than coming last. If you are caught within this mind set then feelings of dysfunctional anxiety can arise.

The feeling of competition has increased for private school principals recently with a down-turn in the economy and therefore fewer parents able to afford the school fees. There is more competition between schools for fewer students. The government schools in Victoria are experiencing similar competition. In the past, students who attended government schools were required to attend their local area school. Now students have a choice of schools and students and their parents are choosing, with some schools winning and others losing the enrolment race. To add to the pressure on the school principals, their previously safe tenure as government employees is being removed and principals in government schools now are employed under a contract.

About What Can We be Sure?

This discussion of paranoia-like behaviour reminds me of a story I remember reading written by a family therapist when he was in training. It was part of a chapter entitled 'Food for thought'.

> Towards the end of the academic year, we were taken to the Royal Melbourne Hospital to interview some real live patients. Dr Jeffrey asked me to see a working class migrant who had come into the casualty ward of the hospital holding a brown paper bag full of sandwiches. He complained that the sandwiches were poisoned; so he was sent to psychiatry. I talked to him. He asked me to look at the poisoned sandwiches. He said he had come from Yugoslavia fifteen years ago; had lived in a boarding house for a number of years; had no family and few friends and he believed that his landlady was trying to poison him.
>
> I asked why he thought this. He replied, 'I know she wants to'. I asked him how he knew and he said: 'She has that look in her face'. I asked: 'What do you mean? What look?' He said: 'She looks as if she wants to poison me'. No matter how much I questioned him, I got no further.
>
> I returned to Dr Jeffrey and our group and said 'I believe the man is a paranoid'. Dr Jeffrey asked me why I thought so and I explained. He then asked me if I was sure. I replied, 'Yes, certainly'. He asked how sure I was. I said, 'very sure'. He asked me if I wanted to go back and ask the man any further questions. I said 'I didn't need any more answers'. He then asked me to get the sandwiches. When I brought them back to him he asked me to eat them. I stopped, then said, 'No thanks!'. (Lang and Lang, 1986, pp. 19 and 20)

I wonder if in schools we ask people to do things that we would not want to do. While we stop short of asking students to eat poisoned sandwiches, we do ask them to learn subjects that may not be relevant to where they are as people. All of this was brought home forcibly to me in a dialogue that appeared in the Methodist Ladies' College staff journal after a staff meeting in which there was a discussion of a 'flexible school day that might begin at 7 am and finish at 7 pm with students free to undertake their studies outside of traditional class groups.' A group of seven staff wrote:

> The scenario of the middle school rower down-loading the maths lesson she's missed and working through it independently in a maths learning centre made

those of us who teach in junior secondary school and middle school smile. It is based on the assumption that students are responsible, motivated and self-directed and, as we know from experience, many students are not.'[2]

I don't want to be too critical of this statement for two reasons. Firstly I want to encourage the free expression by staff of their concerns. Secondly I acknowledge that staff made this statement because they believed what they wrote to be true. Their experience is that some students do not come to the study of maths with enthusiasm. Their experience is of reluctant learners that have to be motivated and supported. However I do want to assert that this is an unsatisfactory situation. As educators this situation should be encouraging us to reconceptualize what we are doing in schools and to question the value of the present curriculum.

Compare this with the statement made by a first year out teacher who has been prepared for this situation by her brother:

What an exciting concept! So much learning seems to be thwarted by timetables, bells and classes. So many students seem to spend their day marking time, waiting for the (end of school) bell to ring so they can go and learn what they want to be learning. For my brother, school definitely got in the way of his education. He would have been much better off travelling the world and coaching a hockey team, and having an individual program within a school etc. . . . But that is just one student . . .[3]

Recently I had to become a learner again. With the introduction of computing into Methodist Ladies' College I had to learn to type, to learn how to use the computer and to master a number of programs. While I admit to experiencing frustration at different times, in general the experience was positive. The process helped me get back in touch with the learner in me. I had no formal classes but my learning was within a community of other learners. It was not a requirement of the job, it was something that I saw would be helpful with my job and so I worked at my learning. New worlds opened up for me. I had success. I could do things that were useful. I had forgotten how much fun it was to learn again. Maybe this is what the students experience with their computer games, the fun of challenge, learning and success?

About what can we be sure? 'Not much' is the truthful answer. Yet instead of this lack of certainty adding spice to our life, it leaves us feeling vulnerable because we feel the need to be on the winning side or at least with the majority. For example, is it relevant to consider that it was a group of seven senior teachers that wrote the critical comments about the ideas floated in the staff meeting?

From Childhood

Then there is the fear and anxiety that comes from our childhood. Psychoanalytic theory has always been concerned with the behaviour of the child as a key to understanding the behaviour of the adult. These fears and anxieties we bring as unhelpful baggage into our adult role as principal. 'As a child I believed that people always picked on me unfairly' can create the victim mentality in the adult. The child whose views were not respected later as an adult may feel that the only views of significance belong to others. As a result that person lives captive in the minds of others unable to make decisions for her/himself. The lurking feeling of being found out as an adult can also be traced back to childhood experiences. As interesting as such a discussion could be I am not qualified to address childhood origins of adult behaviour. However these origins should be acknowledged and so I simply nominate this for completeness.

It needs to be acknowledged that the result of a little self-doubt can be good for a school but not necessarily good for the person involved. Some of the very best principals in the land are driven, always trying to prove themselves by performing new miracles every day. The result is an innovative and vibrant school but an exhausted and sometimes burnt out principal. To the idea of running on empty, I have allocated a chapter, 'The Empty Principal'.

Attentive Listening

As has already been suggested, not everything associated with being suspicious is negative. For example a little fear, distrust or even suspicion could change us from an uninterested audience to attentive listeners. Because we don't believe the story, we listen more closely to what is the complaint in order to discover what is the underlying message. Two personal experiences come to mind where my suspicions led to more attentive listening. I remember being surprised that a recently appointed young graduate teacher, who appeared so enthusiastic and confident at the interview, was having a number of absences from school. Was the teacher really sick or was there something serious happening in the home or at school that needed attention? In sensitively pursuing this I discovered that there was a bigger problem in the staff room where this teacher and other younger teachers were being victimized by a senior staff member who, as an older person, was worried about her continued employment.

Then there was the member of the boarding house staff with the task of ringing the morning bell for boarders to rise. Students reported that she used to ring it in the broom cupboard. She was a vague member of staff and so it could have been that she kept opening the wrong door as the broom cupboard is adjacent to the hall door. This member of staff also was not the most popular staff member and so the students could have been telling exaggerated tales to get her in trouble with me.

At that time good boarding staff were hard to find and so I did not want to lose her through rash accusations. Since I did have a suspicion that all was not well, I called her in to my office and asked a few gentle questions about how she was feeling: 'Was everything OK?' I asked. The conversation was moving along and I was beginning to be reassured when, from nowhere, she advised me that her bed was shrinking. I said, 'Your sheets have shrunk?' 'No,' she said, 'my bed continues to get shorter'. Now I knew that all the beds were iron framed and so I tried again. 'Do you mean that the mattress has shrunk?' 'No it is the bed frame. What is more they keep ringing for me.' Now I was on the edge of my chair. 'Who keeps ringing for you?' She replied, 'They want to get me. They have been chasing me.' My persistent questions continued and suddenly the 'they' became 'me' and I was a member of ASIO, the Australian Intelligence Organization. There is more to tell but I think that the basis of the story has been told. The students whose motives I had questioned were not only exonerated but were to be commended for the sensitive way that they had advised me of a person who was suffering from some form of dysfunctional paranoia.

However, attentive listening prompted by fear of one's own judgment can be paralyzing. Such listening to the voices of others does not inform. Rather it stops us listening to our inner voice, nurtured through those significant experiences that have obtained for us the important and responsible job of principal. Such exclusive listening to others not only impedes our judgments about our first decisions, it stops us taking corrective action after an error for fear of a further failure.

I remember visiting a school and being impressed with an outwardly confident young lady who had just assumed the role of principal one year before. However, I was soon to discover that the outward confidence was not supported by an inward calm. She told me how, just after she had arrived at her new school, she had made a decision that received little support from the staff. At that time she had dared to change the rules and permit students to talk between lessons. While the students had greeted the decision with pleasure, the staff were so angry and voiced their criticism of this decision so unilaterally that she was forced to reverse her decision. 'Now', she said, 'I can't make a decision without trying to work out who would support it and who would be against it. I have got to the stage now that I don't know what I think. It is awful', she said.

I would find her position untenable. Certainly I want to listen to legitimate and authentic voices, to hear the often contradicting arguments and advice, but finally I believe that I must trust my judgment. To do otherwise is to create a situation where there is no leadership. After all the principal is the person who is going to be held accountable and it is very hard to defend positions that you do not understand or do not hold.

> The logic of worldly success rests on a fallacy: the strange error that our perfection depends on the thoughts and opinions and applause of other men! A weird life it is, indeed, to be living always in somebody else's imagination, as if that were the only place in which one could at last become real. (Merton, 1976, p. 330)

Critical Thinking

Critical thinking is essential to a principal. As well as listening sensitively to the talk of others, the principal needs to be able to make determinations based on their merit. Unfortunately we do not come to these moments without baggage. We sometimes are caught up in our own psychic snares, such that we hear or assume things that are not present. Our projections, the framing that we give the message, interfere with what we hear. It is at this point that there is the potential for paranoia. It is when our own psychic weaknesses, often engendered in childhood, start to distort the external message that paranoid-like behaviour occurs. Unfortunately it does not end there. As soon as I become suspicious and threatened, the person with whom I am dealing begins to be defensive and cautious. Such a response then makes the first person feel under more attack and the vicious circle continues.

Peer Support

A principal who had completed nearly thirty years' service in that role announced his retirement. His peers invited him to speak at his last conference. His speech had a powerful but sad beginning. 'This is the first time that you have asked me to speak to you.' The speech was witty and perceptive. He offered good advice to us from his thirty years of principalship. 'Never take your governing body for granted', he said and there were many who were no longer principals who would have benefited from that advice if it had been given to them earlier in their career. As I sat there listening to this interesting and provocative address, I asked myself: 'Why do we leave people out in the cold? Is it this competitive thing again?' Here was a successful principal, as judged by the way his school community valued him, but apparently not valued enough by his peers to be asked to address a conference. What is this fear on the part of principals that excludes those who have different practices and beliefs from being invited to contribute to the debate? Is it anxiety that has become dysfunctional?

With a long history in the Australian Association of Heads I can think back to a number of events where I felt that I had been left out in the cold. In my first year as a principal I left my school to attend a heads' conference, my mind full of questions and dilemmas. How does one discipline naughty students? In particular I was having a bad time in relation to a prefect whose badge I had withdrawn because of her behaviour. The Chairman of my Governing Council, a friend of the disciplined girl's family, wanted me to reinstate her as Prefect. The conference offered me a chance to seek some advice. I looked among those gathered and approached what I estimated to be a successful principal and asked how she handled naughty students. The reply I will never forget. She said: 'I do not have naughty students at my school!' The matter was closed. I did not try asking anyone else. Now I admit in retrospect that the question could have been more specific and more personal. However in my newness and nervousness that was what I asked. Today I would have begun by saying: 'I have a problem. Can you help me? I have this situation . . .' From such a beginning it is clear that I have the problem and not the person I was approaching. Such a beginning does not beget the defensiveness that I encountered.

The truth is that we are a little fearful about how our peers see and evaluate us and this does get in the road of true and open sharing. As a result we talk loudly about our successes and we discuss the safe topics such as the organization of sport, uniforms, government funding.

There is some paranoia-like behaviour in our associations as evidenced by the way we meet so cautiously together. We have shared some good times of fun and fellowship, always there is much to laugh about. We want to be happy and to be seen with a perpetual smile on our faces. Consequently we reveal little about what is really happening inside ourselves except to a carefully chosen few who live in regions remote from our school communities. We have seen what has happened to peers who have talked too openly about the problems that they are having, the hurts that they have experienced. The feeling of vulnerability we may feel is not to be revealed to people with whom we are in competition, our peers. The mutual support that could enliven and deepen our relationships happens for all too few principals. Even worse, this solitary behaviour reinforces itself and so it becomes the norm and the Association redefines leadership, not in association, but as a private affair. Darwin's theory of the survival of the best fit follows and from these successful ones, as defined by the organization, the organization chooses its leaders, ones who are high on goals and achievements.

The competitive marketplace may be delivering better schools but it can also create the potential for the growth of dysfunctional anxiety and suspicion amongst principals and schools. If principals and schools believe that they must fight for the high ground in order to survive, then ownership of good ideas and practices becomes paramount. Recognition as a principal or as a school becomes the critical achievement. 'I was the one who began . . .' Yet the larger goal, to which we all subscribe, is really to improve schools for all students and for the community.

Institutional Paranoia

We have considered personal paranoia. Is it possible that there could be institutional paranoia? Some institutions do take on a suspicious stance and fear that others are stealing their ideas, their programs and even their students and teachers. Visitors are not welcome, and if they come, are treated as a potential threat. In the days before mobile phones, and with no small coins in my pocket, I remember visiting a neighbouring school to make a phone call. I was kept waiting while a person of sufficient authority could be found who would give permission for me to use their phone. When finally after ten minutes this was allowed, the desk on which the phone was to be found was cleared and the owner of the desk stood near to make sure that nothing was . . . I don't know what, stolen?

On the other hand some institutions could do with a little fear. They see themselves as going on forever, maintaining their past traditions regardless of where society is now. Such schools are often focused on outward appearances and give scant attention to the individual and his/her uniqueness. It is management by memory, doing what was done in years before, again and again. Would-be patrons of such schools might welcome the introduction of some uncertainty, even anxiety, into that school about its future. In such a situation, change in thinking and practice might at least be contemplated. Once a crack in the armour of that institution appears, then by careful attention this crack might be widened to create an open door to change.

But what about the institution that is in a sweat of self doubt and maybe even self pity? Beating themselves on the chest, they ask: 'Who are we? Where are we going? Do we have a future? Can we be proud of our past?' Members of such unhappy institutions would probably be quick to find blame for the present predicament. It's the principal's fault, no leadership. It's the ex-student's fault, not allowing change. It's the council's fault, they are not in touch with the community. It's the staff's fault, they won't change with the times. Its the government's fault, inadequate funding. It's the union's fault, they are only concerned about the work conditions of their members and not equally concerned with the welfare of the students. (I confess to being disturbed by how easy it was to put together a list of people to blame!)

The solution to institutional insecurity or anxiety is not necessarily an institutional psychoanalyst, although that would be good as deep-seated fears are difficult to address. However, it is likely that some outside consultant will be necessary to help the people in the institution openly face the criticisms and then move on to some consensus building and strategic thinking. Then we will need a missionary principal to sell this new gospel of hope.

The group dynamics of organization are a proper focus for a principal. It is imperative for the principal to have experience in groups to understand his/her strengths and weaknesses in group situations in order to be empowered and effective.

Unhappy Ending

I wish to conclude this chapter with what I recorded at the conclusion of my walk that morning.

> 'To be or not to be . . .' As I end this dictation I have a sudden image of Hamlet's sad soliloquy. I too feel a heavy sadness within me. I feel drained by talking about my role as principal. Where is the joy that I should be experiencing from my chosen career, a career that has consumed so much of my life, a career that on the first day of my holiday beside the sea sees me writing about it. When I obviously feel so sad, why do I stay in my role as principal? Why do I want to write about that role? I'm not sure.
>
> Part of the feeling relates to the loneliness of the role. How sad it would be if that loneliness is of my own making — that I have unnecessarily chosen to be separate, to be competitive, to be personally cautious in what I have revealed about myself. I remember one day towards the end of a term, three different principals phoned me to talk about problems they were experiencing. I know what they were feeling, I've been there. So where is the joy? Is this why some principals think the best thing they can do during the day is to teach a class? I've heard principals say 'I like the classroom best'. Is the implication that children are more fun than adults? Certainly young people are less critical! For some of us, being with children is safer than being with adults.

However, that is not how I feel. I like the staff room, I enjoy the tussles with staff. I like parents' meetings too and have often come away from them stimulated, rarely bored. I find the community including the press a worthy challenge and mostly an ally. Yet I feel sad. Is this desire to have a happy face to the world one of the occupational hazards of the principalship, one of the signs of our vulnerability that we do not want to reveal? We believe it is necessary to have a joke for all occasions and an omnipotent constitution that allows people to bucket upon us all their garbage while we smile benignly. I desperately want to end this chapter on a happy note, but should I do this when that is not how I am feeling at the end of this session? I am sad and that is how I will end this chapter!

Notes

1 See the chapter 'Reculturing' where this idea is explored more thoroughly.
2 *The Link*, 29 August 1996, **18**, 26.
3 *The Link*, 15 August 1996, **18**, 25.

Chapter 3

The Cinderella Principal

She was the single artificier of the world
In which she sang. And when she sang, the sea,
Whatever self it had, became the self
That was her song, for she was the maker.
(Wallace Stevens, *The Idea of Order At Key West*)

Until a few centuries ago, the 'self' was not even considered as a concept. People
were units of society. They saw themselves mirrored in the social roles and structures of society and its duties. (Dinar Zohar and Ian Marshall, 1994, p. xi)

From Sadness

The last chapter ended on an introspective note. It was a chapter without a happy ending. When a person close to me read this chapter the comment was, 'Where is the
next page? You always end on a positive note.' Well, this chapter is the next page.

I wanted the last chapter to end as I had felt when I had written it. I wanted
to chronicle the event, to be true to how it had felt writing that chapter. It was
difficult to leave it like that. As Principal I do have a particular responsibility for
morale and I have interpreted this as needing always to be positive and constructive
even at the expense of my own feelings. In retrospect I wonder whether I have mis-
understood what constitutes morale. A proper appreciation of morale acknowledges
the negatives while also stating the positives. Being too positive means that the full
story isn't told and the result is that new principals have unrealistic expectations
of what is required of them. I am not suggesting principals' private lives should be
a matter for the school community. What I would like to see in our leaders is a
modelling of openness that allows a more realistic picture of the whole person to
be told. I am reminded that one of the senior members of our staff always makes a
point of saying at the first staff meeting, and at the first student assembly, that she
had a great holiday. She wants people to know that work is only a part of her life,
albeit an important part of it. The issue is not whether a holiday is good or bad but
that people can speak freely about their views.

So, returning to the ending of the last chapter, to the sadness: 'Where do I go
from here?'; 'What do I do with this?'; 'Am I in some sort of Cinderella state?';
'Do I do as Cinderella did — wait, hope and pray for someone to come and
save me or is there some initiative that I should be taking?' In the last questions
I also find my answer. I will consider 'The Cinderella Principal' next. The feelings

described in 'The Paranoid Principal', if ignored are destructive but if they are used to introduce the next set of dynamics, then they can be creative.

Not all sadness is for public discussion or public revelation. Sadness which arises out of difficult role tasks such as correcting someone, maybe even asking someone to leave the school, need to be dealt with in a different setting. The sadness needs to be shared but it cannot be done publicly. Here we could learn from the social workers who have an expectation of always being in supervision. This supervisor has no authority over them. The supervisor is like a mentor, someone with whom they can share their cases, their difficult moments. Maybe as principals we should be looking to create some supervision structure in which we can be nurtured. Maybe it is something that Associations of Principals could initiate. It is not quite the confessional of the Catholic Church although I know that to be useful and positive. Identifying personal loneliness is not the same as being preoccupied or excessively introspective, which might be the way some readers read the last chapter. Rather admitting to loneliness can lead us to talk to others, to enter into relationship whether inside or outside our community. That is the generative spirit that I am seeking, from sadness to action and then to community.

I have one further commentary upon 'The Paranoid Principal'. When I shared this paper with some colleagues who were chief executives in their organizations, only some of whom were school principals, it provoked a discussion about roles and relationships. One person said: 'Are we ever out of a role? We are either in the role of the principal, the parent, a friend, a lover.' This question, comment and subsequent discussion led one person to comment; 'I have a role, therefore I exist.' I have thought about this statement since and believe that it is an accurate description of how I feel. It is hard to imagine myself existing outside some sort of role. When I had my brain haemorrhage twenty years ago, my doctor said that I would never return to work. I was devastated more by this than the thought of death. 'Who would I be if I had no work to give me identity? I have roles, I enter into relationships, therefore I exist.' The philosopher who helps me make most sense of my human condition is Martin Buber. He talks about the relationships of 'I- It' and 'I- Thou'. We do not exist in a vacuum. The 'I' does not exist by itself. 'It is the relationship between the two ("I" and "Thou") which makes the subject and object what they are' (Weinstein, 1975, p. 20). We exist in relationships whether they be with objects, 'I- It', or with people, 'I- Thou'. I also like the way that Buber sees the relationship as being 'in the between', not held by one or the other.

If you are reading this book on the assumption that I am 'the successful principal' then I have to tell you now that your faith is misplaced. I would be more accurately seen as 'the learning principal'. What I can best model is not perfection but openness to learning. By inviting readers to learn about the many 'mes' in my many roles I hope that this honesty and modelling will help others to learn about the many 'thems' in their many roles.

Cinderella

The story of Cinderella conjures up images of fairy tales, of fantasy and of unreality. For this reason some may reject any discussion of the Cinderella principal.

Principals do not work in fairy tale settings. Schools are real places, with real people who exist to help students find empowerment. But there is another sense in which schools exist to make dreams come true, or is this a stereotype too?

And we all have dreams. A grateful and excited member of staff, while overseas on one year's leave from the school, wrote to me as follows: 'The strongest foundation for one's life and the cornerstone for reality is often a dream.' This member of staff had dreamed of this opportunity of travel as a student and planned for it as a member of staff. Now she is enjoying the fulfilment of that dream and she is even able to philosophize about it. But is this the same as Cinderella's dream which appears to offer hope but instead renders Cinderella passive, dependent on a rescue to save her?

On the surface, the story of Cinderella is deceptively simple. It tells the agonies of being a victim; of sibling rivalry; of wishes coming true; of the humble being elevated, of true merit being recognized even when hidden under rags; of virtue rewarded and evil punished — a straightforward moral tale. Without having to do anything herself, Cinderella was lifted above her circumstances and achieved her dream. The story of Cinderella has a number of characteristics that lead us into productive dialogue about the professional role of principals. In the course of this chapter we will look at the status (Cinders) of principals; leadership redefined to include courage; collaboration instead of (sibling) rivalry; victim mentality and the alternative of strategic thinking and, finally, gender stereotyping.

Status

Even the name communicates that Cinderella is of lowly status, literally living amongst the ashes. Linking Cinderella to the principalship immediately draws attention to the status of principals and of teachers. We hear so often that teachers and principals are poorly paid and do not have the status in the community as doctors, bankers or business people. Their professions are the Cinderella professions. Yet their work is not humble. Principals and teachers hold the future of our society in their hands to a significant extent. The roles of teacher and principal could and should be high profile, focusing the attention not only of the school students but of the community on learning, values and possibilities.

So why are we so undervalued? Is it the fault of others or our own fault? Is it, as Fullan (1996) suggests, that we cannot explain ourselves adequately? 'Critics are increasingly using clear language and specific charges, while educators are responding with philosophical rationales (eg we are engaged in active learning). Abstract responses to specific complaints are not credible' (p. 423).

Worse, are we not heard because we are not speaking out? I remember being both horrified and angry that the three most significant recent educational reports in Australia were chaired by people from business and not from education. Yet the truth is that the people who are most regularly being reported speaking on education are business people. When the media looks for a comment upon education, they are not turning to the universities. Why aren't principals using their role, status and education to speak out on issues of importance to the community? Are we in education so demoralized that we do not feel we deserve to have such an important role in society? Or is it a lack of courage? Our culture is such that we fear to be seen as a 'tall poppy' lest we are chopped off.

Is there a link between low status and the fact that teachers have allowed their teachers' union to speak for them? As a profession, teachers and principals have no voice. But as union members their union leaders can speak on their behalf about working conditions, salaries and even direct them to strike action.

Another possibility is that teachers and principals have lost their way in the midst of multiple, immediate, demanding tasks. We are so busy responding to the agenda of others that we have forgotten that our role is to lead, to be prophets, to articulate the new directions. Fullan talks about overload and fragmentation as two major problems for teachers (see chapter 6).

Perhaps we are not heard because we do not identify speaking as our primary task — we do not see ourselves as teaching the organization and the community about our organization and its goals. Charles Handy (1994) discusses the talking role of leaders. They need to be didactic in their message, always seeking opportunities to speak and to explain. They need to help their audience see the larger picture. While principals will live in the centre, they cannot afford to stay there isolated from their constituents. 'The life of the Federal President in a large organization tends to be one long teach-in. Successful Presidents and Prime Ministers know that their main task is to carry the people with them. Roosevelt with his fireside radio talks . . . Churchill with his wartime broadcasts., were all, in effect, running popular teach-ins' (p. 107).

In some ways this book, written by a practising principal, is a departure from the normal role of principal. What does a principal know? Unless the author of a book is an academic or a successful business person, what right do they have to be writing? Yet there can be something rich and stimulating in the personal reflections and readings of a person who lives in the centre and who is prepared to be honest about his/her experiences.

Consider the foolishness of this:

> 'The principal sat glaring rebelliously at the fire, her face animated and fiery. Her bosses were going to the ball tonight, and as a principal, there was no hope of her attending. She had examined their beautiful gowns and was jealous-fiercely angry at fate which allowed some to be chosen, others not. She wished desperately to attend the ball, but how? Should she hope, like Cinderella, for a fairy godmother to wave a magic wand and rescue her, or should she decide to go to the ball uninvited and perhaps even change their conception of what the ball should be?'

Leadership Redefined

Cinderella within her family was completely subordinate. She had no influence over her sisters or her mother. Her role was defined as a slave. There have been principals in similar situations who have responded by grovelling. They have even been known to purchase a hair shirt as a fashion garment. I would rate Cinderella's response as one better than that. She wanted and hoped for better.

Not all situations are as difficult to influence as the one in which Cinderella found herself but we all know the feeling of such powerlessness. Asserting oneself, finding one's voice and exercising leadership is not easy. In fact it is extraordinarily difficult and is often very dangerous personally. Perhaps that is why there are Cinderella principals who escape from the difficulties of the task by wishing for a fairy godmother to save them. From here it is a small step to blame others.

Sometimes it is hard to stay in the difficulties and ambiguities of the present. My experience is that I have a good idea and begin to work on it with enthusiasm. When the idea is good I find that others also like the idea and join in with excitement. The resultant project is off to a great start with support. It appears as if nothing can now stop the project. It is at this stage that trouble begins. First there is opposition, then loss of faith by a few or many. At that time I unfailingly ask myself, 'Why did I begin this project?' Everything was going along smoothly so why did I want to change anything?

It therefore was with some excitement and subsequent relief and insight that I read what was to me a new and operational definition of leadership. Vaill writes about 'leading people out of superficial tranquillity and into anxiety, and then into a feeling of a need for courage and then along the courage filled path itself' (p. 11).

As I thought about my experiences as principal, this description of leadership had a ring of truth. Often there is a sense of calm that is disturbed by the leadership. Maybe that is what leadership is, intervention! I remember well my recommendation that we as a school celebrate the year of the family. At the time it seemed like a good idea as it would bring our large school together with its extended family of ex-students, parents and other community members. The only place that could accommodate our school of 2200 students plus extended family was the Melbourne Tennis Centre. The sense of calm within the community was now disturbed by an idea, an opportunity to do something special and a number of us were excited at the prospect of this family event. The proposal was carefully considered, support to proceed was given and the work began. It was not long before anxiety set in. The venue has a capacity of 12,000 and a stage the size of a tennis court. Could we fill both of these? Then there was the cost of lighting and staging, not to mention the hiring cost of the centre not just for performance but also for the necessary rehearsals. We would need to attract 10,000 people and charge them a significant entrance fee to cover our costs.

This idea to stage a family event was definitely audacious. Critics reminded us that we were only a school and . . . well, schools are not places that could deliver the professionalism needed. Such questioning initially was interpreted as challenge and responded to appropriately but then we had new troubles. We could not get the tennis centre; then we could not obtain permission to perform the music and, always, there was the extreme pressure on those staff entrusted with the task of designing, rehearsing and delivering the production. My anxiety increased when opposition to the idea from within the student, parent and even Council bodies became more vocal. I responded with special presentations to all groups, talking about why we were undertaking this event and how it could be a memorable and worthwhile event for them personally. The critics made an impact upon us. We who were responsible for the idea and its implementation were left uncertain and began questioning the value of the event too. Should we proceed with our plans or cancel the event? Another question that we asked ourselves was why did we ever propose the idea. Situations like this test the courage of the principal because ultimately she/he will have to accept responsibility for a failure and, in this case, the event could have been a huge disaster. It was a moment of truth. At such a time the principal has to call upon personal reserves, both mental and spiritual, to counter the sick feeling of fear that can well up within to disempower him/her at a vital stage. Vaill describes what happens in a leader as she/he tries to manage this meeting of the inner consciousness of self with the turbulent outside world. It is not a quality like strength, or determination, or confidence but an interactive process.

> Our resolve, our faith, our clarity on what we should (must?) do moves: it ebbs and flows, sometimes wavers to the point of disappearance, sometimes rings through us as a powerful affirming chord. (*ibid*, p. 9)

Courage is more like a dynamic process where the leader has to be proactive, in touch with self and part of the real world. It is the opposite of wishing for a fairy godmother to wave a magic wand to make the problem disappear.

Now perhaps the reader can understand the release that I felt when I first read Vaill. This was work worthy of the title, principal, 'leading people out of superficial tranquillity and into anxiety and then into a feeling of a need for courage and then along the courage filled path itself'. Maybe the principal does have to find the lost sand shoe, to reply to the letter but more importantly the test of her/his leadership will be the ability to project a vision of what might be, make judgments and then call forth courage in moments of dilemma and ambiguity.

Robert Fulghum (1986) invites us all, especially those who lead, to consider: 'That imagination is far stronger than knowledge . . . That dreams are more powerful than facts . . . That hope always triumphs over experience' (p. viii). Leadership involves using your imagination for your community's good, for the good of others as well as yourself. Leadership also involves courage to face and deal with the anxiety and ambiguities that follow.

Collaboration

Another feature of the Cinderella story is the sibling rivalry. Dare this be discussed? I cannot speak from experience about government schools but I can say that in independent schools there is significant rivalry among neighbouring school principals. At times when enrolments are short this rivalry will be more open and pronounced. There is not only the quest for students, but there is also competition for the best students academically, musically and in sport. There is competition for staff and for public recognition. While there are professional organizations devoted to collegiality, their attention is given to safe agendas, more peripheral matters or outside threats from government, unions and the like. Furthermore, in these organizations there is significant rivalry for status amongst principals and schools. We would all agree that collegiality among principals is a good idea but it is a soft and fuzzy notion when schools and principals are struggling in difficult times.

As well as sibling rivalry we have sibling conflict. A conflict can be as small as a disagreement or as large as a court case. It is not easy for us to acknowledge that even minor conflicts exist among principals. Many of us have been educated to see conflict as failure, lack of love or respect. I have not found much written about conflict between principals although there is a substantial body of literature about conflict within schools. In this context I found Johnson and Johnson's analysis helpful. They write about conflict-negative schools which assume that all conflicts are destructive and have no value. In such schools, there is an attempt to eliminate conflicts by suppressing, avoiding and denying their existence. In contrast they describe conflict-positive schools where conflicts are considered inevitable, healthy and valuable. In such schools, conflicts are not feared as problems. Instead the conflicts are seen as positive, creating feelings of excitement, interest and a sense of promise. Conflicts, they assert, 'can become destructive when they are denied, suppressed or avoided' (Johnson and Johnson, 1995, p. 15). It would seem reasonable to assume that this would also be true for conflict outside the school such as between principals. Sibling rivalry and conflict are natural, likely to be unpleasant but not something to be ignored or suppressed. They could add a new and positive dimension to our collaborative life.

Collegiality can only happen when there is a willingness and ability to tolerate differences. This can be a problem for principals when their schools have been increasingly trying to differentiate themselves for competitive purposes and, in some cases, for survival. Examples of these differentiations include school size (big is beautiful, small is personal); gender-related issues (single sex or coeducational); curriculum (academic or vocational); values (individual or group) and fees (low fee or high fee). Instead of this promoting dialogue, inspiring creativity and nurturing respect for difference, it becomes one more obstacle to collaboration. There is some similarity here to nationalism and identity. One differentiates oneself and in the differentiation there are gains but one has to be careful that the negatives do not exceed the gains. Two writers recently noted the lessons of Bosnia. Korgaonkar and Jones writing in *The Christian Science Monitor* (19 April 1996) under the heading 'Bosnian lessons: The myths of nationalism', wrote, 'Nationalism is less a matter of deeply entrenched or "natural" differences than exaggerated and politically encouraged differences'. Fullan and Hargreaves (1991) are amongst the few who have addressed in the educational literature the role of collaboration. 'The articulation of different voices may create initial conflict, but this should be confronted and worked through' (p. 93). This is easier said than done but the need for it is becoming more appreciated and urgent.

Unfortunately the role of principal itself conspires against us achieving collaboration. We live a lot of our time in the isolation of our lonely offices. The job is so consuming and the discretionary time so scant, that the time for building trust, for networking, for sharing, for learning from and working together with other principals is limited. Finding time for principals to meet in a collegiate manner represents both a problem and a possible solution. An individual principal working alone in her/his school will not be able to solve the problems confronting her/his school let alone the problems confronting society. Yet when principals come together with time for joint planning, assisting each other professionally, collectively reflecting on what is happening and undertaking action research, answers will be found. A new inclusive culture in and between schools is needed that sees collaboration as a help not an obstacle to solving the problems in individual schools. Schools are not just places where young people learn but are places of learning in their own right. Traditionally, there has been an intellectual gap between the researchers or scholars (the so called 'gatekeepers' of knowledge) and the teachers and principals who were the recipients of knowledge and this has been a significant reason for the inferiority that teachers and principals feel as professionals. Today a new type of teacher and principal must emerge, one who can generate new knowledge and not be simply a transmitter of knowledge. Within Methodist Ladies' College we are addressing this through a learning network. Directed by a member of staff, Mary Mason, the network sponsors research into learning, the sharing of this knowledge and the rethinking of the fundamental tasks of schooling.

The organizations for principals could be structured to nurture collegiality. This is not currently the case. In fact a recent decision of the Association of Heads in Australia shortened the duration of the National Conference. The reason for this was that we are 'too busy' to give time to sharing, building trust. Perhaps the time has come to change this. Our individual way forward is becoming more dependent on successful collaboration. So it is that schools need to think about strategic thinking not just for their individual school but for all schools. Our joint organizations need to give priority to collaborative planning. While in schools there is idealism, energy and inventiveness, it seems that between schools this is harder to harness in a collaborative process. Supporting each other could help make a difference in our own schools and in society, but we have to believe this before we will resource it with our time.

In considering sibling rivalry, to this point I have considered it only between principals and schools. It exists also within schools among staff. A member of staff wrote to me:

> You say that you want collaboration and collegiality between all staff, that we are to work together, yet when conflict arises your default mechanism of hierarchy always overcomes these words. The subconscious is always stronger than the conscious. You cannot domesticate this new vision of collaboration into past methods of teacher control.

To address this there has to be a new openness of individuals where they are free to express their views such as we have just read. There needs to be a focus on attempting to develop a collegial atmosphere in which conflict can be handled in a constructive way such that it introduces new ideas, even excitement. There needs to be a focus on the whole and less on the parts. The literature notes that 'improving schools' are characterized not so much by meeting the individual needs of staff members but by 'promoting staff development that has a whole school focus, that supports and extend collaborative processes' (Russ, 1995, p. 5). We school principals need to remember the important role played by many.

> Principals are important: they may even be critical; but they are not the only initiators of change. They are not our last and only hope. Leadership is interactive. A school shapes a principal as much as a principal shapes a school. (Starratt, 1986, p. 7)

Tolerating differences is not a universal truth. This will be one of the tests of our ideal of a democracy in the near future. There are certain truths that we hold about individual liberty that should not let us tolerate certain behaviours that are tolerated in some other societies.

Strategic Thinking

Cinderella sees herself as a victim — within the family and within her culture. She does not believe that she can save herself. She believes that she is dependent on others and, in the first instance, her saviour has to be supernatural. Principals who have been unable to assert their leadership sometimes end up feeling the victims in a power play in which they had little authority. From here it is a small step to blame others for the predicament in which they find themselves. The government has not provided the money; the council does not understand; the staff are ruled by the unions; the parents have the wrong values or the students are lazy. None of these groups can be equated with powerful fairy godmothers who can grant wishes. Having said that, it is not asserted that principals of schools, working alone, can achieve all their goals.

Consider this alternative version of the Cinderella story, written by a year 9 student:

> But no one could suppress the Fire-ella principal. A hessian sack was quickly converted to a ball gown, elegant in its basic simplicity. Her hair brushed and shining, she looked quaint, beautiful in her own way. Undeterred by her lack of transport, she set off for the ball, trudging many miles through sludge and bog.

Schools need this Fire-ella principal. It needs to be emphasized that schools are institutions and, as such, are social technologies. With them we can manage our social activities so that children are educated to maturity, economic activity is promoted, social cohesion is fostered. Thus those who accept leadership within these institutions have great trust placed in them with consequent responsibilities. Foremost among these responsibilities is the future.

A future is chosen and then it must be worked for. Even the decision not to act is in effect the choice of a future which is an extrapolation of the present. Thus the role of the principal is primarily a proactive one. You cannot afford to sit back and wait for someone to save you. If someone is going to save others then it is reasonable to expect that those entrusted by the community with leadership would be the ones to do that saving. This implies that a particular skill required of a principal is that of strategic thinking.

If a particular environment is stable, then there exists little need for strategic thinking. The managers in such a situation can respond by ensuring that the organization is doing what it has always done more effectively and more efficiently. A classic example of this was Henry Ford's manufacture of the T-Model car. The T-Model was an extraordinarily successful invention. Ford was rightly proud of his car and he resisted every attempt by his staff and by his son to change to a new model. He improved the quality and cheapened its price by introducing assembly line manufacture and improved his marketing of the car. Eventually, falling sales and the greater success of his competitors forced him to acknowledge that a new model was necessary. Ford's environment had changed and he was forced to change with it.

The environment today is not stable. Yesterday is different from today which is again different from tomorrow. Our society has to cope with new values, new technology, multiculturalism, changing job opportunities, multiple careers, an ageing population, changes in family structure.

It is unfortunately true that we all have a tendency to look backwards rather than forwards, running more on memory rather than on imagined and chosen futures. Strategies for today and tomorrow need to take advantage of these new realities and convert the present turbulence into opportunity. Not only success, but survival, demands that schools take the long range view. When we think of education, it is therefore particularly inappropriate to be looking back. Toffler (1970), in *Future Shock* said, 'All education springs from some image of the future. If the image of the future held by societies is grossly inaccurate, its educational system will betray its youth' (p. 3)

Unlike many institutions, schools have their primary impact in the distant future when students will be graduating from school. Programs in the early years of school have to guess at the nature of the world in twelve years time. Consequently schools must operate with a long-range perspective in mind. Strategic thinking in schools will envisage therefore a planning horizon of decades rather than days. Furthermore, to be consistent with the calling as educational professionals, the future is not just what is predicted. It is a chosen future that is worked for tomorrow, shaped and created from what we believe, want and can envisage.

Thinking strategically is even more important as we approach a new century and enter into a new paradigm where the focus is no longer on teaching but on learning, no longer on classes but individuals in different size groups, no longer on separately resourced schools but on multiple sites that are community embedded where learning can occur. What we seek now is a conceptualization and practice in schooling that does not yet exist.

Drucker (1995) takes this challenge further.

> As knowledge becomes the resource of the post-capitalist society, the social position of the school as 'producer' and 'distributive channel' of knowledge, and its monopoly, are bound to change. And some of the competitors are bound to succeed . . . Indeed, no other institution faces challenges as radical as those that will transform the school. (p. 203)

It is hard to think of the future when our mind is limited by our past experiences. Furthermore we continue to define the present in terms of the past. The car when it first emerged was described as a horseless carriage. The word 'wireless' continued well past the time when wirelesses ceased to have wires. We have had electronic funds for more than ten years but we persist in describing this as 'the cashless economy'. Until recently mobile phones were called 'cordless telephones'. For twenty years numerous groups have been practising leadership from within the group. The groups are still referred to as 'leaderless groups' on the assumption that all groups must have one nominated leader. In education when we talk of the school of tomorrow, we use descriptions such as 'a school without walls', 'the virtual campus' and 'the dispersed campus'. Once again we are attempting to define the future by the past. The search is on for a new word for school that will not look back to what has happened before but relate to the new tasks and the new settings. Is it possible, then, to describe and define what will be the principal's task for tomorrow? It is in the identification of the new role that the real challenge lies for those who would lead.

The principal has a primary role, not just in wishing for, but in shaping tomorrow. He/she needs information from all sources. There are the soft insights from personal experiences and from the experience of others on her/his council, from parents, staff and students. Then there is the hard data from academic and market research. Strategic thinking requires all this information and will use it to broaden the consideration of issues rather than to discover the one right answer. Strategic thinking also involves intuition and creativity. The outcome of strategic thinking is an integrated perspective of the enterprise, an articulated vision of direction but unfortunately a conception that is, at this stage, relatively imprecise. Real strategic change requires not merely rearranging the established categories but inventing new ones. Such is the magnitude of the challenge that confronts principals.

Unfortunately it is not possible simply to extrapolate from the past. While certain repetitive patterns, such as seasons, may be predictable, the forecasting of discontinuities, such as technological innovation, events in other countries or competitors cannot be predicted. While something will be gained by such an extrapolation, and this needs to be done, a bigger jump is needed if a principal is to think strategically. The larger picture needs to be seen. Once that is done, then the principal is in a position to begin the complex and time demanding task of strategic planning, of articulation and elaboration of the strategies that will deliver the chosen future.

Backcasting (Hooker, 1994) offers a new way to view the principal's role. With this method one chooses a future, such as establishing a learning organization, and then works back from there in stages. The methodology involves placing yourself in a suitable time in the future and then considering imaginatively what alternative possibilities are available, examining what are the constraints and considering the stages that have to be passed through to reach the present. At the beginning of each stage it is necessary to identify what must be done to ensure that by the end of that stage the desired outcome will be achieved. This process is repeated for each alternative future that is considered. Then comes the task of choosing the most appropriate alternative future designs for their feasibility, costs and benefits. And then you work your way forwards in time to realize that design. Periodically it will be necessary to revise the plan. We must check regularly that the environment has not changed in ways not anticipated.

Hooker notes that backcasting surfaces the values that are inherent in every choice and integrates these with facts.

> Every design, every choice among future alternatives, is an integrated choice of a set of values realised as particular facts, as actual features of our future world. But when the world is an artefact made by us this separation is no longer possible and we must teach ourselves to think through both together.

There are other good features of this backcasting approach. It sharpens the capacity to critically extract information. It empowers and motivates people.

It is important that we do not take a narrow view of education, say as purely skills acquisition. The challenges to any society are not confined to economic ones. A professor of philosophy, C.A. Hooker, in a paper entitled, 'Brave new world or grave new world? Education for the future/futures in education' lists four challenges that will have a profound effect on the future of Australia and its people. Firstly social unity and cultural diversity. This is not just a superficial challenge but, in fact, a fundamental one because Australia needs to give serious thought to what the underlying social agreements are to be that will make diversity tolerable without producing chaos. For example, 'I can tolerate your different religious practices as long as you do not wish to use them to suspend the due process of law when you and I have a conflict'. The second challenge is economic prosperity. The third is the social quality of life with a particular focus on family, neighbourhood and community life. The fourth is the environmental quality of life. Hooker makes the point that our children will have to pay both the environmental and economic costs of decisions taken in the past.

Gender

Is it significant that Cinderella is a female?

I am aware that this is dangerous ground on which to walk. My reason for choosing Cinderella was not to examine gender but to contrast active and passive leadership and to consider stereotypes. Colette Dowling (1981), the author of *The Cinderella Complex*, believes that we are talking about a female Cinderella. Females are taught that they have an out — that some day, in some way, they are going to be saved. The author describes this as the Cinderella complex. 'Everything about the way we, as women, were raised, told us we would be part of someone else. That we would be protected, supported, caught up by wedded happiness until the day we died' (*ibid*).

Any chosen future surely will reject most of the social distinctions we now draw between women and men. It is important to dismantle those social practices which maintain any dominance of one sex over the other and address the social inequality that generally exists. Segal has argued that gender difference is not true difference at all. The good qualities that are described as masculine such as courage, strength and skill, for instance can be found in women. The good qualities ascribed often to women such as tenderness, the ability to feel and express feeling exist in men too. All good qualities are available to all and should be recognized and acclaimed wherever they occur regardless of the sex of the person. 'Any society we set out to organise anew would surely be a celebration of multiplicity and individual difference' (Segal, 1987, p. xv).

In management theory gender has come to the fore. Today there has been almost a rush to claim new ground for values that have been stereotyped as female — sensitive listening as opposed to high talking, horizontal networks rather than hierarchical structures, family and community not individual selfishness, collaboration and not competition, process (enjoying the journey) and not product/goal focused. Yet the reality seems to be that both, not either or, are valuable. We need competition and cooperation, listening and talking, collaboration and hierarchy together with process and product.

It would appear that for women, the glass ceiling and the glass slipper both have been broken! This is a fact to be celebrated. Yet it also needs to be noted that the crashing of the glass is only the first step. Identity does not automatically follow, a fact that modern men would admit as they are struggling too, with the task of finding a new identity.

Chapter 4

The Empty Principal

We cannot spend in good works more time than we have earned in meditation. (Rabbi Moshe Leib)

Are there any school principals who have not felt at some stage, and maybe many times, that they have so depleted their energy sources that there is nothing left, that they are running on empty? Fullan (1996) writes:

> Overload and fragmentation are two major barriers to education reform, and they are related. Overload is the continuous stream of planned and unplanned changes that affect the school. Educators must contend constantly with multiple innovations and myriad policies and they must deal with them all at once. Overload is compounded by a host of unplanned changes and problems, including technological developments, shifting demographics, family and community complexities, economic and political pressures and more. Fragmentation occurs when the pressures — and even the opportunities for reform work at cross purposes or seem disjointed and incoherent. . . . Overload and fragmentation . . . take their toll on the most committed, who find that will alone is not sufficient to achieve or sustain reform. (p. 420)

In My Emptiness

With depleted energy resources, I was attracted in 1994 to a conference, 'Sources of Renewal for Educators' run by the Friends' Council on Education at their retreat centre in Pendle Hill, Pennsylvania. The conference theme was to explore the sources of spiritual vitality in our personal and professional lives. I decided to attend the conference and to stay for a week after the conference as a 'sojourner' in this Quakers retreat. This had to be one of the best decisions that I had made in my life. This conference gave me a new sensitivity to myself, a new awareness of others and a better understanding of the educational task. The conference was led by Dr Paul Lacey. Paul was a quiet, gentle person, open to others, not afraid of showing personal emotion, being present in discussions and bringing not only his personal experiences but richness from his study of English literature. The style of the conference was simple: some introductory comments, a reading or two, an invitation for us to spend time writing and then, subsequently, to share our writing if we felt we would like to do this. There were no prizes for the best written material or the most original presentation. Nothing was collected afterwards but I am pleased to have copies of my writing, upon which I can now reflect. Furthermore Paul did not carry a briefcase of reading home that night. He was free to think and prepare.

As I reflected on my writing experience, I thought about the students' experiences of writing. The things many students like least is having their work marked. The thing teachers like least is marking students' work. Yet the strange thing is that schools seem to be organized around the setting of assignments and their marking rather than the personal discovery that students may achieve from writing.

Initially I found writing difficult. I thought about what others might say when they heard it read to them. After all, most of my writing to this point had been for other people — a report for Council, a letter to parents, minutes from meetings and, of course, exam papers. This writing was for me. I was to be the audience. Furthermore, in this case the value was more in the process of writing, as I sorted out my thoughts and feelings, than in the product. The word 'writing' was not to be a noun but an active verb! This writing was a chance to explore some personal issues. If I felt that there was something to be gained for me or the audience, then I could choose to share these insights by reading my writing.

The writing task was to be enjoyed for itself and in the process of our full participation we will get in touch with ourselves, with others and with the universe. I remember Paul Lacey saying that, if we only think of meaning as something which must be distilled from our daily lives, we will be frustrated and unhappy much of the time. The secret is to find the meaning diffused in our lives, not separate from the living. The metaphor used was of fish breathing water, drawing the life giving oxygen from the medium in which they live and move and have their being. This is a metaphor for living life, focusing on the being rather than on the doing and by this means getting in touch with self, others and the universe. Each moment is important for itself.

> In Buddhism, there is a word, apranihita. It means wishlessness, or aimlessness. The idea is that we do not put anything ahead of ourselves and run after it. When we practise sitting meditation, we sit just to enjoy the sitting. We do not sit in order to become enlightened, a Buddha, or anything else. Each moment we sit brings us back to life, and therefore, we sit in a way that we enjoy our sitting the entire time. (Thich Nhat Hanh, 1994, p. 243)

As I reflected on my school days, once again a contrast was apparent. It is not the grade at the end of school but the learning as you make your way to your finals that matters. How often as a principal have I been more concerned with the destination and ignored the journey, with doing rather than being? 'I will take time for myself when the holidays come', has been my attitude. But is this good enough?

One of the readings that Paul Lacey gave us was from a poem by Michael Pettit, *1000 Cranes*. I have extracted some of his words:

> What if, in answer to need or pain,
> you were to fold 1000 cranes?
> . . .

Believing with each motion
you move closer to your wish,
. . .

Doubting, for that is human,
for the moment what you have begun
. . .
What would you ask to happen
that had not happened before then,
when you were at long last finished and knew
your longing and journeying are never through?

My reflection on that poem was: 'Be careful that this is not you, David. All this trouble for what? Now is a good time to rethink what your life is all about.' The notes continued: 'I wonder if, in a few years' time, I will reflect on my time as principal and wonder if it was like folding 1000 cranes — that I lived for extrinsic goals, for deadlines that in retrospect do not seem all that important? Will I consider that I was blinded by the lights in other people's eyes?'

One Hour

While in the community I learnt to appreciate the truth in some of the Hasidic tales as reported by Martin Buber. One such tale is ascribed to Rabbi Moshe Leib. He said 'a human being who has not a single hour for his (her) own every day is not a human being'. Now here was a personal challenge. My mind set, my upbringing, tells me that I am there to serve others, that enjoyment comes through ministration and commitment. I am not sure if I can blame the Protestant ethic for this mind set, but I am sure that I bring this attitude to my work. When I do things for myself like having a haircut, shopping, reading a book, meditating, it feels as if I am stealing time from my work. Even when on holidays or weekends — and a significant part of this book has been written during these times — I have work to do. I see this as normal. I even feel fortunate that my job is so interesting and absorbing! But how can I continue this way? I can rationalize this by noting that unless space is created for renewal, it is difficult to imagine how there can be any freshness or receptiveness to others. I don't want to be a leader who, when asked a question, gives the same tired old answers over and over. People who show no freshness from reading or reflection bore me. But Paul Lacey wants me to go further than this. He wants me to enjoy a moment of meditation, not for the benefits that it might bring, but for itself. What kind of person would I become if I did this?

There is a Zen story that makes a similar point.

Nan-in, a Japanese master during the Meija era (1868–1912), received a university professor who came to inquire about Zen.

Nan-in served tea. He poured his visitor's cup full, and then kept on pouring. The professor watched the overflow until he no longer could restrain himself. 'It is over-full. No more will go in!'

'Like this cup', Nan-in said, 'you are full of your own opinions and speculations. How can I show you Zen unless you first empty your cup?' (Reps, 1957, p. 17)

Recently I stood for reelection to the Standing Committee of the Association of Heads of Independent Schools in Australia. I was unsuccessful. If this had happened earlier in my life I might well have looked for explanations as to why I had not been reelected — may even have blamed certain circumstances for the event. This time I decided not to look for excuses and chose instead to feel, as I had been taught by the Quaker conference. I allowed myself to go internal, to feel what it was like to lose, to be passed over by my peers, to be placed after others on the ballot. What I attempted to do was to integrate my feeling with my thinking. I was upset. 'So this is how my peers feel about me.' On previous occasions of personal loss I would not have spoken openly about my feelings. However, this time I decided to say to some of my friends how disappointed I was, and how sad I was feeling. Their response, which could well have been mine to them on previous occasions, was to say, 'Don't worry about it, you should have been elected. I don't understand why you weren't'.

I found it interesting that my friends did not want to stay with my sadness. They wanted to hurry me past this point and have me think positively about tomorrow and even today. Yet it was at this time that Rabbi Moeshe Leib's statement came back to me — 'a human being who has not a single hour for his (her) own every day is not a human being'. I needed to feel what it was like to be elected one year and not reelected the next year. I wanted to feel the loss of role, the disappointment of failure, because this would extend my knowledge of myself and would assist me in the future when I would work with other people in similar situations. There is a sense in which, unless you have an inner life, you have no resources upon which to draw in times of need. Without an inner life you have neither the experience nor the energy to deal with the inner lives of other people.

Paul Lacey (1993) has published a book called *Running on Empty*. In this book he rephrases Rabbi Lieb's expression as questions.

'You who draw on resources of your inner lives to care for, comfort and teach others, what help will you be able to give, if you never refresh your inner lives?'

'Are you so sure of your humanity, your inner resources, that you can take them for granted?'

'What practical care do you show, in institutional terms, for the spiritual health of those you work with? Do you respect and protect the hour for oneself they, and you, need?' (p. 4)

In our group discussion of this personal hour, some members drew attention to the fact that they cannot begin the day without a cup of coffee. I know there are some who, as part of their religious communion, spend a half hour in a quiet time with scriptures and in prayer. Others spend time in meditation. All of this tends to be in private. What would happen if someone came to school and said 'The next half hour is mine. Please do not disturb me.' Could we accommodate this?

I remember Paul Lacey challenging us at the conference about not being first to school and not being last away. I remember laughing at his story, yet when I returned to school I noted that I was disappointed if I wasn't the first in the office and was making an excuse if I wasn't the last to leave. Even more disturbing was the fact that another senior member of staff was making a similar excuse when she left 'early' at 5.30pm. Where is the time for self-renewal, for family, for friends? Running on empty is a definite possibility when one behaves in that way.

Silence

Not being a Quaker, one of the most surprising things that I discovered was the value of silence. At the conference Paul would read a poem, make a statement and then there was silence. There was no embarrassment at the silence. As I looked around the group, people had moved inside themselves while they were thinking, feeling and reflecting. Five minutes might pass, sometimes even longer, then someone would make a statement. The first statement may or may not elicit a response from another member of the group. Alternatively another person may make a statement. Members of the group did not have to say 'I hear what you say' and then make some supporting comment of 'That's interesting.' or 'That's good'. It was taken for granted that people were listening and did appreciate the honesty and the significance of the statement by the speaker. To me this was a new and exciting world. I found this a wonderful opportunity to understand more about myself, to integrate past events with present experiences and future aspirations. I also found this a community in which I could share, unself-consciously, some of these revelations about myself.

What was most surprising about this experience was that it wasn't egocentric. Even though people often closed their eyes and breathed deeply, apparently isolating themselves from others, there was a real sense of a joined community. While the eyes were closed there was a sense of being part of a larger whole and that the other members of this whole were known intimately. What sense would a community like this make of those statements, 'eyeball to eyeball', or 'one on one'? The idea of not speaking directly and personally would not have occurred to them!

I was so excited by this discovery of the integration of personal space with community that I was determined to bring this back to Methodist Ladies' College. I have to report that I failed miserably with this task. I lacked the courage to carry it off effectively. It always seemed that there was a lot of resistance and, of course, practical issues to be dealt with first! When I set the agenda for meetings, I nominated time for reflection but I did not follow through and provide it. I was too aware that people were in 'action' mode, that they had only enough time for the work that we had to accomplish. In one school meeting the staff even articulated this feeling: 'We do not have time for being, only for doing'.

At the Quaker conference, one of the Hasidic tales we examined was *Silence and Speech*. It was written about the period of Napoleon. It too was gathered by Martin Buber.

A man had taken upon himself the discipline of silence and for three years had spoken no words save those of the Torah and of prayer. Finally the Yehudi sent for him: 'Young man', he said, 'how is it that I do not see a single word of yours in the world of truth?'

'Rabbi', said the other to justify himself, 'why should I indulge in the vanity of speech? Is it not better just to learn and to pray?'

'If you do that', said the Yehudi, 'not a word of your own reaches the world of truth. He who only learns and prays is murdering the word of his own soul. What do you mean by "vanity of speech"? Whatever you have to say can be vanity or it can be truth. And now I am going to have a pipe and some tobacco brought for you to smoke tonight. Come to me after the Evening Prayer and I shall teach you how to talk'.

They sat together the whole night. When morning came, the young man's apprenticeship was over.

What caught my attention in this tale was the communication that occurred just by sitting together. So my reflection looked at the idea of silence, its power and in my case its unused potential.

When other members of our group came to share their reflection on this tale, I was initially shocked at how different their reflections were and then saddened by their experience. One person described how she had been silenced by the education that she had received too. Another person said that his schooling had deadened his spirit of learning. Another person said, 'I have no wisdom to add to the world of truth'. Another person spoke about how life had gone out of the young person. What kind of educational system have we created that graduates could feel like that?

One of the crazy things I did on my return to school was to set up a room that was to be used by people who wanted to have some time by themselves. The room was established and yet no one used it. I was surprised by this fact until I reflected that I too had not used that room. Another idea I tried was to create a half-hour on one day each week which was to be personal time for all staff. I set up a committee to explore the possibilities of this. The committee was enthusiastic. The staff as a whole saw merit in personal time. They were delighted that I was acknowledging the pressure under which they work. Under the guidance of the committee, we even got to try personal time on one day. We closed the whole school down for staff but we did not try to do it for students. That was to come next! We chose a lunch time for this experiment and had only a minimum staff on for supervision. Once again this was an idea that did not work. People said they would prefer to choose their personal times when they were in the mood. While the staff are used to my crazy ideas, these ones they felt were too much!

Upon reflection I now acknowledge that the best chance I have for introducing personal change is to model these changes within myself. It is interesting that, as

I have been writing this section, I have got back in touch with the experiences I had with the Quakers. I am remembering and valuing time and commitment for writing and reflecting. I am once again resolved to personalize the time we have together as a staff. This time I won't try for an organizational change. Instead I will focus on some personal behaviour modification. I resolve not to be the first to school, to take time to have lunch in the staff room, to talk openly but not boringly about my need for some personal space and actually take some time for it. In addition we could try some organizational changes. One such change, which I know that staff would like, is the provision of mental health days for staff who are stressed, days that can be taken without having to claim that they are physically ill.

In response to my initiatives, one subject coordinator wrote:

> I feel much more in tune with the notion of creating time for teachers in their working alone and together than for providing them with a personal space for half-an-hour. I want them to have space to reflect, learn, interact and 'to be' in their work. From this could follow personal growth as they become receptive listeners to themselves and to others.

What is Our Work?

If we can reconceptualize the nature of our work then the need to run on empty may be avoided. It is so easy for us to be busy. More than likely we will do the easy things first as that provides the satisfaction of having at least some things finished. But are these the important items? Will they have the most leverage? Senge defines leverage in organizations as 'small, well-focused actions (which) can sometimes produce significant, enduring improvements, if they're in the right place' (Senge, 1992, p. 64). A friend of mine has the expression 'keep the "think" to "work" ratio high'. Another person tells me to 'work smart'. But what does this mean in practice? Professor Judith Chapman has helped me make more sense of this dilemma. Speaking at an educational conference, Judith suggested that the work ethic of the twentieth century might be replaced in the twenty-first century by the learning ethic. At present I conceive of work and learning as separate and try to do my work and then, in my non-existent spare time, I undertake my learning. As a university student, learning was my work. As a school principal, learning continues to be my work, yet I find it hard to give it the priority in my office.

To give more priority to my learning, and the learning of the staff, means that someone else has to undertake the tasks that will be left unattended. But there is no money available for increased staff. Around the world we are seeing a proportional decrease in the money being made available to education. Governments are being made smaller, the population is ageing and this ageing population is much more interested in money being spent on their health rather than on the education of youth who do not seem to appreciate it. Yet the task in education is becoming more complex and more demanding. Where will we find the resources? The need for ongoing professional development, for time for professional dialogue, must be met partly within the school day. How do we do this without increasing staff?

One way is to rethink how teachers spend their time. We are trying to do this at Methodist Ladies' College with varying degrees of success. Our major focus has been to question the assumption that all learning and teaching is to occur in a class setting of twenty to thirty students. We have introduced lectures to the whole year level of 300+ students and staff in which all, staff and students, learn together. This has reduced preparation time for staff and introduced stimulating ideas from people outside the school. Two classes working together means that students enjoy two teachers, their different ideas and interactions and the teachers can specialize in different parts of the curriculum. As well it means that one teacher can be out of the classroom researching, or talking with a small group of students. One teacher wrote: 'I cannot tell you the joy I have working with another teacher.' Then there are times when the students do not have to be supervised on a class basis. Once the focus is on learning and not upon teaching, students take more responsibility and teachers find that they have time to meet, plan and learn too.

We are also trying to rethink the roles of teachers and of students. We have a situation where there are 2000+ computers in the school, most of them privately owned as mobile computers. When we changed our internal mail system from CC Mail to Pegasus, it meant that every computer had to have new software added. People needed to be taught how to use the new software. We initially planned that the technical staff would gradually work through the school calling in computers, so many a day. This meant a long period of time would pass before everyone was back on the internal e-mail — an intolerable thought for those locked out. Employ more staff, was one suggestion and, in fact, additional staff were employed. This still didn't solve the problem because these technical staff had to deal with other issues like printers, networks, failures in different computers.

The greatest resource available to us that we had not really utilized was students. Why did we not think immediately of them or, even more importantly, why did they not immediately suggest this solution to us? Is our culture to ignore the skills of students? The reality is that many of our students would be delighted to help and have the technical skills and knowledge to do it. We have created a culture in schools that does not provide us with a way of easily accessing this help. To state this more strongly, we have created a dependency culture with the adults as experts. To help us change our culture at Methodist Ladies' College, we gave two of our students scholarships to travel overseas to an American setting where the students do more than load software. In the chosen American schools, students run the network, repair computers, design and maintain the home page. It was easy to choose competent and worthy students. There were lots with the knowledge and skills. Our students returned, excited by what they had learnt, yet they found it very hard to make changes at Methodist Ladies' College. Staff regarded these young experts as students to whom real authority could not be given. We also provided a scholarship for an American student who had been a senior student manager, on networks and on the e-mail, to come to our school for three weeks. At the end of the first week the American student saw me and said: 'You have wasted your money bringing me out here. While I have been entertained, I haven't been able to do any work.'

I was upset by the relative failure of what seemed like an inspired idea. Why couldn't the staff have given students more space? Yet staff were taking their responsibility seriously. After all, they would be held responsible if the system failed. Yet would they be held responsible under a new student-staff partnership? As I thought about it more, I decided that the failure was more my fault. I had misread the school culture. I had seen it as more flexible, more open to change and more accommodating of initiative than it was. In retrospect I realized that the students needed a staff sponsor or advocate in our current culture. A staff member needed to accompany the students so that, when the students returned and began working on the computers and training other students in this role, the accompanying staff member could be working with our staff to help them understand the changing roles for students. In retrospect this makes more sense and fits with the idea of reculturing, a topic that I take up more fully in chapter 9. A major plus with initiatives such as this one, had it worked, is that they would not only be self-funding but that they would release staff time for other work including staff learning.

The reality is that in schools we need to be looking for some bold new initiatives that are cost-neutral. To find them we will need to take some risks. It is imperative that we create some time for thinking, dialogue and planning by our staff. We need to look for initiatives that will leverage this scarce resource. In that way we may be able to break out of our present practice of running on memory, which we end up doing because there is no time for planning alternative ways. We need to make the rhetoric about both students and teachers as 'learners and teachers together' a reality. Unless we can do this, we who lead will continue to run on empty, and many young people will continue to be silenced by their education.

Living Community

Since my Quaker experience I have changed my educational goal from the 'intentional creation of a learning community' to the 'intentional creation of a living and learning community'. I wish to place a greater emphasis on our living together, our sharing, our interdependence and our individual lives within that community. Education is more than academic learning. It includes four essential elements: learning to learn; life skills; personal growth; community experience.

A family community, for example, has meals together, shares tasks and responsibilities, spends time together in relaxed settings, goes on outings and pays attention to individual happenings such as birthdays. Why can't we accommodate some of this within our structure? As a school we need to find new ways of celebrating our life together. The church with its seasons and feast days suggests to us that we could have days and events that have particular meaning for us as a community.

Such a family image will not please all. Some people choose to live alone. Others are very private. It is not being asserted that staff must make the school community their life. But it is asserted that what is expected of an adult in a school situation is more than coming to a class period and 'teaching a subject'. Real participation in community is important.

A look over the horizon in education might well see schools as dramatically different places. Their task will go beyond the present narrow confines of academic curriculum and the staff of these community centres will have new specialists including doctors, physiotherapists, dieticians, religious leaders, sports and music specialists as well as teachers and social workers.

The Potlatch

Within the Quaker conference, Paul introduced us to the story of an Indian Potlatch of the Kwakiuti Indians, as described by the anthropologist Ruth Benedict:

> A chief wants to prove that he has more riches than anyone else, so he invites all his rivals to a potlatch, a giant bonfire. They all settle around the fire and the chief says, 'the fire needs more fuel' and throws on one of his most valued possessions, a canoe. The fire flares up and the heat gets intense but the chief is not satisfied. 'It is still too chilly', so he tosses on a couple more canoes and a few buffalo robes. His rivals are pretty uncomfortable with the heat but they have to continue to sit close to the fire, to show that it is not much of a blaze. And so it goes, until, over the hours, he consumes everything of value that he owns, knowing that the size of the fire, the heat, the discomfort of his rivals will be remembered as the measure of his wealth and greatness.

I found the story very distressing and had some trouble moving to it as a metaphor. The thought of all that waste of resources going up in flames particularly when, at the end, all is consumed! How will his people cope? Then there was the foolishness of the chief worrying what his fellow chiefs were thinking of him. One has to live in one's own mind, not in the mind of others. As we sat in silence at the end of the story, I had a feeling of immense sadness.

Paul interrupted our thinking with the simple statement: 'You are the chief in that story.' 'Not so', I heard myself say quietly. Paul said that we can read this as a story of professional burn-out. He reminded us that we had told him how we were determined to work harder and longer than anyone else, that we responded to practically every request without demur, that we gave our all. What is more, by doing this we were inviting others to burn both their work canoes and learning clothes when we set an example of commitment that our fellow staff had to match. When you have burned up all that you have, you will be running on empty.

Chapter 5

The Learning Principal

When I told people I wanted to live with an Amish family everybody laughed. . . . I didn't know when I first looked at an Amish quilt and felt my heart pounding that my soul was starving, that an inner voice was trying to make sense of my life. I didn't know that I was beginning a journey of the spirit, . . . I thought that I was going to learn more about their quilts, but the quilts were only guides, leading me to what I really needed to learn, to answer a question I hadn't formed yet: 'Is there another way to lead a good life?' I went searching in a foreign land and found my way home. (Sue Bender, 1991, p. xii)

Within the demands of a pervasive and overwhelming profession, finding and managing oneself is a challenge. This chapter describes work in progress. As such it is the story of a personal quilt in the making.

The Task

Just how difficult it was to be a surviving principal let alone a successful principal, I was not acknowledging. As the professional demands increased, I gave more time to my role as principal. As the pressures increased, I tried to take that pressure and use it as a creative force to pursue outcomes that seemed desirable. Fellow principals commented that it was harder to be school principal today, more dilemmas, more demands, more events, more need for complex strategic planning and more paperwork. I agreed that there was more pressure but tried to turn the negative into a positive by emphasizing that our work is very rewarding. I was determined both to be successful in the job and to enjoy it. I worked hard to train myself to focus on the task and ignore some of the personal consequences. My wife, family and friends tried to hold a mirror up for me to see a stressed person in the reflection, but I saw past the reflection to other incompleted or more important tasks.

In describing my role, I am not suggesting that only school principals are busy. Unfortunately the pace of everyday life for many people is like this. One business person describes his busy life:

Most of us work very hard and long. A day, beginning with a breakfast meeting is filled with rushing here and rushing there — telephone calls, meetings, conferences, one on one. The daylight is gone before you get to the pile on your desk. You handle the items in the red file and then head home, your briefcase bulging with required reading for tomorrow's activities. Even on the way home you are so busy on your cellular phone that you hardly notice the scenery.... Weekends disappear in a blizzard of paper work and phone calls. (Belasco and Stayer, 1994, p. 295)

A Personal Quilt

If ever there was a subject waiting to learn, it was me. My job had become so challenging, demanding and fulfilling that other parts of my life were beginning to look pale and relatively insignificant. But how was I to learn to place this work within a normal living context?

Among others, Sue Bender (1991) entered into my life. Here was a woman who had discovered the plain and simple life when she had lived in the Amish community. She described herself as a harried person who was wanting some change in her personal life, a life that had become so busy with

hundreds of scattered, unrelated, stimulating fragments, each going off in its own direction, creating a lot of frantic energy. There was no overall structure to hold the pieces together. The Crazy Quilt was a perfect metaphor for my life. A tug of war was raging inside me. (p. 4)

I could identify with the 'frantic energy' and the tug of war within. Her search for a simple integrated life was also my search and so I was drawn to read more. For Sue the search began when she saw and was deeply moved by a display of Amish quilts. Sue saw in these quilts a tension and yet a harmony and wondered about the people who had made them. So she sought out the Amish community and lived with two Amish families. There, instead of the chaos of her life, she found calm rituals and inner quiet. Most importantly she noticed that there was no distinction made between sacred and everyday events. There was a unity and a coherence in their lives. Sue recorded her experiences of living with the Amish and her feelings in her delightful and honest book, *Plain and Simple, A Woman's Journey to the Amish*. She noted that her goal in spending time with the Amish was for the 'old me' to disappear magically and be replaced by a 'new me' in its place. She noted that this transformation did not happen. 'Nothing of the old me disappeared. I found an old me, a new me, an imperfect me, and the beginning of a new acceptance of all the mes' (*ibid*, p. 148). Sue describes her book as her quilt. Her book captures and acknowledges tensions, everyday and special events and achieves a new acceptance of all of these.

Unlike the Amish, but like Sue, I will be living in a more complex multi-dimensional culture where there are many mes. Yet I resist the conclusion that some of the Amish peace and integration is unattainable in Western culture. My search for self, personal authority and understanding, unlike Sue's single journey, took me to many places and into diverse and different programs. The result was a combination that has some unique individual features that I would like to share with you. In the chapter, 'The Empty Principal', my Quaker experience was discussed. Issues of emptiness and turn-out, silence a personal space, together with the idea of a 'living community' was explored. In a later chapter, 'The Journeying Principal', I describe how I move from fear of self-disclosure to 'coming out', talking about my feelings while undertaking leadership.

Now in this chapter I want to talk about my personal growth. I will talk about the PAL program which I found so helpful in enabling me to see what I was doing to myself and my family and which gave me some desperately needed collegiality. Then there are some programs that helped me understand organizational life including Bion type groups, some outside the school and some as study groups within the school. For the business and financial parts of my role, there were business management training programs. While these were important in developing my skill and knowledge base, I will not describe them as they are package courses that can be purchased from a number of sources. However, I will describe a little of the beginning journey with computers. School visits, particularly when I was overseas, were important. Then there was the important and stimulating reading.

PAL

With a mind set of achieving some balance in my life I came to PAL, a professional program for principals designed to give (p)eer (a)ssistance with (l)eadership. Principals were to be trained as PALS. Two peers would work together as PALS visiting each other's school, observing and helping the observed to see what was happening in her/his school.

While this program did not have the extended immersion factor that was so important to Bender when she lived amongst the Amish, it did begin with a residential period of five days. As it turned out these five days were five of the best that I have enjoyed of peer fun, stimulation and support. The residential learning period was in a small conference centre well away from school. The centre was comfortable and relaxing and so we were in the right frame of mind. The goal of the residential period was to introduce us to the partners with whom we would be working during the next year. It also was to be a focused and intensive training time. We were trained as listeners so that we could hear what was happening in the school that we visited rather than going as missionaries preaching about what we were doing in our schools. It trained us as questioners so that we did not become preachers or prophets but simply observers whose only means of comment was through questions. We were also trained as note takers so that, when we departed from the school, we left behind the notes of our observations.

We could choose our partners. My partner and I chose each other on the basis of similarity of school, both large, single sex girls' schools and, most importantly, in different states. We believed that by choosing partners out of state, competition between our schools would not exist and so we could be more honest in our dialogues.

The outcome of working in a PAL environment was unexpected. It changed none of my educational views although it has challenged some. It did not change the way I organize my day or week, although I am hoping that it still might. By involving myself in another school and hearing what is happening in that school, I was able to gain a new perspective on my school. Like many people who have exciting and demanding jobs, I had become too closely identified with my work and had lost a sense of perspective. This experience reminded me of my different perspective on planet Earth when I first saw pictures of it from space. Earth from space was not large and all pervasive but small and fragile. My role I now saw differently.

On a recent visit to my PAL's school, I observed the large number of activities in which the principal was involved — days, evenings and weekends. 'How does the principal manage all this?', I thought to myself, 'Where is the time for her?' Yet when I came home and thought about my week, I suddenly discovered it was just as busy as that of my PAL principal. Neither my observation, nor the mirror that those close to me held up, had revealed how time-demanding is the role. I had to go to another school, to be outside my situation, to see just how busy life is in a modern school which is attempting to give a contemporary education.

For me another personal outcome from participating in the structured exercises that are part of PAL was equally unexpected. It involves some kind of bonding. My experience of about twenty-six years as a principal of independent schools was that fellow principals were peers but rarely colleagues. In the early years my experience of principals' gatherings was of information and ideas but very little togetherness or real sharing of experiences other than, of course, the achievements! We were competitive people. Survival and identity were amongst our foremost thoughts. Yet the PAL experience was different. An openness rapidly developed and sharing occurred at a level that I had not experienced except sometimes when overseas. The structured exercises and program gave me a previously unknown feeling of community with other principals. So significant was this experience that I approached my membership of the Association of Heads of Independent Schools of Australia differently. I even offered myself for a leadership role within the organization. Suddenly, I could see the creation of a supportive community as possible.

Taking Responsibility For Self

It is very easy to blame the school, the system, my employing Council, the parents who have paid a significant amount of money for their daughters to be educated. To explore the extent of apparent powerlessness, a study group of influential teachers representing a cross-section of the school was set up. The task of the Group was 'to explore the institution of our school in our minds and its implication for our role within that school'. We employed a consultant whose experience was in the psychic and political relatedness of organizations — how people and organizations connect.

This approach to our research follows on from the action research that is a feature of the Tavistock Institute of Human Relations in London and of other groups such as the Australian Institute of Social Analysis (AISA) in Australia. The philosophical basis for this research is that people have minds and are capable of managing themselves in their organizations. People are not objects of research as would be the case in some scientific experiments (Lawrence, 1986, p. 49). The goal was to find out what are the real issues for people living and working in our school.

This group that we established was designed as a leaderless group yet this lack of leadership was one of the first concerns the Group had. 'Why isn't the consultant doing more, controlling the meetings, making sure that our time here together is profitable and efficiently managed?' There was also the belief that the principal, who was also a member, ought to take more responsibility for the working of the Group. After all: 'He called the Group together.'

In the early stages of the Group most of us, myself included, arrived late for the Group meetings. Those late were not always the same persons, and always the late people came with 'valid' excuses. Since there appeared to be problems with our meeting times, on two occasions we changed to a later meeting time in the expectation that this would solve our tardiness problems. Despite these changed times, we continued to arrive late to the meetings. When confronted with this lateness by the consultant, our reaction was first of embarrassment and then guilt. As one person said: 'I am driven by my conscience. I have a black belt in guilt.' Subsequently the Group's reaction was of anger to this continual confrontation of our lateness by the consultant: 'We have other important things that we have to do like attend to students' needs.' When we discussed this inability to be on time, as we did always and mostly with emotion, we concluded that this lateness was not so much a reaction to this Group as a general reaction to meetings at school. As staff members in school meetings, where we do not control the agenda, we feel powerless. Furthermore, in staff meetings, staff felt that much of the time is wasted on irrelevant matters. Instead of attending these meetings, staff felt that they could be getting on with their 'real' work, the work that was generating the personal pressure and stress. I concluded that part of the reason why staff come late to meetings is as a silent protest against the irrelevancy of meetings.

The events of the Group encouraged reflection. Arriving late was something that I did when I attended meetings of our Association of Heads of Schools. I was more aware of the pressure of leaving work incomplete back at school than of arriving and of new opportunities in such a meeting. Clearly the Group had already identified an issue, the feeling of powerlessness that many feel in large group meetings. Passive aggression, as we came to call this behaviour, we saw as more acceptable than open conflict. It was a learned behaviour from our school student days when we did not oppose the government, but were reluctant to comply with all that was requested of us.

This Group met over ten weeks. Its agenda was generated by members of the Group within a structure established by the consultant. In the group's early stages it was clearly easier for a member to use a statement by someone outside the group to make a point rather than to commit oneself personally. One teacher reported that another teacher in our school told her friend: 'My school is a good place to enrol your daughter but don't apply for a job. They make you work too hard.' Personal statements were considered to be dangerous for their authors. Consequently there was a reluctance to make 'I' statements, to take responsibility for one's statements.

In our study Group there was a culture of politeness. Difficulties were dressed up with happy faces. This was particularly evident when we were invited to draw a picture of our experience of the school. While many of the drawings depicted painful experiences, all the people in the drawings wore smiles. The principal and those in authority, including parents, were treated with a respect that had its origins in fear of authority figures. We asked ourselves; whether we could say 'no', and if we could, did we do this very often; whether we had to be infinitely available to students; whether agendas could be influenced by teachers or were agendas out of teachers' hands? While describing the culture of the school as supportive, friendly and warm it was also clear that it was unsafe and one had to be guarded in what one said. While this response disappointed me as the principal of the school, it was also my experience of authority as in my employing Council and in meetings of the Association of Heads.

The problems of dependency and leadership exist in the community as well. We keep looking for the perfect leader who has our interests at heart. Many thought when John Kennedy was President of the United States that they had such a leader. His period in the White House is still referred to as the Camelot period, that period when the King was in the castle and all was well.

Martin Luther King Jr. made an interesting observation. When the Ku Klux Klan was performing all sorts of atrocities, King said that he could forgive the members of this Klan more than he could forgive the millions of silent Americans who have not spoken up against what was happening. Why was the majority silent? Had their experience of school, their images of the ruler and the ruled, so affected them that they believed their voice to be insignificant? 'I often wonder whether or not education is fulfilling its purpose' (King, 1983, p. 26). This question is an important one if our democracy is to survive and, for those in schools able to influence the next generation of leaders and responsible citizens, critical in the formulation of curriculum.

The meetings of this staff Group prompted reflections about school matters and about connectiveness in general. I thought about my normal social interactions. I tried to imagine a situation where I was seated with seven other people around the dining room table enjoying a meal together. The person opposite me wants to contribute to the conversation so he raises his hand. If this happened I am sure there would be laughter and someone would probably even indicate the direction to the toilet. Raising one's hand to speak at a dinner party is not usually done. Possibly the dinner party might be better organized and controlled if there were a chairperson and people were invited or permitted to speak at times determined by the chairperson. But that is not how we normally converse.

Then I thought about a group dynamics course that I had participated in outside the school. One of the elements of this program involved sitting in a large group of sixty people with no leader. We were arranged in a helix shape. Initially conversation was dominated by a few. My response in such a large group was to let others have their way until at some stage I became so bored and/or so annoyed that I spoke up. At that point I took some responsibility for myself. It was difficult.

I wasn't heard by everyone and it didn't influence the direction of the group. Like all leadership attempts, this was risky and unsafe, as I was quick to find out. In one meeting I dared to move my chair. Suddenly this was the topic to be discussed and I discovered that, in the views of others, I had committed a mortal sin. I had dared to take action without full consultation and the consequences for me were emotionally severe. I learnt that the only safe thing to do is to be quiet. But is quiet what I want to be or, even more importantly, is being quiet possible? Furthermore, if I remain quiet the group does not have my wisdom available to it. No doubt this fear of others is why we invent ways to influence the direction of events while trying to keep a low profile.

As I reflected on this experience, I thought about the times when students have sat in classes and not been heard, or worse, of students sitting in large assemblies and being told to be quiet while someone else droned on. Large groups aren't our normal experience of life, but when they do occur, how do we handle them? We talk to the person beside us or we read a book or we go to sleep. We opt out of participation in large groups. These are coping mechanisms but not membership activities. Our educational system needs to address these problems rather than reinforcing inappropriate group behaviour. Despite the absence of large group experiences in our adult lives, the major experience we give to students is of large groups, albeit dominated by a caring and benevolent leader. Does such an experience create an educative environment for our young people? Does it lull them into sleep or complacency, leaving leadership and responsibility to others? Is this how the victim mentality begins? Does it encourage students to take responsibility for their own lives? Worse, does it create anger and annoyance which expresses itself in a passive aggression. In some students we know it creates overt anger as expressed in disobedience, rudeness, and other disruptive behaviours.

Why do we place young people in such large groups? The answer that most frequently is forthcoming is that it is efficient and effective. But have they been effective in helping us to grow into adulthood or have we been emotionally compromised?

Consider the effectiveness arguments. The metaphor that comes to mind is of the factory with batch processing. The factory is effective when the desired outcome is identical products. But are we looking for identical students? By setting up a structure where there are thirty students facing one authoritative person who has responsibility for these thirty students, we are modelling a structure that places responsibility on the person at the front and deemphasizes the role of the individual member of the group of thirty. Does such a setting encourage the student to take responsibility for his/her own learning, or more importantly, take responsibility for his/her life? Is it effective if it does not deliver important social consequences? The teacher's assignment has been: 'Be silent while I interrupt what you are thinking.' The teacher's role has been compared to that of a sergeant in the army, to a police officer enforcing rules and to a factory manager delivering products. All of this is fine if dependency is what we want but if our democracy depends upon people taking responsibility for themselves and for others, then this model may not be effective. Apparently schooling is not preparing students for their working life either. On the front page of the newspaper, *US Today*, on 6 April 1995 was a story headed 'Diploma'. The article presented statistical evidence that demonstrated a lack of faith in public schools. A national survey revealed that: 'Only 4 per cent of business teachers think schools do a good job preparing students for work compared with 44 per cent of teachers and 68 per cent of superintendents.' The survey sampled 5000 public high school teachers, 5000 superintendents and the presidents of 5000 of the largest companies.

The efficiency argument is also suspect as has already been argued in our discussion of passive aggressiveness. For the money we are spending on schooling, could we achieve better results by educating students in their homes with home tutors visiting; might technology be offering new ways of delivery of educational products? These arguments will be considered later in the chapter 'The Frog Prince'pal'.

It would be interesting to know how much time a student spends sitting in a larger group setting. Currently, educational theory encourages teachers to break students up into groups to encourage cooperative learning and there is considerable commitment to the personal development of students. In contrast the examination system is still competitive and assignments prepared for assessment at graduation actively discourage any cooperation between students. The current class (group) model of instruction for students needs to be revisited. For the same outlay per student, could we give a better experience to school students that would enable them to take responsibility for their lives in a constructive and empowering way?

Teachers are caught up in this dependency model too. The authority structure within schools often leaves teachers powerless. I don't believe that principals or senior management are inherently power hungry. Are they simply going into default mode and reproducing what they have experienced in their teaching days? Then there is the default mechanism of teachers. Has the closed door syndrome of the past, the classroom belongs to Mr and Ms Chipps, meant that teachers have little experience of collaborative work groups? Our training as teachers did not address these issues. We were taught, and that is the correct word for what we received, about knowledge and this included a little about psychology, philosophy and sociology. What we experienced was a reactive and stimulating peer group.

Schools are not the only ones concerned about people failing to accept responsibility for their actions. The leaders in the business community are concerned too. In a discussion of the problems of upward delegation, assigning responsibility to the boss to make decisions, there is this assessment:

> One of the biggest problems in transferring ownership is that 'being responsible' runs counter to most of our training and education. Because we have been trained to look to someone in authority for direction throughout life, most of us are constantly looking to avoid responsibility. Furthermore, avoidance worked for most of us in the past . . . This trained response creates the victims . . . (Belasco and Stayer, 1994, p. 58)

To live in an upward delegation mode creates the victim mentality.

> I love being a victim. It's so easy. After all, why be responsible when I can blame someone else for all of my misfortune? I have often heard myself say 'they won't

let me do it. "They" are the problem. If only they would get out of the way, everything would be all right.' I have also all too often heard other people in my company say the very same words. (*ibid*, p. 35)

The book from which these quotes are taken is an interesting one. The authors examine the analogy of the buffalo herd. Apparently there is one leader and the herd is absolutely loyal to this leader. This loyalty made it easy for Indians and settlers to kill so many of these wonderful creatures. Their task was to direct the leader, and the herd followed and often this was over a cliff to their death. The authors of this book see in this the old leadership paradigm with the head buffalo out in front planning, organizing, commanding and controlling. The authors comment:

I realised eventually that my organisation did not work as well as I liked, because Buffalo are loyal to one leader; they stand around and wait for the leader to show them what to do. When the leader isn't around, they wait for him to show up. (*ibid*, pp. 16–17)

Those of us in schools have attempted to change our classrooms but not our personal circumstances. We have carried with us our life experiences from many years in classes at school and university — years when we have had to sit at the feet of authoritarian teachers. We have been told what to study, when to have it completed, what is important and we have been rewarded with graduation and subsequent employment but the personal results have not all been good. In our work situations we feel powerless. We have in our mind the idea of a 'we' and 'they': 'we' the workers and 'they' the administrators. We feel the pressure of their request for performance, of endless duties. We find little time for ourselves. Some of us are angry and others simply emotionally opt out.

There is a growing interest in the study of the social defences that we set up to protect ourselves against the anxiety that we feel in the course of carrying out work duties. (AISA and Tavistock are two groups involved in these studies.) These defences include role definition ('this is not my task'); procedures to be followed ('first you must talk to . . .') and culture ('always smile even when it hurts'). These defences are not conscious creations of bosses or workers. They rise from the unconscious of members and groups. The study of these must be a priority so that behaviour can be considered rather than repetitive. When we are aware of the processes operating, then we can begin to control the consequences of our group life together.

Lest the reader think that I am against schools, let me emphasize an important and positive feature of schools. They provide physically safe havens for our young people, giving them contact with mature and caring adults who are concerned for their welfare. The alternative of setting students loose in the community or even on the information superhighway is a dangerous one that does not give proper and due regard for our young people's safety.

If schools are to continue they need to change. The initiative for this change needs to come from within the school, from students and staff. Schools need to become places of inquiry, and that inquiry must be both about intellectual curriculum — languages, humanities, maths and sciences — and about the social setting for this learning. The possibility of creating a space within the curriculum for reflection is a priority. In such a space students and teachers can acknowledge their anxiety and reflect upon potential responses to this. In such a space they can study the conscious and unconscious behaviour of themselves as well as others and this could lead to a better learning environment, to reflective and integrated persons, and to a greater democracy.

Some of these ideals were set in the 70s but unfortunately the 70s couldn't deliver these ideas. The presence today of computers and related technology means that we have a vehicle that may enable us to deliver both the content and the process in education and so free school time for more reflective and social activity. The more repetitive and factual curriculum can be delivered by technology at any time of the day and in many places. But those personal and group encounters, so precious and so important, can be assigned to the limited hours from 8.30 am to 3.30 pm in that setting that has been described as school. With such a focus, the nature of that place we call school might change. As professionals we are taking responsibility for creating new student learning environments. As persons we must take responsibility for our lives in all settings, a task much harder but equally important.

Technology

To this point I have been writing about my personal learning. Other learning of a less personal nature is also important. While the topics change, the need for continuous learning does not change. When I was searching for a personal example of skill learning, I found an address that I had delivered at an end of year function for year 7 parents and students. I include it as it describes my predicament, one that I share with other people who had to start from scratch in learning to use a computer.

In contrast to my deficit knowledge, students within my school have grown up immersed in a world of computers and other information technologies. They play video games; they listen to music on digital compact disks; they help their families program the computerized controls of videocassette players. These experiences have given children a different way of interacting with information compared with previous generations.

> My story: Once upon a time there was a school principal who could not type. Can you imagine such an incredible happening? This principal was so embarrassed that in the school holidays he borrowed a program called 'All Fingers Go' from his school. That holidays he worked at that program for about an hour each day for most days. He was very frustrated that at the end of the holidays (and they were the long Christmas holidays), he could only type at thirteen words a minute although at least he could type now and could use all his fingers.
>
> When school resumed the principal visited a year 7 class. He was pleased to note that not all the year 7 students could type faster than he could. During that year the principal typed his speeches and reports, including the very important Strategic Plan for College Council, and some letters. At the end of that year the

principal had increased his speed to about twenty words a minute — a definite improvement but there was still room to improve further!

All seemed to be going well for this principal until he made another visit to the year 7 classroom. This time the principal was asked by a student to help with a problem in logowriter. This again was embarrassing. It looked as if this principal would have some work to do over the next holidays!

That same principal now finds out that he cannot live without his computer. He takes it on holidays and even types in the car when his wife is driving. He has his personal notes on it. This year he has even begun to complete his tax return on it! I don't suppose anyone has guessed the identity of this principal?

Our need to learn technical skill never abates. All that changes are the skills to be learned.

Learning

The final word goes to Richard Gordon (1989) whose description of learning I like:

I want to portray learning as an action-packed, hustling, bustling process, by which each of us adapts to changes in our environments. Learning in such a personal context, is the transformation of our direct experience into knowledge as meaning, as a precursor for action. As a process it involves us intimately with our world around us — encouraging us to feel and to sense and to value, as well as to reflect, and finally to act. Above all, it is a creative process. We can portray it as a flux between finding out about our world (and our relationships with it) and taking action to change our relationship with it. (p. 10)

Chapter 6

The Transformed Principal

We could see him down there in the choir, in his dark secular clothes, which made him easy to pick out, among the uniform white of the novices and monks. For a couple of days it was that way. . . . Then suddenly we saw him no more. He was in white. They had given him an oblate's habit, and you could not pick him out from the rest. The waters had closed over his head, and he was submerged in the community. He was lost. The world would hear of him no more . . . strange. . . . To say that men were admirable, worthy of honour, perfect, in proportion as they disappeared into a crowd and made themselves unnoticed, . . . the one who was best was the one who was least observed, least distinguished. Only faults and mistakes drew attention to the individual. . . . The logic of the Cistercian life was, then, the complete opposite to the logic of the world, in which men put themselves forward, so that the most excellent is the one who stands out, the one who is eminent above the rest, who attracts attention. . . . The logic of worldly success rests on a fallacy: the strange error that our perfection depends on the thoughts and opinions and applause of other men! A weird life it is, indeed, to be living always in somebody else's imagination, as if that were the only place in which one could at last become real. (Thomas Merton, 1976, pp. 325–6)

Riding a wet slippery log down a fast flowing stream using only innate skills is one way of describing what it is like to be a new principal trying to maintain your balance in your new role. A committee charged with the selection of a new principal should also be charged with the responsibility for ensuring that there is assistance for his/her professional growth. There is a misconception about the readiness of new principals for leadership. This misconception arises from, or is supported by, the metaphor of growth. Newly-appointed principals have not had time for growth. They have to learn a new role. They may have been fully grown as teachers but as principals they are as tender young plants, vulnerable, needing support in the early stages.

How can the experiences of future school leaders be constructed so as to contribute best to the development of effective orientations to the role?

Principal Task

The urgent phone call from the junior school receives priority over scheduled interviews and tasks that are demanding attention on the desk. The Acting Head of the Junior School tells me that the grade 1 teacher has left her class in tears. She was so upset that she is being counselled by another member of staff before having the rest of the day at home. I am also advised that a replacement teacher has been found and so the students are being cared for. What has happened, why has it happened and what is to be done, are now issues for the principal to attend to immediately. Through telephone conversations and interviews I quickly piece together what has happened. I learn that the morning's incident is not isolated and that the teacher was feeling harassed by the parents. This morning's incident was the last straw. I phone the teacher to offer support and I talk to the Head of the Junior School to see how further support can be given to that teacher. I phone the parent who was involved in the incident and ask for an interview and, at the same time, arrange a meeting with all parents in grade 1 so that they can express their concerns, and the school, through me, can explain what has happened and how the problem can be resolved.

I begin this article with a junior school story but I could have chosen many alternative stories of events in the life of a school where the principal is expected to show leadership. I could have talked about the tragic death of a year 12 teacher and the impact this had on teachers and students. I could have talked about the negotiations with teachers about trying to extend the class period from forty minutes to eighty minutes or the discussions between the school and the union over salaries. Dealing with these events is my job, not interruptions to my job, as I sometimes feel when I have a diary full of appointments, correspondence and reports to write, not to mention some new skills that I need to achieve with technology and important reading to complete.

Like many of my peers I wonder how I can gain more control of my time. I realize that a major part of my role is a reactive one, dealing with the situations as they arise. I recognize also that if problems can be anticipated, then they can be prepared for and sometimes avoided. Similarly, opportunities need to be searched for and time made available to grasp these opportunities. But where does the time come from?

More Than Time

Time is not the only problem. A picture of how secondary school principals in an Australian state system felt about their role is provided by Pusey (1976).

> My first and strongest impression of the principals was that they seem to be plagued by feelings of insecurity and depression. Only one or two of the secondary principals with whom I have spoken seemed to enjoy what they are doing. Most of the principals were very pessimistic about the schools and also about the state of the world . . . Another described his work as a gut-tearing business. Yet another said with vehemence that his was a rotten job . . . you get no thanks and all the blame from every side. Many principals spoke with pleasure about tangible physical and curricular improvements in their schools . . . But for the principals these satisfactions seemed to be outweighed by diffuse uncertainties and anxieties concerning their own role as well as less tangible social and moral aspects of school organization. (pp. 73–4)

When I read this I wanted to dismiss the conclusions as being extreme. It is not my experience of the principalship. Perhaps in a state school system principals' roles are more restricted. Consider then the view of one of Australia's most outstanding headmistresses from the independent school sector, Betty Archdale. In her delightful book, *Indiscretions of a Headmistress,* she wrote: 'The life of the headmistress is full of pressures and worries. Every day there are complaints, frustrations, demands, unpleasant interviews, worrying incidents, all of which have to be coped with by the Head . . .' (Archdale, 1972, p. 164).

Both these assessments were made in the 1970s. Is being a principal as difficult today? A more recent assessment is given by Roland Barth in his book *Improving Schools from Within.* He vividly describes how a 'once very stable profession is now facing unprecedented turnover'[1]. He cites the reasons for people leaving the principalship as excessive time demands 56 per cent, stress 52 per cent, heavy workload 51 per cent, desire for change 40 per cent, fatigue 37 per cent, lack of support from superiors 35 per cent, court/legislation 35 per cent, lack of teacher professionalism 35 per cent, student discipline 29 per cent and student apathy 28 per cent (Barth, 1991, p. 65).

Barth makes another interesting statement. More disturbing than the loss of principals, is the fact that 'the very best principals appear to be the ones most likely to abandon their positions'. What he is referring to here are those committed, conscientious, caring principals who seek to meet all the demands of their students, parents and council. In another sense they aren't the very best principals because they haven't been able to stand back from their principalship and see these stresses, give some priority to the tasks and, most importantly, manage the person who is the principal. But how does a principal do this? It is all very well for those outside to say, 'Take time out. Give yourself some space in the day! Allow some time for personal renewal!' What then happens to the things left on the desk, the people at the door, the new projects not begun, not to mention the family at home? There is no money today to employ additional staff. Work smarter we are told.

What seems to be missing is the preparation for being a principal. How is a principal prepared for her/his task?

Principal Growth?

Principals of schools today, if their experiences are anything like mine, would while teaching have proved themselves in administration through managing a timetable; running a boarding house; directing a curriculum area, managing pastoral and discipline issues for a segment of a school and then been promoted to the role of principal.

This change from teacher into the new role of principal has been described as one of continuous growth and development. This conjures up an image of a plant growing and flowering. While it is a beautiful image, and perhaps flattering to the teacher who becomes a principal, it is not an appropriate image as it disguises the truth. Furthermore, such an image suggests that those teachers who never become principals are failures. One can grow as a teacher but one only becomes a better teacher through this growth — one is not transformed into something else, a policeman or a principal or a social worker. As well as becoming a better teacher, a teacher can grow and become a mentor teacher or a master teacher supporting or even supervising other teachers. In the distant past the headteacher was the principal. Now the role of principal has changed. If the principal teaches, it is to escape, it cannot be a regular full task. Today a teacher cannot grow into a principal as there is no direct continuity of role between these two different positions.

This does not mean that it is irrelevant whether a principal can teach. In fact the opposite is true. Principals will be called on to do some teaching, sometimes with students but mostly with staff and parents. Similarly it is important for the teaching staff to know that the principal understands what it is like to be a teacher, to spend a night marking papers, to deal with difficult situations in classrooms and the like. The credibility of the principal with some people to some degree rides on outward signs such as teaching skill even though teaching is not the primary role of the principal. As useful and important as these are, good teaching skills do not automatically translate into good principal skills. A principal needs a different set of skills, works with different priorities, requires less curriculum and more general and business knowledge and these are not derived from teaching.

Principal Metamorphosis

If the growth metaphor is inadequate, what metaphor captures the change that is to occur before a person is transformed into a principal? One possibility that comes to mind is that of metamorphosis. This is a process where something is changed from one state to another. A good example of this is a tadpole that is transformed into a frog. This transformation is visible, it has definite stages, and the result of the transformation is functionally different from its beginning.

In the inorganic area, there is also metamorphosis. Rocks that are subjected to pressure and temperature are transformed. So we have limestone transformed into marble. For some principals this imagery might sound familiar as they think about the pressure of work and the temperature sometimes generated in various events and discussions although as a person, I don't wish to see myself hardened by past experiences. I would prefer to think that my years in the role of principal have made me more sensitive and open because of my contact with energetic, effervescent young people, dedicated professionals and caring families.

Neither of these metamorphosis images is very attractive although I did give a passing thought to a further transformation of the frog into a princess or prince through some fairy tale process. An interesting metamorphosis is of a caterpillar into the butterfly or the silkworm into the moth. These two changes, besides drawing attention to short life spans, suggest a new idea, that of an in between stage, a cocoon period. If there were a cocoon period for all principals when they could withdraw from daily life in order to study, reflect and plan without distraction or interruption, then they might be better prepared for their new role. If the greatest asset of a community lies in skills, knowledge and developed values then a cocoon time space may not be a luxury, but an appropriate investment. Whether by withdrawal or by on the job education and training, the principal does need time for further education in order to 'fly'.

Growth After Transformation

I reject the growth metaphor which suggests that a teacher naturally matures into a principal. What happens is some mysterious transformation of the teacher. Then new growth must occur. To provide for this growth, some form of pre-service education is important. It is amazing that this has had so little attention and it is therefore not so surprising that we have the high loss rate from the profession. While there are some basics that can be taught before a principal begins work, the rate of change in both the role of the principal and society is such that the only effective preparation will be continuous on-the-job education, in-service education. This needs to be made a priority. Good leaders need time to understand and interpret the big picture as well as to become familiar with what is happening with curriculum, structures, educational and business trends. This is more than a maintenance role. It is a strategic task. The time commitment is significant and should be at least one day in ten. If we want good principals, salary inducement is important but, equally, provision needs to be made for principals to attend to their continuing education.

While the need to engage in one's personal and professional development is apparent and urgent, most principals feel an even more compelling need to answer the telephone calls and letters, to write the policy statements, to be visible at a range of school events of which there seems to be more and more. For most of us the consequences of not doing these are worse than the consequences of not participating in our personal learning.

While the pressures of work have restricted my professional development, if I am honest, my attendance at many in-service functions has also discouraged me from further participation. At many of these functions I have learnt nothing. This has even occurred when we have had eminent international speakers. I would have gained more from a succinct written statement which I could have read in a few minutes. Instead of wasting a scarce resource — my time — travelling to a remote destination and listening to a presentation that had been prepared possibly for a different setting. To make things worse, during the presentation my mind would keep going back to what I had left unattended in the office.

Perhaps this criticism of the speakers and courses that I have attended in the name of in-service is a little unfair. Perhaps I should be more critical of my choices. Increasingly, I am acknowledging the different learning styles of the students in my school. Perhaps it is time that I acknowledged that my learning style might be different from the next principal and possibly to the presenter of the in-service for principals. The answers that I need may not be found in attending talks but in conversations, reading and structured exercises such as the PAL and Tavistock programs already described.

The Changing Focus of In-service

When in-service for principals was first introduced, it was geared more towards informing the principal about changes — the introduction of new curriculum, legal matters, union and professional issues. It was like many classes. We came and sat in rows in front of teachers who instructed us and we duly took notes and subsequently applied this new material to our schools. The wise principals were those with long experience who could speak from this experience. The focus was upon beginning or updating the data bases of principals.

In this rapidly changing society, principals need more than the professional development of their data bases. We need to grow and change as people in concert with the changing society. While we are all challenged, some more than others, by technical tasks such as understanding the legal implications of such legislations as harassment, even more difficult are the challenges for us to grow as people and to increase our personal skills. With the diminution of authority according to rank, principals have to learn to accommodate new structures where power is associated not with status but with knowledge, sensitivity and planning. As schools change from places where individuals stand out, to collegiate groups and teams, new personal skills become necessary if one is to exercise leadership in these new settings. The necessary personal skills can and need to be taught.

A very important role for the principal is that of strategic thinking and forward planning. The school community expects from the principal some guidance and direction and increasingly this is becoming a major leadership function for the principal. In 'The Journeying Principal' chapter I will assert that leadership is that part of executive action that may be directly attributed to the inner life of the leader, to such personal characteristics as her/his beliefs, visions, ways of being and acting. For this reason personal growth is an imperative. It has been said that the worst thing for a school is a principal with vision — such a principal may not be very sensitive to other people's visions, holding on to her/his own vision at all cost. It could also be asserted that the second worst thing for a school is a principal without a vision, for such lack of leadership at the top means that the school is probably going nowhere. As well as having a vision, the principal has to be able to hold on to that vision through good times and bad.

Two Growths

In our school we distinguish between personal and professional growth. In the first there is an emphasis on the person growing and changing. In the second, growth is more about developing the professional skills necessary to carry out the role effectively. While the distinction between these two can be arbitrary as they are referring to the same hopefully integrated person, it is important to identify both learnings, as in some programs the personal growth development is neglected.

Personal growth, as the name implies, is individual, varying according to the life experiences and traumas that a principal brings to the role. In a general description such as this one the more common problems and opportunities for growth are the only ones that can be described. So there will be no discussion of personal growth needs of principals, such as those of one principal who is currently before the court for sexually interfering with children in his care.

At the time of writing I am encouraging our school council to make a commitment to two major projects that will impact significantly on the school. Both projects received early enthusiastic support and then they seemed to come to some impasse. In each case I moved from the commitment to an important educational innovation and the excitement that generated, to the despondency associated with opposition and with goals not being met. Unfortunately there are no pills that one can swallow, no education courses that one can take to eliminate such despondency. There is plenty of advice, such as that given by Susan Jeffers: 'Feel the fear and do it anyway.' The feelings will come and while they may not be pleasant, it is important to be able to feel these emotions. It is not a matter of becoming masochistic nor is it a matter of so inuring ourselves to the pain that we don't feel it. Indeed the ability to feel, to read one's heart, to see the omens in the environment are important elements in leadership. To dull this ability to feel, to be insensitive, is to reduce one's potential for effectiveness as a leader. To be aware of the emotional impact on yourself and others of events and actions allows you both to be empathetic to others and also more able to support them. So often the problems that are presented in the office are not the real problems of concern to the person presenting these problems. A staff member who comes to talk about the timetable may really be wanting to talk about his/her personal inability to cope or even about problems at home. It is easier to talk to the principal about the timetable than about more personal matters. If the principal hears only the discussion of the timetable then there can be no growth or resolution. The feeling of empathy is important and my emotional intuition is often my best guide. For this reason, this empathy has to be educated.

There are preparations that you can make to enhance your ability to be more sensitive to yourself and to others. Case studies of other people's experience are important. This was important to John F. Kennedy in the so called 'Bay of Pigs' drama. His brother Robert writes that John's reading and research for *Profiles in Courage* (Kennedy, 1957) helped him make the difficult decision that took the world to the brink of a nuclear war and then to peace. Robert Kennedy described *Profiles in Courage* as 'a study of men who, at risk to themselves, their futures, even the well being of their children, stood fast for principle. It was towards that ideal that he (John) modelled his life' (p. xi).

Experience Reflected Upon

One does not have to go outside one's experience to learn. All of us have had to make difficult decisions. The problem is not that we have no experience but that we have conveniently forgotten painful experiences and thus have lost the learning from them. This is a pity as reflecting back on our past personal experiences provides rich source material for our learning. The amazing thing about principals, and probably all professional people, is that we are unable to see how dramatic these incidents are in our lives. After nearly twenty-six years of principalship, I could not see this for myself. To see it I had to participate in a peer assisted learning project, PAL. In this program you visit another principal, observe and attempt to reflect something of what is happening in that principal's professional life through structured questions and observation notes. That principal then visits you, observes your behaviour and attempts to hold up a mirror in which you can observe yourself. In our case we managed 'observations' of each other about three times in one year. One of the amazing learnings that I obtained from this experience was how dramatic the life of the other principal was. Each time I visited there was a major event of substantial consequence happening. Was this just a coincidence, my visit and these happenings? Then I thought about the times when that other principal had visited me. On one occasion I was in conflict with the union, on another I was trying to resolve a conflict between two staff members with the issue finally having to go to an arbitrator, on another I was making a complex and traumatic decision on a multi-million dollar commitment to a computer supplier. All of these incidents were highly emotionally charged and yet those of us experiencing them thought they were simply an everyday event. We have so hardened ourselves to the stress that we accept it as a matter of course.

It would be good if in times of stress we could reflect on previous practice and use this reflection to give a perspective on the new challenges. I often wish, when I am in the midst of some significant event, that I had kept a diary describing previous 'challenging' events, my reactions to them, other people's reactions and subsequent outcomes. Unfortunately, I didn't keep that diary because I was more determined to manage the day-to-day problems. That got me through yesterday, but it hasn't helped much today nor given me additional insight to cope with tomorrow. From a proper reflection on past practice I might have hoped to have been able to learn something of my style as a leader, the complexity of the management of schools and the forces that exist within these communities.

An example of memory deficit was when we had to make a change from a DOS operating system to a Windows operating system on our mobile computers. The decision seemed so difficult at the time. Amongst the staff there were strongly held contradictory views. If we changed, what was to happen to those students who could not make the change? If we did not change, we would be disadvantaging all students, holding back their opportunities for learning and restricting curriculum development that was only available on a Windows platform. This problem was not unlike the one we had when we introduced mobile computers and decided to make them compulsory for students and staff. The introduction of mobile computers, now that it has been achieved, seems sensible and appropriate. Past difficulties with their introduction have been forgotten. Today we have new problems, challenges as some would have me say, of how to improve the quality and decrease the price of the computer and how to increase the rate of curriculum change to properly utilize this wonderful learning aide.

Recently there has been an increased interest in portfolios that keep records of work in text, picture or graphic form. We are being encouraged to look at the potential of portfolios as an alternative to scoring students with number grades. In our school we are also encouraging staff to keep portfolios of correspondence received, new initiatives taken, joint projects and their outcomes, to use in their application for advanced standing (and increased pay) in their professional life. Perhaps a principal should keep one of these portfolios too, for assessment but also to remind her/him of what has been achieved and, more importantly, of the difficulties and uncertainties on the way. It is so easy in the hurly burly of daily life to forget what has been overcome. It is as if the past counts for nothing — everything seems to have to ride on the next decision.

There is always the possibility that, having written about our life events and achievements, we would not have time to read them. At least the event has been acknowledged and can be read about and, you may be surprised, you may just find time to read the writing that you judge to be helpful! It is important to note that writing is both a process and a product operation. Only when we analyze our work, write about it and engage in conversations with others about that work can we begin to understand ourselves and our leadership style, the complexity of schools and the pressure of the tasks confronting us. The more we are able to articulate what is happening in our schools, the greater the chance that we can improve our practice and contribute to the learning of others.

The problem I find is that when one is in the midst of doing something one doesn't appreciate how significant it is. I didn't believe that when we introduced personal computing into MLC that it would be as big nor as dramatic as it has become. From that early decision so much has followed. At this time a new consequence is emerging. We are introducing a 'Compass Centre' into the junior secondary school. This program is for gifted students across a number of year levels who will come together to share and work. These students need a larger peer group than can be found in our school. To create this peer group we are augmenting the MLC group with students who live geographically remote in many countries. These distant students will 'visit' this centre using technology such as e-mail and video-conferencing. In this way we will create a virtual community of students. This technology will also be used to bring appropriate mentors to this Compass community. We see this centre as our first 'no-walls' classroom working uniquely with old technology of books and pencils as well as with new technology of electrons, software and networks. Is this the classroom of the future?

Good School

This chapter began with an implied discussion of the 'good' principal and so I would like to conclude this chapter with a brief statement about a good school, of excellence in education. It is important to dispel the idea of perfection that lurks not far below the surface in schools. Does any school enjoy a singleness of purpose, a unity of mind among all in them? Unlikely! Equanimity, perfect harmony are utopian ideas yet because these utopian ideas exist, they create impossible expectations and thus enable despair and disillusionment to prosper. Good must be seen as a relative term, something better than something else.

In a long career I have been fortunate to have been able to visit many schools. I have seen some impressive, innovative, exciting, traditional, different schools. I have not seen a perfect school. Every school has its imperfections and uncertainties. The schools that I liked were the honest ones that could acknowledge their imperfections and could talk about what they were doing about correcting these. My good schools were involved in self-analysis, encouraged rather than squashed differing staff and parental views and saw the need to take action, not just talk about the problems. Good schools were yeasty, vibrant challenging places. There was no complacency there. The good school, as a consequence, is a constantly changing school (Loader, 1984, p. 51).

Note

1   See also the discussion of teacher stress in the beginning of the chapter 'The Reculturing Principal.'

Chapter 7

The Stumble Principal

When change is discontinuous, . . . , the success stories of yesterday have little relevance to the problems of tomorrow; they might even be damaging. . . . Certainty is out, experiment is in. . . . Everything could be different.   (Charles Handy)

I Stumble

It was from a stumble that this book began. I never set out to write a book but I did have the assignment to present an academic staff seminar at the University of Alberta. My task was to describe how personal computing (laptops) became adopted as a policy at Methodist Ladies' College. I was on study leave and so had more time to ponder my topic than usual. Furthermore, the seminar was to be an important trial of my ideas for a keynote paper at an international conference in Australia, on my return from leave. I was looking for a connecting idea to hold the seminar presentation together and the notion of serendipity kept reappearing. Initially I rejected this notion. After all I am a principal who practises strategic thinking! However the more I thought about this the more I was confronted with the fact that I, and my staff, had stumbled onto this major initiative of introducing personal computing. The consequence of this stumble was that laptop computers became compulsory for all students and staff.

At the same time as I was writing this paper, I was teaching myself the computer software presentation package, Powerpoint. The result was that I decided to deliver the seminar using this software. The first presentation to the University staff seminar went well. I received good feedback, not only about the ideas in the paper, but also about the presentation method. As a seminar group, we tried to find a better word than 'stumble' but could not. I was so encouraged by the positive response to the idea of stumbling that I worked hard on both the topic and the software. The result was well received when delivered at the international conference, Leta '94 as 'The Stumble Principal and The Vanishing Classroom; an Epic Journey in Real Time'. Now if all this had not happened I would not be writing this book now. From that first 'stumbling' presentation has flowed invitations to speak and now this invitation to write!

In this chapter I will restrict the discussion of stumbling to five examples. While there will be much discussion of technology and of classrooms, the topic is really about a principal leading through stumbling. I want to emphasize that not all the leadership was by the principal; many people contributed. However, the focus of this chapter will be the principal who, as was suggested in the book's introduction, could be any leader in any setting.

The Principal

When I first presented this topic, I looked for a graphic with which to begin. Words are for talks but a multimedia presentation should at least create some 'imagescape' into which to project the necessary words. I searched with my limited skills for a graphic. In the clipart I found some unsatisfactory masculine images. I had nothing else and so I worked on these and managed to convert one of them into an image that could be male or female. By the time I had finished mutilating the image, all that I had left was a person that existed only from the waist down. I showed this image to my son (family is always a source of honest assessment) and asked his opinion of the image. He asked me what it was supposed to represent. I explained that it was a school principal. He thought for a moment, actually a very short moment, and said: 'Oh, I understand. Yes, I see. It is a school principal. It has no head and no heart.'

Having disposed of the principal as a person with feelings and intelligence, an issue to which we will return, the question remains as to whether a principal can actually stumble. There was a time when we thought principals were very powerful figures in the community, even godlike. Today some people continue to regard them as powerful. Could such a powerful person really stumble? A fellow principal recently placed an advertisement for a new member of staff. As is the custom, he added to the advertisement the badge of the school. The day after the advertisement appeared, an ex-student of the school phoned this principal and began the conversation angrily: 'How dare you change our school badge.' When the principal subsequently checked the advertisement in the paper, he found that the newspaper had attached the wrong school badge to the advertisement. As the principal reflected ruefully: 'Oh that I was so powerful!' Unfortunately this stumble by this principal did not lead to some new vision of what might be for his school.

In order to depict this stumbling hypothesis, a case study of Methodist Ladies' College will be presented later in the chapter. In retrospect I can describe my experiences as an epic journey and, in prospect, I hope that my telling of this journey will encourage courageous adventuring and stumbling in other schools. Before describing the events that occurred, I want to provide some background theory.

Stumbling Theory

Firstly there is a need to define 'stumbling'. Like Alice, I have given a specific meaning to this word. Since there are the three Rs of education, I am nominating the three Rs of stumbling and adding one more R for luck. In life there are constraints and regrets and so it is natural that we find them in stumbling theory. These will be considered. Then there are the rules. We could not have a leadership discussion without rules! The result, when put together, is a stumbling theory.

To 'Stumble'

Now the word stumble is perhaps an inadequate word but I can't find a better word. Stumble can mean flounder, blunder, bumble, lurch, . . . In our dealing with technology we have managed all of these. But that is not the sense that I mean. By stumbling I mean that as I venture forth into the unknown, I chance upon something unexpected, maybe even fall over it. But it does not end there. Having fallen, I don't lie passive or angry, but get up and reflect on this fall. If in this reflection, a glimpse of some new possibility results, then follows decisive action which capitalizes on that stumble. This process is repeated by venturing out again, stumbling, reflecting, glimpsing and then taking considered action.

Three Rs (And One More)

The three Rs, associated with good stumbling, are relevance, risk and responsibility. The additional R is that of resistance. Together they give us the basics of good stumbling.

It might be interesting to teach students about the kings and queens of England but how relevant is that to someone whose parents are separating and s/he must choose with whom to live? Similarly how relevant is it to talk to your child about making her/his bed when s/he has an important maths exam tomorrow? Useful learning needs to begin where the student is at that time and then builds on what that person knows. The biggest challenge to an educator is what to forgo from the 'old' curriculum in favour of something more relevant.

Then there is risk. I remember as a new principal returning from a lecture by a lawyer who spoke about a principal's responsibility of care. As I walked from my car to the staffroom I spied a young fellow up a tree. Now, I thought, I am responsible if I leave him up that tree and he subsequently falls and hurts himself. I hesitated just long enough to remember the times when I have climbed trees and the fun that my sons had in trees. I walked past and left him in the tree. To climb a tree, fly in a plane, walk across the road all have risks associated with them. The first question is not whether there is risk, but how much risk is acceptable? The second question: Does the risk have the potential for improving learning? If we are to improve our schools then we must risk making some changes. At our school we have tried to break out of the cautious culture that would have us tied to what has happened in the past. We have risked a school evaluation, and we knew that this had the potential to show us inefficient, ineffective, or worse. We have introduced structural changes which have the possibility of destabilizing a functioning system. We introduced personal computing at a time when others were laughing at the idea.

Writing this book is a risk, according to some of my friends. To not risk is to not learn. Or to state this more positively; risk taking can make one open to learning and can ensure that this learning is retained. Genuine leadership involves taking risks, grappling with uncertainty, containing contradictory information, and taking action under ambiguous conditions. Policies and practices that we inherit are not final; they need to be continuously reviewed and new ones tried.

The third 'R' is responsibility. At all times we must accept responsibility for our actions. I visited a technology school while I was overseas on leave. I had heard about this school and had seen the plans for it. It had the potential to be a model school, given the care that went into its planning and the budget that it had. I went to that school with a great deal of anticipation and excitement. What I found was devastating. In its first year of operation, the founding principal was replaced by a new principal, two of the staff were in hospital with stress leave, ten of the staff were leaving at the end of the year and I have no idea how many of the staff had left the school already. Parents were hostile about the situation and divided among themselves. This beautiful, new, well equipped school was a fearsome place. This should never have been allowed to happen. People were hurt and they may never recover from this. Responsibility in planning and implementation is paramount. There is no escaping responsibility for our actions. And so it is that stumbling has relevance, risk and responsibility.

The additional R is that of resistance. When you bring in changes there is opposition from those who do not want to have change. This is to be expected, and yet we continue to be surprised by this resistance when it occurs. In the 'Cinderella' chapter I talk about leadership disturbing the equilibrium. None of us want to be disturbed, particularly if we built the present model. In the case of computing, many teachers were not enamoured at the thought of learning to use the computer, nor of developing new curriculum. Then as staff became more familiar with the computer, developed some skills, perceived the long-term value of it for the students and for themselves, they began to reappraise its value. I chose not to force the issue too quickly allowing time for staff to become acclimatized, while at the same time heading off any reactionary responses.

The Regrets

That last story leads us into a discussion of principal regrets. These regrets are of two kinds. There are the regrets such as in the last story, regretting something that has happened. But there are important regrets of another kind, the regrets that we have about opportunities not taken. For some principals, the second kind can be greater than the first. Such principals regret not undertaking further study last year, not undertaking a fire drill before the fire occurred, not introducing computing earlier into the curriculum, . . . These are opportunities forgone, and some of these opportunities will not occur again! When we next stumble, which of the two regrets will we have?

The Constraints

Amongst the constraints are our mental images or mind sets that we bring to our thinking about what is school. While those of us in schools may wish to blame others for imposing constraints, many of our constraints are self-imposed. Are we able to escape from these and respond to what we believe is best for our students?

One of the most difficult constraints is the burden of old curriculum. Do students have to study what we studied while we were at school? A principal phoned me just after he'd started a laptop computer program and he said to me: 'We're not getting through the work.' I asked what was this work and he replied: 'All that we were teaching last year!' I remember that fear. Will the students 'fail' if we don't teach them the contents of the old curriculum? When we started with laptops we tried to do all that we had been doing and then all the new computer work in addition. It was absolutely crazy! Before we can add new material, we need to discard old curriculum.

It is not just curriculum, it is the ideas that we bring that constrain us. Must we have classes or could we move to more flexible groupings of students? Is it constructive to think of school as a place? Must senior students attend school or could there be more flexible delivery systems of courses? Could we have teachers who visit and teach in the homes through computer technology? I understand this fear of setting out in new directions. It is not easy to embrace uncertainty.

Then there is the inertia emanating from past or perceived successes constraining us. All is going well so why make changes? Business leaders have the same worries. To invest in new factories when they are doing well, to launch a new product when the present product is selling well — or do they attempt nothing new?

The constraint that is usually listed first is money. In certain cases this is the most limiting. But it is not so for all schools. Schools, in general, are well staffed according to established ratios of staff to students. Yet it is this staffing that limits the flexibility. By providing those teachers and those classrooms, other opportunities have to be forgone because there is no money left. This is not the absence of money but the commitment to a mind set of how the money should be spent.

The question of inequality has not been addressed. To give according to need is not an established procedure in resource allocation and our future society will reap the fruits of such foolishness and selfishness. Then there is the constraint of uniformity; 'look-alike' schools; schools offering the same courses; students in a uniform.

The 'Stumble Principal'

Let me try to gather this together in my 'stumble principal' principle. The stumbling is within an educational philosophy, in accordance with the strategic intent of the organization. What is being advocated is not an ad hoc policy where anything goes. For the stumble to have significance it must fit into our present policy or lead us to rethink this existing policy. While stumbling suggests erratic behaviour, coherence is given to it through the active process of attempting to integrate it back into the system. After the stumble comes those important questions of 'why' and 'what', questions that are not just important to students but equally vital to us in our role of learner and leader. These questions are an essential part of our leadership tool kit. We need to be modelling a culture of inquiry and building a community of learners. The 'stumbling principal' is to be seen within the context of choosing a future, not just accepting what is being given to us or, even worse, doing what we think people are telling us to do. In stumbling theory we are capitalizing on the unexpected in order to find new solutions. We are assuming that there are no sacred cows, that all policies and practices can be questioned and, if necessary, be changed.

Stumbling has many consequences and foremost among these is the need to discover and nurture new talent. To us who have been in schools a long time, it is a scary and sobering thought that a new graduate teacher may have skills more valuable to the school than the mature and experienced teacher.

It is important that any reformer notes that a criticism can also be a stumble from which you can learn. It is important to be analytical of criticisms, not hiding from them nor walking away from them. Criticisms, of what we are doing, need to be understood and explored. The criticism may lead to new learning and, in addition, by listening to this criticism we will be encouraging participation and ownership. Alternatively the criticism may not be about new ideas but emanate from my mistake. While I regret and want to minimize mistakes, mistakes can have some positive consequences. Take heart, mistakes can be used to model that it is OK to make mistakes in the course of taking initiatives.

The Rules

The first rule of 'stumbling' is that leadership needs to be both proactive and reactive. To be proactive involves taking the initiative and then using some form of strategic planning to deliver the desired outcome. Because expenditure is involved, this planning needs to be supported by a cash flow statement, looking not just at this year but up to five years in advance. Reactive leadership is important too, as expressed by: 'This program is not going too well, students are unhappy and staff critical. We need to look at this.' This does not mean that we have to collapse. Our reaction, after considering the situation carefully, may be to press ahead.

The second rule is that leadership needs to be inclusive of the whole community. It is not a matter of making decisions in the privacy of your office and then leaving the selling and implementation work to others. If the decisions are yours, then you must sell them to the community. This involves a significant commitment of time and a willingness to face personally any criticisms. If the decisions are made by a group of people, then that group has to argue their case. When we at MLC told parents in 1989 that we were going to introduce laptops in 1990 for their daughters and that it would be compulsory, the news was not universally well received. We scheduled meetings to talk about this and parents scheduled a few meetings of their own. There were protest letters to which we had to respond, interviews with parents and their 'expert advisors' and even protests from a staff member. Then the matter was referred to the Parents' Association where, in a volatile meeting, the laptops won by one vote. It would have been easier for me personally to have made the hard decision and then to have said to the staff: 'Now it is your job to sell this policy.' To do that is not leadership but abdication! Leaders need to 'work the community' and the community has a right to debate the ruling with the people responsible for that ruling.

Including the critics in the dialogue is essential but not easy. The task of the leader is to be able to state the criticism more clearly than the critic. Then it is possible for the leader to answer the criticism. With the laptops I remember one staff member who aggressively opposed the introduction of laptops. I spent a lot of time with this critic. It is a matter of pride to me that, when this person received a promotion into another school, she immediately set about introducing laptops!

An important 'stumble' rule is not to rest on your laurels. In our changing society, it is not safe for any organization to be complacent. For this reason it is good to be constantly reviewing all that you think and do in terms of engaging expertise to assist with this. Our experience with consultants has been good. When we started with computers, we needed all the help that we could get. The other important ingredient for success is time. Any new project needs lots of staff time for planning, for review and for implementation. When staff ask for more time, the request needs to be taken seriously and budgeted for in the cash flow.

Good leaders are sensitive to morale. This is so important. Today's enlightened view is of learning communities in which it is not just outputs that are valued, but also the process in itself.

Another important 'stumble' rule is that you need to make choices. One cannot sit on the fence for too long. To not make a decision is to make a negative decision.

The Theory

So 'The Stumble Principal' theory begins with the stumble. Then comes the reflection. This then needs to be discussed, decisions must be made and planning undertaken. Once adopted, a review follows (together with possible new stumbles) and the process begins again.

MLC Case Study

Theories have a basis in events. For me, these events were a number of significant stumbles. These occurred at the Methodist Ladies' College and so the school will be described briefly. Then five stumbles will be examined.

Methodist Ladies' College was established in 1882 as an independent, fee charging school linked with the Uniting Church. Students are all girls and provision is made for students from kindergarten to year 12, year 12 being the last year of school before university. There are 2200 students in the school in four schools within the college: senior school with years 11 and 12; middle school with years 9 and 10; junior secondary with years 7 and 8; and junior school, year 6 and below. There is an open entry policy and so the school, while being predominantly academic, provides vocational courses and a broad curriculum, and is best described as a comprehensive school. From 1994 each student in year 5 or higher and each staff member had a personal laptop computer. In this school there are 2000 plus laptops! There is also a fifth school, community education, which operates primarily for students and adults out of normal school hours.

The 'all girls' nature of the school is interesting. When the school first introduced laptops in 1990, the girls would take their computers home and their brothers had to humbly ask their sisters if they could borrow their computer. So in a whole host of families in Melbourne the girls received computers before the boys received them.

Before we moved into personal computing we had a philosophy that sought to follow John Dewey in working towards a more active, self-directed student learning process. The goal was to give back to students the control of their learning. We wanted to go beyond that stage where a teacher comes in to the class and begins: 'Have I got some great news for you. Today we are going to do . . . and you will love this.' To this, many students respond unenthusiastically: 'Oh?' The idea that students might have some ideas of their own or even that they might want to learn is not the first consideration. At MLC our long-term goal is to place the responsibility for learning, and the choice of content, back on the student.

Stumble One

I, along with many principals in Victoria, received a letter describing a 'Sunrise' experiment. The author of this letter, Ms Liddy Nevile, asserted that schools are not really good places for student learning and so she had decided to set up a different learning environment in a museum. '. . . students and teachers in conventional schools are subject to the culture of their schools and generally this does not support autonomous learning by the students.' Well, such a letter made this school principal interested to the extent that I had to accept the invitation to visit the museum. I asked myself; 'How could a museum of dead artefacts be a better place than a school? At least in the school, the exhibits are alive!' So I had to visit to see what Ms Nevile was doing. What I found were some interesting highly motivated people, a constructivist philosophy and a technology-rich environment. Each student had a computer, not one machine between twenty or thirty students or even between two or three students. Each student had access to a machine. While it was the learning, not computers, that was to be the focus of this class, the computer's presence provided the opportunity for the new formulation of the classroom, the means by which a new form of learning could be achieved and the trial of some different roles for teachers.

So here was the first computer stumble. I was not thinking about computers. I stumbled on them. As it were, I picked myself up from this stumble, this provocative letter, agreed that computers were consistent with our chosen future, acknowledged that they offered a new solution to student-directed learning and began to think about how they could be incorporated into the school. I was out of my depth now. I needed to involve some consultants and to nurture new talent if we were to emulate this bold innovation. There were risks involved in this new commitment as we intended to walk where other conservative schools were yet to walk. As well, I needed to prepare for criticism for this will surely follow when one steps outside conventional practice. Where would we begin? We decided to set up a trial class of volunteers at the year 7 level and to monitor what happened.

Stumble we did, but fall we didn't. We shared the vision with our community. Staff debated it and then supported it. Enough parents and students wanted to participate so that a class was established. Computers needed to be found, staff training provided, curriculum developed, consultants engaged, time found, morale monitored and assessment was to be ongoing. It all seems so easy when you look back on what happened those eight years ago. But it was not easy. I remember meetings where there was a lot of anxiety expressed by staff about the correctness of what we were doing. We were aware of criticism within the community. Questions such as; 'What happens if we don't get through the syllabus?'; 'How will these students cope in external exams when they cannot use a computer?'; 'What happens to the students who do not get this opportunity?'; 'What happens if parents withdraw their children?'

After eight months, when it was considered that the trial was a success, we began to consider what we were going to do the following year. It would be impossible to give each of our 2000 students and staff a computer! We debated our options. The first option was the cheapest. We would ignore computers. While the trial had been successful, it would be impossible to provide a computer for every student. The second option was a home solution. We would say to the students that computers are important and, since the school could not provide them, parents would need to buy one for the home. The next option was to provide a computer at school for each student. This would be an expensive option for the school, not only to fund the computers but also to 'wire' the school. How could this be funded? Another problem would be that the school computer would only be available for limited hours, during school time. The fourth option would be for there to be two computers, one at school and one at home. This would be the most expensive option but it did give students access to computing power at home and at school. The problem seemed too hard!

Stumble Two

As we were pondering this problem Julian, a member of our technical staff, convinced me to go to a computer exhibition. At the exhibition he introduced me to laptop computers. I did not know that they existed before this. I came back to school thinking that laptops might be the answer to the problem that we could not resolve. Each student could have a laptop computer that would be available to the

student at school and at home. Remember, all stumbles do not have to be acciden-
tal, a 'friend' may have stage-managed your stumble!

To explore this stumble further, I gathered together a group of staff that I
thought would support this idea. To this meeting I introduced a computer consultant
and asked him to convince the staff about this new idea. Unfortunately this was not
successful. Those carefully selected staff rejected the idea of laptops. They talked
about students putting the disks down the toilets, computers being dropped, left on
trams and students being robbed of their computers. I wasn't giving in. 'This is a
good idea', I told the consultant. 'We will have some more meetings. I will invite
different staff to the next meeting.' And so I did call another meeting and the result
next time was positive. Some staff liked the idea and it was agreed that these staff
would introduce laptops into the school the following year. From that stumbling onto
laptops at the exhibition, we moved to introduce laptops throughout the school. All
this happened in 1989. There were lots of questions that followed and there is not
space to consider all of these. However, it is important to mention that we decided
that the laptops would be owned and paid for by parents. But how do we get parents
to do this? At the year 7 level, where we had 300 students, the solution was easier.
We offered parents a choice — to be in a laptop program or continue in the traditional
program — and we ran both programs. However, at year 4 where there were only
two classes, the parents of these students were informed that there was to be a dramatic change in the style of education to be offered to their daughters. As from the
beginning of 1990, their daughters would be required to have a personal laptop
computer, together with pens, paper and books.

From the introduction of laptops, monumental consequences flowed. A school,
its culture, curriculum and its teaching-learning paradigm began to be transformed.
Unlike previous technologies such as projectors, radios and TVs that supported the
traditional teacher-centred classroom, computers are a transforming technology in
that they make the student-centred model more accessible. This is why Papert
(1993) describes the computer as a subversive element within a traditional school.

One of the difficult problems that MLC confronted at that time was the myth
that schools should provide everything including computers. We did not intend to
provide the computers. Another issue was whether to provide computer laboratories. The cost of these laboratories is not just the computers; it would mean additional rooms, additional equipment and additional staff for this room. A more
fundamental criticism of these labs is made by Seymour Papert. He sees them as
'immune responses by the school to a foreign body' handling the intrusive subversive element in such a way as to control it (*ibid*, p. 54). Again we decided against
providing many laboratories for all students although we did provide two specialist
laboratories with very powerful computers.

Stumble Three

In requiring each student to have a personal computer, we stumbled onto a philosophy
of 'personal computing'. This is not the usual way of coming to a philosophy, or

is it? While the critics, and there were many, saw the words 'personal computing' as conveying the idea of a computer with only one owner, it was not the computer that we were discussing. It was the use to which the computer was to be put. On a personal computer, students create their knowledge space with their ideas, data, software and within their skill level. It is ownership, not just of a machine, but of enhanced skill, knowledge and power. I find that I am particular about what goes on my computer. I don't want any software, no matter how highly recommended. It has to be useful to me and within my skill level.

Personal computing gives significant and meaningful control of learning back to students. It addresses the two interconnected myths that have restricted change in schools. The first is that schools are the work places. I visited a school that had an astonishing computer laboratory with powerful machines and exciting software. But this lab was only open for limited hours, mainly between 8.30 am and 3.30 pm. When it was open there were classes in there most of the time. What kind of work place is that? Apart from this practical problem, there is the theoretical issue that homes, community libraries and places of employment are also work places. The second myth is that teachers are the controllers of students. Are students not able to control themselves? This 'myth' is discussed in a couple of chapters including chapter 12.

Personal computing introduced new learning opportunities to us. Through discovery, using a computer, students discovered new ways to understand abstract concepts in maths and science. Students developed simulations and built micro-worlds to study phenomena in science, maths and social studies. Students accessed information that had not previously been available to them. A new curriculum, based on the skills and needs of our information age, was beginning to emerge which utilized the computer's ability to be a multimedia controller.

These new learning opportunities encouraged us to rethink some of our conceptions of knowledge and learning. In adopting personal computing, we were supporting Dewey's idea of a child as a person 'with the right to intellectual self determination' and as a student who is 'active and self-directed' (*ibid*, p. 5). We gave credence to Papert's view that learning will come about through 'an epistemological reversion to more concrete ways of knowing — a reversal of the traditional idea that intellectual progress consists of moving from the concrete to the abstract' (*ibid*, p. 137). This has been called constructionism and is based upon Piaget's constructivism where knowledge is built by the learner and as such is temporary, developmental and socially and culturally mediated. Students are invited to construct knowledge and understanding. Knowledge is seen as something personal, not something out there that you gather.

In *A Dialogue For Liberation*, Shor and Freire (1987) are disapproving of school knowledge that is produced at some distance from the classroom by textbook writers and official curriculum committees. They want this changed with students and teachers creating and recreating knowledge in their classrooms (p. 8).

John Abbott, in arguing that knowledge is constructed by the learner, reminds us that these new approaches are not just about different bases of authority and style. Abbott believes that there is important new work on the brain about which we need to be informed. He writes about the work of neurologists, evolutionary psychologists, and a broad array of cognitive scientists (Abbott, 1996, pp. 2–3).

When I showed a member of staff what I had written abut the movement of MLC towards a learning community, she responded as follows:

> You make it sound so effortless, and we certainly haven't reached this point. I doubt that many teachers could articulate what you have written here. Many still see the laptop as a tool for doing what was done before. You have set people on their journey but there requires much more work to be done before they reach this level of knowing.

Yes, I agree that we have a long way to go. However the travel has begun and this is often one of the hardest parts of the journey. As a school, we are seeing the learning task differently. We have a 'learning research group' and this is seeding the community with its research findings. We are asking different questions, not only about content but also about method and inviting students to ask questions too. We are less afraid of deviating from traditional studies, as you will read when you come to chapter 9. We are on our way to removing the 'culture of silence' that Freire speaks about:

> One element is the students' internalising of passive roles scripted for them in the traditional classroom. . . . After years in dull transfer-of-knowledge classes . . . many (students) have become non-participants . . . These students are silent because they no longer expect education to include the joy of learning, moments of passion or inspiration or comedy, or even that education will speak to the real condition of their lives. They expect the droning voice of the teacher to fill the very long class hour. (Shor and Freire, 1987, p. 122)

Stumble Four

What began as a challenge to upgrade staff computer skills led to the unexpected outcome, a new stumble, of a transformation in the thinking about our community. Instead of seeing ourselves primarily as a teaching institution, we now describe ourselves as a learning organization. This is not just a change from inputs (teaching) to outputs in education (learning). Rather it is a paradigm shift in conceptualization of the school where everyone is a learner and even the organization is allowed to make mistakes and be a learner. This shift began before we had computers, but it is the computers, that by facilitating and accelerating this movement, has forced us to confront this change.

With the increased use of laptops, staff find many dimensions of their occupational roles changing, including the cultural setting, work standards, required skills, hierarchy, salary and career opportunities. The introduction of laptops has meant that staff need to be supported in ways that enable them to cope with their changing professional environment. Consequently MLC is being redesigned to make it into a learning place for teachers as well as for students. Time for professional development, for planning and for curriculum evolution is being provided and it is very hard to find this time. This time deficit is driving us to look at our teaching methods to see if all this face-to-face teaching time is necessary. Can time be saved by reducing the amount of time teachers are in classrooms? How would students' academic progress be affected by this reduction? Can the face-to-face teaching be replaced with some form of distance education? Might such a reduction in 'class' time be good for students too, forcing them to be more independent? It is clear to us that only when teachers have time for research, reflection and discussion will teachers be able to consider fresh approaches to teaching and learning which will take advantage of the expanding electronic medium in which their students are working.

The above is rather clinical and does not do justice to what has happened at MLC. There is a lot of excitement, and feelings of achievement and professional pride amongst teachers. Visitors often comment upon what they see as a shared feeling of pride amongst both the staff and students. They hear such statements as: 'This is the only way to go and we are getting there first'. There is a sense of unity as 'learners together' within a school setting. There is less of 'them' and 'us' and it feels good.

We now need a new metaphor to describe the role of the teacher. Teachers are: significant people interacting; co-learners sharing; co-workers creating; curriculum experts directing; researchers reflecting; coaches guiding and encouraging; adults evaluating and community representatives.

So we have stumbled onto something else. It would be good to be able to say that, in advance of experience, we envisaged this learning together. But we didn't! We stumbled onto it. Now that it has been found, we intend to plan the development of this concept.

Stumble Five

As we have stumbled on we began to notice that the classroom that is contained within four walls was beginning to vanish. The reality of a personal mobile work station, today a laptop computer, has given significant and meaningful control of learning back to students and in places remote from school. The classroom is no longer containing the learning, and the teacher no longer the sole transmitter of knowledge. As the students move out into the community and access the Internet from home, school and many other settings, the class, as the basic unit in schooling, is beginning to break up. Seymour Papert talks about a knowledge machine that opens up opportunities for learning outside of school. 'America's school system was once a radical invention, an information revolution itself!' (Mecklenburger, 1994, p. 3). Now we have a new information revolution. Students can work alone or in groups of their choosing. Could it be that as students take more control of their learning we will see the mental model of the student as the reluctant learner being replaced by the image of the student as the motivated constructor of meanings.

Not only are students freed from the necessity of joining a classroom to learn, other information vendors are appearing on the scene. Technology is 'empowering new people and new institutions to be interested in doing some of the education work long expected only of formal institutions such as schools and colleges' (p. 2). Computers and related technologies have brought us to the brink of a revolution in schooling and the possibility that the classroom might yet disappear.

Technology does not deliver all that we want. There are important educational ingredients that technology cannot deliver. These include: the custodial care of young people whose parents are at work; the cultural, sporting and other group activities for which students need to be present; a protective haven for young minds; a social context in which to expose young people to the mature knowledge of adults.

But as work increasingly becomes possible from home, perhaps these needs will recede. In America the fastest growing segment of schooling is home schooling. Home schooling numbers are greater than private school numbers in America today. Perhaps this is the basis for the next stumble? Instead of 'going to school' where we have a virtual community, we may become part of virtual schools and experience real communities.

Theories of Leadership and Management

When I first presented this stumbling theory, I was asked whether I was presenting a leadership or a management theory. My initial response was leadership. However, on reflection, I think that it is both leadership and management. Leadership refers to the articulation of the mission of the organization, setting directions, providing the vision, shaping and holding the strategic intent. Management, on the other hand, is about the administrative functions of achieving goals, administering policies and procedures and monitoring and controlling. I have heard it quoted, and I do not know the source, that 'leaders do the right things while managers do things right'. If we accept these definitions it would seem impossible to have effective leadership without having effective management. There is no heroic leader, no saviour, who is going to save an organization by inspiration, by vision, . . . To see a better future, and not be able to deliver it, is of little value. Similarly there is no salvation, in times of dramatic change as we have today, in effective management. Management, by concentrating on doing what has been done before better, will inevitably ignore the changing environment, and thus not address the bigger picture. There is an essential link that must be made between the ideas and their delivery and between leadership and management. It is not an either or but a composite, not an opposition or conflict model as we will see in the chapter 'The Reculturing Principal', but an organic, collaborative, hierarchical whole.

This stumbling story is therefore about leadership and management. Stumbling is about falling upon new ideas and directions and integrating these into the existing organization. It has both rational and imaginative aspects. Shelley in 'A defence of poetry', quoted in *English Romantic Writers,* wrote:

Reason is the enumeration of qualities already known; imagination is the perception of the value of these qualities, both separately and as a whole. . . . Reason is to imagination as the instrument to the agent, as the body to the spirit, as the shadow to the substance. (Perkins, 1967, p. 1072)

It may not be one person who delivers both elements and it also may not be the principal who provides either, but it is the principal who must endorse and support the actions taken. Implicit in this discussion of leadership and management is the idea of 'the self as tool'. It is because the principal has a head and heart that s/he might stumble with good effect. Starratt (1996) argues:

Our sensitivity to issues, our ability to carry around the whole school in our head, our ability to remember . . . our ability to read the unspoken messages . . . and our ability to see the connection of the present decision to the long-range plan — all these enable us to become this 'primary tool'. (pp. 7–8)

In reflection

There is a history in all men's lives
Figuring the nature of the times deceas'd
The which observ'd, a man may prophesy,
With the near aim, of the main chance of things
As yet not come to life, which in their seeds
And weak beginnings lie intreasured.
(*Henry IV, Part II*)

Chapter 8

The Reculturing Principal

It is surely not difficult to see that our time is a time of birth and transition to a new period. The spirit has broken with what was hitherto the world of its existence and imagination. . . . This gradual crumbling . . . is interrupted by the break of day that, like lightning, all at once reveals the edifice of the new world. (Hegel, Preface, *Phenomenology of the Spirit*)

Cultural Conflict

Once again I was confronted by the need to look deeply at the culture of schools this time when I read the morning newspaper. Here was a sad and frightening picture of the deep hole into which schooling has fallen. On page 2 was the head-line: '20 per cent of teachers suffer stress disorders'. The article under this heading reported that 'almost one in five NSW teachers has been diagnosed with a stress disorder and nearly 40 per cent of teachers reported taking legal drugs to cope with the pressure of their job'. These horrifying statistics were found when a survey was conducted at the end of 1995 and included 2360 NSW teachers (*Sydney Morning Herald*, 1 July 1996, p. 2). Here was evidence that all was not well in our schools, that urgent attention needs to be given to reculturing these important communities.

There were two photographs that accompanied this 'teachers suffer' headline. The first was of big union leaders with arms folded looking very determined. The reader was left with no doubts, the teachers and their union viewed this state of affairs as a significant industrial issue in which confrontation, including strike action, was an appropriate means of resolving the argument. There was a second photo-graph and it showed a large number of the 600 delegates at the teachers' annual conference looking very serious and very much of one mind. On their conference agenda teachers had such resolutions as: to end school one hour earlier each day; bans on the marking of end of year exams; bans on such items as school excursions, drama and music performances and sporting activities. The State Government had been warned by this conference that it faced a 'policy of non-cooperation' by the teaching profession who will jettison 'unnecessary roles and extra responsibilities' from their duties (*Sydney Morning Herald*, 2 July 1996, p. 3).

As happens in so many of these public confrontations, attempts were made to 'personalize' the dispute. The news item carried quotations from the President of the Teachers' Federation attacking the Government's Minister of Education: 'He is not much of a man.' The President of the ACTU warned that unless the government intervened in this 'dispute over teachers' salaries', it would lose office in the next election. The Minister of Education is quoted as saying that such remarks 'do not warrant a response' (*Sydney Morning Herald*, 1 July 1996, p. 2).

Should such an important dialogue be carried out as a public acrimonious debate? What kind of role modelling is occurring here for the young people in the care of these teachers and elected government officials? What real chance is there that the stress issue for teachers will be addressed through such means? Not only will the teachers and the government be losers but so will the whole community.

This lamentable state of affairs requires urgent attention. The Teachers' Federation has a solution: increase teacher's pay, reduce the teachers' workload and provide more supportive management (*ibid*). The Government's response is to offer a salary increase of 7.1 per cent. Oh, that it were so simple or that either of these solutions would satisfy! It is unlikely that a salary increase or reduced work loads would resolve the stress situation. To grant one or both would at least be an acknowledgement that there is a problem but the problem lies deeper. We must ask some basic questions about the nature of schooling as well as looking at the culture of schools. In this chapter I will look at the people in our schools and the culture of which they are a part, leaving to another chapter a discussion of the nature of schooling.

Deep Listening

In our schools, something is drastically wrong when our teachers are suffering such disorders. So much stress, absenteeism and medication is not good for teachers and it cannot be good for the students they teach or the community with which they work. Are we principals, and those with some authority in schooling, going to listen to the rhetoric which management and the union use to avoid dealing with the problems, an action incidentally which keeps the system within their control and which keeps the teachers passive? Alternatively are we going to spend time with teachers listening in depth to their stories about the pressure that they are under or will we dismiss teachers as whingers? Are we going to reject their cries with responses such as 'You teachers ought to work in the real world and then you would know what hard work is about, not just for forty weeks[1] in a year but forty-eight weeks in a year'? Are we going to try to address the task of reconceptualizing the teachers' professional task with them as active participants or just give them some of what they say they want, more salary and a few less students in their classes? I acknowledge that salaries should be higher and that class sizes need to be smaller. But to see that as the only, or even the main problem, is to miss the point that the old factory model of schooling is no longer relevant. The imprisonment of teachers within the system, and their demoralization, are two of the bigger issues.

On the same page of the newspaper, placed there by a thoughtful editor or serendipity, is an article by a staff reporter who is reviewing an article in the latest *American Journal of Public Health*. She reports: 'People who have little control over their jobs and who get little social support at work are almost three times as likely to die of cardiovascular disease.' The reporter interviews a senior lecturer in psychology whom she quotes: 'If you are doing the physiological equivalent of running from a bull in the paddock every day, week in week out, the body finds that extremely taxing.' Her final interview is with a spokesperson for the Australian Psychological Society and she summarizes his argument: 'The new findings should encourage companies to move towards collaborative decision making, which a recent study had shown was also important for corporate success . . . In Australia the rhetoric is fairly common but the actual implementation is a bit lacking . . . Some of the work that has been done on Australian managers suggests that their level of interpersonal skills is low compared to comparable managers in other countries' (*Sydney Morning Herald*, 2 July 1996, p. 3).

As I read and contemplated this, I was reminded of an article 'Dismantling the walls that divide' that I had found personally challenging and which I had kept to read again in the hope that I could internalize some of its teaching. The article tells the story of a group of people who had all experienced deep hurt and who had come together to fashion a submission to the Government concerning mental health and the lack of it.

> As people shared their stories of suffering, sorrow and oppression, a new world of human experience opened to us. . . . Through speaking so openly it seemed our friends were leading us back to places deep within ourselves which we had not acknowledged. . . . We were brought face to face with some basic vulnerabilities of human existence . . . These people with their spirits crushed reveal to us the essence of what it is to be 'poor in spirit'. 'Blessed are the poor in spirit for theirs is the kingdom of heaven', when poor in spirit is linked to the basic vulnerabilities of the human existence. (Brown, 1996, p. 4)

Now here was a different response. Before an outcome was suggested, there is a real attempt to hear the stories, to allow the hurt to be talked about, to search within as a listener for synergy. There is no denying the experience, nor trivializing it by suggesting that it can be solved by money, nor coming up with simplistic solutions. This is a situation that did not have to be 'personalized' in some acrimonious way, as was the case in the teacher dispute. Here people began by listening to other people. They were hearing personal stories of suffering and not just being confronted with the suffering of others, but becoming aware of their own personal hurt. This was a joining, not a confronting situation.

This is a challenging idea. Those who are suffering are not just problems to us, obstacles to the work that we had planned for the day; they could be our guides. People who have been 'crushed in spirit' and are in touch with their suffering have the capacity to help us identify our sadness, our despair, even our poverty of spirit. The sensitivity, openness and honesty of these suffering people are in sharp contrast to my usual rough-and-tumble goal orientated day in the office. I need to be reminded that my important work is in the 'I — Thou' dimension and not in the 'I — It' alternative. I need to be led back to places deep within myself as well as to the outer parts of the universe and to the inner parts of the atom. Our human existence with all its vulnerabilities needs to be acknowledged. May we, to whom much has been given, be encouraged to 'risk deeper human encounters; recognize how we develop protective barriers; loosen our attachments to self centredness, to temporal comforts, power, status and position'. Then we would be able to extend 'love, solidarity, comfort, mercy and justice' (*ibid*).

This aspiration is not over the top! It is possible to ask those who teach and those who are responsible for the teaching process to be learners too. The content of our teaching is more than knowledge of 'out there' facts, it is something deeply personal. We all acknowledge that reading, writing and arithmetic are to be taught but is there not something even more important to be communicated, our humanity?

Schools are peopled places. It is important to focus on these people. We teachers and principals work with people and not organizations even though it is the organization, which is the community entity, that appears to pay our salaries and to accredit the students. There is a tension here which needs to be held between the organization and the people in it. The organization is the public utility and it is also the cultural artefact of the people in that institution. The people are not just its constituents but they are what gives the organization its meaning. The people of our school organizations include those who work there, students and staff, together with parents of the students attending, governing council, the community which partially or fully funds the school and which will receive the graduates from the school and the people in the statutory authorities. All of these people have human needs and it is important we see them in this light and not as obstacles to our goals or pawns in an organization.

A New Quantum Community

The adversarial model of democracy, as described at the beginning of this chapter, and as we find in our political parties, was initiated in an earlier time as a way of balancing the conflicting interests of a community of individuals. But does it serve either our community or our individual interests today? I suggest that it is an inheritance, based on some outmoded way of seeing the world, that hinders rather than helps us live together. What we need is something that allows for more personal expression while at the same time permitting more joining rather than confronting within the community. This is possible if we build upon the quantum theory rather than upon a more atomistic model of reality.

It is argued in an interesting and challenging book, *The Quantum Society*, that our current perception of social and political reality has its origin and basis in the mechanistic thinking that emerged from the philosophical and scientific revolutions of the seventeenth century. One of the greatest of the figures of that time was Isaac Newton. Newton described the basic building blocks of the physical world as atoms that bounced around in much the same way as billiard balls do. Political thinkers compared these colliding atoms to the behaviour of individuals in society. Society is but a collection of individuals with their personal trajectories. Collisions follow much as they do for atoms. Thus we are to accept confrontation as the norm. The main paradigm for thinking about society was mechanistic physics. Mechanism stresses not only isolated and separate individuals but also isolated, separate and interchangeable parts. Neither the whole nor, more importantly, human conscious-ness has a role or place in Newton's atomistic and mechanistic world. As the French biologist, Jacques Monod, describes it, we live 'like gypsies . . . on the boundary of an alien world' (Zohar and Marshall, 1994, p. 5). In such an understanding of the 'real' world, the expert, the observer, the detached individual became important. Fixed roles, rigid bureaucratic organizations emerged as they met the criteria of mechan-ism. There was an emphasis on the unchanging and the certain, rules embedded in stone, ambiguity was not acceptable. 'In Newtonian physics there is only one reality at a time. The either/or of absolute choice becomes the favoured way of dealing with reality.' The Rational Choice theory is built on this paradigm; 'individuals will always choose to act in pursuit of their own self- interest' (*ibid*, p. 4).

It is the view of Zohar and Marshall that quantum physics together with com-plexity theory (which includes chaos theory) should be the basis for a new social vision. At the heart of this is to be a shared reality. Today 'we lack a consensus about meanings, values, customs and symbols. We have lost what sociologists call the "taken-for-grantedness" of social reality. We must learn to reexperience this reality as an integrated whole' (*ibid*, p. 7). The authors list some characteristics of this vision:

- it must be holistic and not isolated mechanistic units;
- it needs to go beyond the individual/collective dichotomy to something that mediates between these extremes;
- it must be plural, no more either/or of absolute truth, but a shared inclusive way;
- it must be responsive as opposed to fixed roles and rigid structures;
- we must relocate the sources of authority and decisions, no longer at the top of a pyramid of power;
- it must be green, there is no need for a dichotomy between us and the material world;
- it must be spiritual, have a teleological dimension and potentially provide some answers to questions such as purpose and meaning, the nature of reality and what it means to be human;
- it must be in dialogue with science and, I would add, the arts (*ibid*, pp. 5–10).

What is being argued here is a case for a new wholeness, a gestalt, that will replace the classical emphasis on separate parts. As well there is a call for us to move out of isolation and away from collision type relationships and to enter into new patterns of dynamic connection and interaction. 'Living systems have integ-rity. Their character depends on the whole' (Senge, 1992, p. 66).

More Than Caring

Initially this chapter was to have been called 'The Caring Principal', caring for the students, staff and for what the institution stands for such as standards and values.

But caring did not seem big enough to hold all the ideas that I wanted to convey. Caring is within a culture and I wanted to question this cultural context. Secondly, caring can have some patronizing overtones. While it is not suggested that caring is always this way, 'our approach to serving others can make people dependent and ourselves indispensable, and can be a concealed form of the love of power or domination' (Brown, 1996, p. 9). It is important for us to remember that people who are suffering deeply can become sick and tired of 'good' and 'generous' people who come to do them good. '... love is not to give of your riches but to reveal to others their riches, their value and to trust them and their capacity to grow' (*ibid*, p. 9).

Effective caring requires that we understand how the other person is feeling. A proverb claims that 'to walk in the shoes of another person, one must first remove one's own shoes'. This is quite a challenge and to accomplish this we will have to employ some deep listening both to others and to ourselves and the latter may well be the harder. 'As our listening became more intent, the strangeness of this world began to evaporate. What first had appeared alien began to sound more and more familiar' (*ibid*, p. 4).

Choosing Leadership

In the question time following an address that I had given at a conference, I was surprised to be asked whom I admired most as a leader. I replied that I was wary of any personality cults and that no one person held all the answers for me. As the person was not to be put off and asked again, I responded, if there has to be one I would nominate Martin Luther King Jr. Since then I have had a chance to consider this and my answer remains the same. King is someone whom I admire greatly. King could see the big picture and did not let himself get distracted by the minor problems. He had a mission that was for others but they were others in whose shoes he had walked. The problems that he addressed were real to him and he did not flinch from the task which he believed to be so important, even knowing that his efforts would bring personal danger to him and to his family.

King could have shown practical helpfulness to many people. He chose instead to see the larger picture and to give his energy to those activities that would have the greatest impact. The result of this commitment the world knows and acknowledges.

In telling this story I seek to illustrate my belief that the principal's primary commitment is to the big picture. It is important that the principal finds time for meaningful interaction with students and time to be involved in the full life of the school. This is to walk in the shoes of others although the evaluation of effectiveness of her/his role as principal, by those who employ the principal, will not be based on these criteria. The test of success will be based upon whether the principal had an overview of the whole school and used her/his time with maximum leverage to deliver the best possible educational outcomes for all the students. Within that big picture, there needs to be some kind of commitment. Tom Peters (1988) asserts:

'. . . the very essence of leadership is that you have to have a vision. It's got to be a vision you articulate clearly and forcibly on every occasion. You can't blow an uncertain trumpet' (p. 399).

In reviewing some literature for this chapter I looked at the contents of some of the secondary school principals' publications. In an old one of these I was surprised to find an article entitled 'The principal's weekly spelling test' (Smith, 1966, p. 33). This is an article describing how a principal spends two hours a week with students teaching and testing spelling. Now that is something that I would not do! I can imagine that there might be an occasion when a principal may want to make a point about the importance of spelling, or some other critical curriculum matter, and personally initiate an appropriate program. I am also aware that the principal's lessons were highly valued and remembered. However, I cannot see how this could continue to be a priority for her/his time today. Similarly in a school of 2000, the principal knew the names of every student (Zainu'ddin, 1982, p. 287). Again as important as this is, I could not see that as a priority for me. The tasks today confronting a principal are about managing change. In the past the challenges were about doing what had been done before better. It was not easier in the past. Principals had no time then and they have no time now. Of one principal, and I am confident that it could be said of most in such a rewarding profession, 'this man gave all that he had and then was anxious to give a little bit more' (*ibid*, p. 350). There is not sufficient time in a principal's day to accomplish all, some items will have to be given priority over others. The tasks chosen to be accomplished need to give leverage. With a lever long enough, a single person could move the world (Senge, 1992, p. 13). For these reasons I have tried to focus on analysis rather than implementation, on developing shared values within the whole community as opposed to imposing my view, to providing time for professional development for all staff so that they could keep up to date too and to look for organic, collaborative ways of structuring rather than using a rigid hierarchy. Schools are big businesses with multi-million dollar budgets which need to be managed efficiently and effectively through budgets. By funding priority areas there is leverage. The whole budget, and not the individual program costs, are the principal's concern.

The culture of the school also provides leverage opportunities. By virtue of the role, at least in an independent school, the principal can change the culture by the appointment of staff, the allocation of resources, restructuring, school evaluations, ceremonies, etc. Since these are so critical I will look at some of these opportunities later in the chapter. There is no recipe for reculturing. My method is instinctive, intuitive, reflective[2] and informed by listening and reading. Where I began and what happened next reflected an organic response to what I found rather than some significant formula that was being followed.

In order to be more effective in my principal's role, I have committed myself to personal and professional development. I have worked hard to understand my ideological presuppositions and to develop my leadership skills. I have chosen to attend business programs and been supported by my school to attend such courses as a two week residential strategic leadership program at Ashridge, UK. I have given priority to my membership of and participation in the Australian Institute of Management. Listening was an important skill to develop so I attended such residential institutes as are provided by Tavistock in the UK and AISA (Australian Institute of Social Analysis). I have written articles for professional journals on the school matters that were being researched and implemented within the school. For example, prior to introducing a teacher appraisal process, I researched this topic and wrote about it in professional journals. In that way I not only informed myself and, I hope, introduced better programs but I invited comment upon them from within the school and from outside. Writing has been a valuable way for me to reflect on, as well as to guide, my professional practice. In my theoretical reading and research, philosophy came ahead of curriculum studies, or psychology because philosophy is concerned with such big questions as those dealing with purpose and meaning.

School Restructuring

In my second year as a principal I called together a committee to consider the possible restructuring of the school. It consisted of representatives from different parts of the school and included senior and junior members of staff. At its first meeting a senior teacher described the authority structure in the school as the principal at the top, the principal's secretary next, then other secretaries in the school followed by the maintenance staff with students coming next and teachers last! This was reason enough to look at the existing school structure. Whether the structure was as described by the senior teacher or not, this person believed that she lacked authority and that those who had the authority were not teachers in what we then regarded as a teaching institution.[3]

This committee was to meet over thirteen months. Members of the committee searched the literature and looked at other schools for possible models but for our school at that point in its history, no one model worked for us. The search and review process was open and inclusive. Time was taken to hear the various opinions and consider objections. For a new principal it was a wonderful way to learn about the culture and complexity of the school even though the more time we spent on this task the more complex it became. I remember being frustrated with the process taking so long and at one point wondered if a satisfactory structure would ever be found. The careful process also afforded the staff a chance to meet their new principal in a work focused situation. Staff not on the committee had regular reports and finally came to adopt the committee's recommendation.

From the perspective of fourteen years later, it is interesting to look back on those extensive deliberations. While we were not conscious of it at the time, we were introducing a new model of staff collaboration. I remember the initial scepticism of some staff: 'Administration already knows what it wants and the committee is only a smoke screen.' This conclusion was not surprising since a previous principal in a different era had been more directive about outcomes. 'If staff meetings ever expressed conclusions contrary to Dr. Wood's wishes he would simply say "Thank you," but I would point out that the final decision is mine' (Zainu'ddin,

1982, p. 351). This new collaborative process showed that there were opportunities for participation in decision making, people's views were listened to and there was a real search for a new answer that fitted a unique school. Subsequently we were to adapt this successful model of consultation when we changed the school uniform through a similar open and comprehensive process, this time involving students and parents as well. At that time, as a school, we were also accustoming ourselves to change, something that was initially hard for us as a community although, without that beginning, later changes might have been impossible. The first changes are the hardest although change is never easy. There is always the temptation to stay with what we know even though it is not satisfactory.

Fourteen years ago we responded to the perceived needs of our school and the changing educational emphases of the period. Our school was large and we wanted to make it more personal. We decided to break it up into sub-schools, into more personal communities. Another problem identified was the difference in the maturity of students. Our school starts in the kindergarten and continues to year 12 when students can graduate to university. We created age-related sub-schools, senior, middle, junior secondary and junior schools. At a later time, when we expanded into adult education, we added a fifth community school. In the early 1980s, when this restructuring was occurring, questions were being asked about the ability of a kindergarten to year 12 school to cater adequately for all students in the same setting with the same rules. In Australia in the 1970s there was a great deal of interest in the students in years 11 and 12. It was noted that students at this level were closer in age and maturity to adults than to the junior students with whom they were joined by school uniform and school regulations. Senior colleges had emerged at the beginning of the 1980s and were given a good report (Anderson, 1980). In the 1980s the focus moved to the middle school years where it was noted that many students felt a great deal of unhappiness about their education (Fawns and Teese, 1980). A survey of students in this level both in our school and in the community showed that a large number of our students in years 9 and 10 were alienated from the school and its goals. The curriculum for these students was not adequately providing for their needs. By providing a separate school, a middle school, we expected that these concerns would be addressed.[4] Other problems to be addressed included pastoral care for students, professional development for staff, time release for teachers to spend time with the parents of their students.

An indication of how much our school culture has changed is shown in the attitude to authority. Fourteen years ago there was a fear about the decentralization proposed. Sub-school heads and their staff executives had initially been given more discretionary authority by the structure committee. A subsequent regulation was introduced to restrict this power. Decision-making groups were only properly constituted when two of the following three people were present, principal, vice principal or head of sub-school. Today even the head of school isn't always present and the principal and vice principal only receive the minutes of the meetings. I have been know to question decisions but, to this date, have not asked for any reversal. The result is a school setting where more people are taking responsibility for decision making, there is more innovation and greater responsiveness to individuals and change. As principal it has sometimes been hard to keep up with all the changes occurring throughout the school.

It is time to look at this structure again. Much has happened in those intervening years. Currently we are looking at the institution of Methodist Ladies' College 'in the mind of staff'[5]. It was asserted, and we were to prove this, that what the institution of Methodist Ladies' College says about itself and how staff describe it would be different. We are using an outside consultant to work with us. Again a working group of eight was chosen to represent the community. An examination of the unconscious, as evidenced by this group, threw up some interesting data. Staff seem to be programmed by what they bring to the situation more than by what the situation is demanding. One of the aspects of the 'institution of the school in the mind', which became evident through the group's exploration, was of a strong dependency culture where the principal is regarded, as one member put it, as 'the ultimate authority'. In this culture the principal is expected to have 'the answers', and there are corresponding expectations of magical solutions. When the principal resists this, passive aggression emerges from members of the Group' (Bain and Loader, 1996, p. 3). As a result of this study a new one has begun involving those staff in authority positions. Because of my imminent departure the task of this group has changed to become an examination of transition in leadership. Where will all this lead?

School Evaluation

A major task of a school principal is to bring a school community together to open up their issues and conflicts. There is no future in trying to sweep these problems under any school carpet. While keeping the community looking forward, the principal will focus their attention on conflicting issues, the resolution of which will lead to better outcomes for all members of the community. In 1983 I thought that one of the best ways of bringing these issues to the surface would be through a school evaluation.

This view of the role of the school principal, of opening issues for full and open discussion, has not always been held. In an earlier period, 1972, one of my predecessors wrote:

> Managing staff meetings . . . called for more tact and skill than any church meetings over which I had presided. I generally steered contentious issues away from any immediate decision and often resolved the matter afterwards. (Zainu'ddin, 1982, p. 267)

Evaluation is an integral part of any program. It is more important when there has been significant change such as had occurred in my first five years at Methodist Ladies' College. In that five years eighteen of the thirty-two Council members who had appointed me to my position had retired. Under my principalship, the College had been divided up into four schools each with its own Head of School, together with a new administrative structure which provided a greater voice for staff in decision making. Curriculum had also changed at all levels but most dramatically at the middle school level following the creation of a separate middle school within the College. This curriculum change was directed by a new Board of Studies.

But the evaluation did more than bring issues to the surface and provide a review of changes. The evaluation identified what was happening and how this fitted into the total school program. As a consequence of this, our evaluation allowed the school to be proactive by facilitating the clarification of purposes and future objectives and, because of its inclusive nature, we secured the commitment of the majority of the community.

The method chosen by Methodist Ladies' College, through its steering committee, was to invite staff to undertake an honest appraisal of sixty-one areas in the school. These areas included all curriculum areas: administration, including health and finances; special features such as innovation and the single-sex nature of the school; Council and Parents' Association. This evaluation by staff was subsequently validated by an outside visiting committee of 100 professionals who spent two days in the school. Self-study was chosen because it offered an opportunity for total staff involvement and for ownership of the process. A self-study also ensured that the assessment was in the context of the school's aims and objectives.

Not surprisingly, given the extensive nature of this evaluation, it generated 1000 recommendations! The implementation committee charged with examining these and ensuring that they were addressed, reported twelve months later that 600 were implemented, 150 were yet to be implemented and 250 were not to be implemented. In my report to council I noted that the process had been a collaborative way of examining every aspect of the school's program and structure. The result of this evaluation was a number of changes — not least of which was the introduction into the school of a more self-critical note. Surely an important characteristic of a good school is that it is self-critical!

I have retained from that evaluation, among the many memories, one vivid recollection. At the conclusion of the evaluation process, I proudly delivered to Council members a 'book' of the commendations and recommendations of that evaluation. It was to be discussed at the Council Weekend. I went to that first meeting of the weekend very proud of the achievements of that evaluation. Imagine my surprise when Council member after Council member condemned some aspect of that report. Not one word of commendation did I hear — there may have been some but, if they existed, the roar of the criticism in my ears was louder. One Council member submitted the following written statement. 'Commendations and Recommendations from the School Evaluation 1984/5 provides Council with an almost indigestible volume of comment and from the very (evaluation) process revealed details prior to Council having opportunity for its own assessments.' If that was not bad enough, it was also clear that there had been much talk about this report between Council members before the weekend of which I was not aware. Instead of becoming paralyzed about this assessment of our work of evaluation, which I might have done given different circumstances, I became 'righteously' indignant. Sometimes when I am emotional I lose words, but on this occasion, my memory was that words came fluently and strongly. At the time I blamed the Council for insensitivity. In retrospect it was I who was not sensitive. 'I should have known what the concerns of Council were in advance and have addressed these.' That is the role of the CEO, in this case the principal.

Despite the success of the school evaluation in changing us as a school, we have not been back for a second evaluation. As I reflected on this, the process was something like an electric shock process, sometimes necessary but not to be used on a regular basis. The process put a lot of pressure on all involved because the school had to continue through it. At one point the pressure became so great that the staff association met to express concern at the lack of time available for staff to achieve the goals indicated.[6] However, I do not think that this is the reason for not repeating the evaluation. It relates more to changes that have occurred since.

In the 1980s we were more concerned with the performance of individual teachers and departments. We also had an idea of a gentle big stick to encourage change. In the 1990s the focus has changed and we are now interested in teams, collaboration, interdisciplinary learning, student initiative and other concerns that are encouraged by support rather than by formal evaluation. The emphasis is now upon encouraging innovation and encouraging staff teams to work on the problems that we know about. Today greater prominence is given to empowering teachers to work together. Instead of the writing of evaluative reports, a major challenge facing Methodist Ladies' College is how to provide more time for teachers, administrators and other professionals in and out of the school to engage in conversations about theory and practice, to plan collaborative ventures in curriculum and to share their visions for the future. What is sought is a process that releases the creativity, professionalism and energy of all in the school setting. The dynamic nature of a school in 1996 cannot be sustained without priority being given to continuous learning by all members of the school community. The school belongs to the whole community who take some joint responsibility and not to administrators who exercise authority through supervision processes such as evaluation.

Teacher Stress Study

Teacher stress is a reality, as we have read, but what to do is not clear. Attentive listening is the first step. With this in mind, in 1991 Methodist Ladies' College initiated a two-year study with funding from the Felton Trust. The study focused on teacher stress and student learning. The assumption was that if the existing conditions and structures under which students learn and teachers work could be modified, then teacher stress would be lowered and student learning would be improved. In the light of the newspaper report quoted at the beginning of this chapter, it is important to note that the Felton Trust viewed the project as one of national importance.

The project had Judy Mitchell as full-time director. A steering committee of Methodist Ladies' College staff and an advisory group of people external to MLC gave guidance and direction to the study. It is worth emphasizing that this was a school taking both the initiative and responsibility to undertake research into its own practices; no university was called in to do this study.

Judy's research provided some staggering statistics. The average number of students for whom a teacher is responsible is 124. The median is 116 and the range is sixty-one to 330. Teachers of students in years 11 and 12 have smaller classes and more periods and so they are the ones who teach fewer students. In subjects such as music, physical education and religious education, where teachers only see the students for a few periods a week in larger classes, teachers are meeting with over 200 students. It is difficult, under these conditions, to know individual students well (Mitchell and Loader, 1994, p. 7).

The study revealed that, while Methodist Ladies' College had many positive features, it was a stressful place for teachers.

> Expectations of maintaining standards while introducing significant changes increases the pressure on teachers. For teachers to move from a focus on teachers teaching to students learning, is not only professionally challenging but also personally demanding. Additional time for staff to meet and plan, both individually and in collegial groups, is needed but is not available in sufficient quantity. The expectation that technology will be used in all subject areas creates stresses associated with both learning and operating the technology. There is a need to develop new curriculum that takes account of the new technology within the school and the changes in society. While consultants have been employed to assist teachers with this, most of the development work still falls to already busy teachers. Then there is the VCE[7]! With all these changes throughout the school, there is a need for more time for professional development to allow staff to gain new skills and knowledge. Since MLC is not in a position to increase staff, all of the above has to be achieved with existing staff numbers. Hence the stress under which teachers work. (Mitchell and Loader, 1993, p. 5)

The study gathered some important data.

> Over the study period (8 May-19 June 1991) the average number of hours worked per school day was 8.7 hours (range 5.2 to 13.4). The average number of hours worked on weekends was 5.9 hours (range 0 to 22). The average percentage of time spent teaching was 31 per cent. The average percentage of working time spent marking was 17 per cent. The average amount of time spent planning was 12 per cent. Besides teaching, lesson preparation and marking student work a teacher might, in the course of a day, also be involved in:
>
> | | |
> |---|---|
> | Finding resource material | Recording order marks |
> | Contacting guest speakers | Consulting the Student Counsellor |
> | Booking venues | Talking with school visitors |
> | Writing subject /pastoral care reports | Typing reports, worksheets |
> | Collating reports and references | Setting tests |
> | Parent /teacher conferences | Preparing lists |
> | Attending curriculum / information evenings | Attending rehearsals of student productions |
> | Attending meetings | VCE consultations |

Organizing meetings	Filling in forms
Telephoning parents	Working with individual students
Communicating with other staff	Planning new curriculum
Organizing competitions	Filling out requisition forms
Responding to VCE changes	Sending information to Student Accounts
Professional reading	Collecting money
Helping a student with a personal problem	Ordering materials
Chasing late work	Checking departmental financial records
Photocopying	Helping students with social service activities
Pastoral care	Attending House practices /functions
Reading/responding to internal memos	Attending social events
Planning for open days	Printing computer material
Attending open days	Attending assemblies
Learning about new computer applications	Writing an article for an MLC publication
Planning excursions	Attending a course /seminar /conference
Roll call	Planning exhibitions of student work
Yard duties	Being involved in staff appraisal
Covering emergency classes	Interviewing new staff
Evaluating staff	Previewing computer software
Consulting with staff at other schools	Organizing student lockers
Organizing seating for speech nights	Preparing name tags for school photographs
Counting money	(*ibid*, p. 11)

From this research a number of initiatives have followed. Academic funding was introduced. This funding allowed a teacher or group of teachers to apply to do some research at the school into curriculum development. Innovative approaches to professional development were funded. The funds available for professional development were increased and opportunities to participate during school time were extended. Use has been made of non-teaching staff to support student learning. Flexible grouping of students for different types of learning has been introduced throughout the college. Teacher collaboration has been emphasized and the new Advanced Skill Teacher III award that provides both status and higher salary requires evidence of collaborative work. Substantial support has been provided to assist staff with the introduction of computers as a ubiquitous part of the learning environment. New facilities are being added that support flexible groupings of students. Two major classroom blocks have been gutted of classroom and new flexible learning spaces created. The timetable has become more flexible (Mitchell, 1993, pp. 2 and 3). A major current initiative is the Learning Centre. This is the initiative of a senior member of staff, Mary Mason. Through this centre, the nature of learning will be researched and new models of learning developed.

While these and other consequences are significant, the teacher stress continues and the hours worked are probably longer today. The way forward is significant change to the working day and to the way students are grouped. Must we continue with classes? Can the idea of the school day be expanded to include seven days a week and twenty-four hours a day? Can teachers play a different role to instructing? These are some of the questions. In all of this, our best hope for significant change is in the potential of teacher collaboration for changing teaching and learning and provision of funding and support by school leaders for these changes.

All of this activity is a long way from teachers echoing passively, Cinderella-like[8], the demands of the unions for smaller classes. It is also a long way from employers seeing increased salary as sufficient motivation. We need to move away from the Newtonian position that encourages unions and management to politicize the debate, to move into combat mode. The quantum whole needs to be seen, deep listening on both sides is necessary. We need that new kind of physical holism that replaces 'the classical emphasis on separate parts and we need new patterns of dynamic relationships (to) replace the old tension between isolation and collision' (Zohar and Marshall, 1994, p. 10).

Collaborative/Hierarchical Culture

Is it possible that in one community you can have both hierarchy and collaboration? Not if you follow Newton who would have us choose between them. That is part of the reason that I am attracted to quantum theory which allows a more complex and interactive whole in which to work.

In describing the process we went through with our school restructuring, it combined the hierarchical 'We will do this' with the collaborative, using a representative committee. For example, subject coordinators were not convinced that I understood what kind of new staff they needed so I made the decision to allow subject coordinators to choose staff for their departments. To support this staff selection process I introduced a human relations specialist who was to have responsibility for normal HR functions, as well as assisting with the selection of staff. In the early stages of this, it was my view that some staff were choosing people who mirrored their pedagogical approach. To counter this I introduced some rules, one of which was that new graduates were to be employed, although exceptional circumstances could be instanced that would allow for senior staff to be appointed. I had other reasons for this rule, including the desire that the average age of staff should be closer to thirty than fifty. Initially my intervention was angrily opposed by some but the new graduates, with their different perspectives and the fervour of youth, have persuaded the staff that a mixed-age staff has advantages.

It is my view, although I am sure that some staff would disagree, that the enlightened intervention by hierarchies is important. It is my view that the school urgently needed the first evaluation. But did it? Would we have been just as successful without it? Is the hierarchy always enlightened and do we not have some school graveyards as evidence of this? Every good hierarchy works better when there is open and frank dialogue.

I believe that it is important to acknowledge up front that hierarchies have and will make mistakes just as staff and committees will make mistakes. Currently the staff at Methodist Ladies' College are unhappy about my statement that in 1998 some sort of extended day will be introduced. As principal it is my duty to set the agenda. Equally it is important for the staff to disagree and to be given space and opportunity to do this. I may be wrong. If I am wrong about 1998, it will need to be acknowledged. But in the meantime I will press for what I believe and staff need to be in there arguing and justifying their case.

Incomplete

When I planned this chapter I had intended to discuss many more topics. There is not space and so I will content myself with a list that at least gives some inkling of one school culture. The items that I had considered include: the importance of multiple visions (not just that of the principal); risk taking and flexible roles; the difficulties for a principal to stand back after something s/he has initiated has begun is passed into the hands of another; curriculum reviews, the life blood of the educational process (and to this can be added the informal curriculum of ceremonies and their importance which in our case include awards, gifts, morning teas, winter celebrations and birthday cards for staff); the importance of communication and story telling through our weekly newsletters to staff, parents and council; constraints and opportunities such as school fees, budgets, long-term cash flows, professional development, outside consultants; creating a learning culture and delivering customer service, . . .

Reculturing

Reculturing refers to the process of developing new values, beliefs and norms for systematic reform. It involves building new conceptions about instruction (for example teaching for understanding, and using new forms of assessment) and new forms of professionalism for teachers (for example building commitment to continuous learning and problem solving through collaboration). Restructuring concerns changes in the roles, structures and other mechanisms that enable new cultures to thrive. . . . To put it bluntly, existing school cultures and structures are antithetical to the kinds of activities envisaged by systemic reform. (Fullan, 1996, p. 422)

Reculturing is a journey and like all journeys has its difficult moments. At Methodist Ladies' College we have not arrived but we have set out. We are facing the problems and not pretending that they do not exist. We seek staff ownership of this process of reculturing. We are trying to break free of our mental models, to see afresh what is the task. An important part of our process is to provide time for reflection, to discuss what has happened and what may yet happen. Sometimes this is facilitated by an outside consultant because by ourselves we can become prisoners of our past. We value and support initiative, diversity and stumbling. All of these take us beyond our present mind sets. Failures we try to see in a positive light, not emphasizing that someone got it wrong but appreciating that someone dared to be inventive. We have too many meetings and we are only too aware that a think tank can quickly become a talk fest. We are aware of the need for implementation committees and the people for these are often different from the inventors. But we are attempting to set our 'lands in order'.

Notes

1 In a year of fifty-two weeks, the normal working period, allowing for annual leave of four weeks, is forty-eight weeks but teachers are required to attend school only forty weeks in a year. This is not to say that forty weeks is all that they work. Most teachers would work a lot of their holidays in preparation and marking. This 'home' work, because it is not on public seats, is not counted by some!
2 This position is discussed in 'The Alchemist Principal'.
3 Today we see ourselves as a learning institution.
4 A major innovation that followed was the development of a remote residential site especially designed for year 9 students. This is described in 'The Dreaming Principal' chapter. Other innovations included extensive curriculum and pastoral care initiatives that dramatically changed the nature of the middle school years.
5 This is discussed more fully in the chapter 'The Learning Principal'.
6 It should be noted that the staff association had indicated support for the evaluation but was simply expressing concern about the lack of time available to undertake the task.
7 VCE is the Victorian Certificate of Education, the final assessment at year 12 level. The results from this determine university entrance.
8 See the chapter 'The Cinderella Principal'.

Chapter 9

The Dreaming Principal

This was the tenour of my waking dream. (P.B. Shelley, *The Triumph of Life*)

Dreaming

Dreams probably have been part of human beings' experience from the beginning of our time on earth. I have met people who say that they do not dream. My experience is that I dream a lot. I also find that my dreams tell me a lot about myself. As a young person I used to be afraid of some of my dreams. There was one recurring one that I can remember but fortunately have not had since my youth. It was a vivid dream about someone trying to enter my parents' home and, in particular, my bedroom. In the dream I run to check that the house is fully locked and when I am satisfied that it is secure, I try to hide from this person who keeps trying to look through the windows.

Revisiting this scary old dream, thinking hard about it so that I could record the details, had an interesting consequence. The very night after I recorded this dream, I had another dream. In detail the new dream was remarkably similar but, in its impact upon me, very different. The new dream was about a frightening electrical thunder-storm. My wife and I were in bed in our first home, a wooden framed and clad house, with the window blinds open. We lay there watching and fearing the electrical strikes, counting the seconds between the light and the sound to see how close each strike was to us. We decided that it was as safe to stay in bed as to go anywhere else in the house. At one point some glowing coals from a strike landed on the bed and I moved quickly to remove these. Then the storm was over as quickly as it had started. I checked the house and found no damage, then went outside and found our neighbours outside safe and relieved that it was over too. As I write this I am feeling comforted by this dream. It is as if my unconscious has spoken and said that the dream of my youth has been superseded, there are scary things to be experienced but fear not, you are no longer alone.

Not all dreams are quite so personal. There are those dreams that we have for others and for the future. Often these dreams or visions drive us forward into new ventures. Martin Luther King Jr. is someone whom I admire and I particularly delight in his dream for others and for himself. He said in that famous speech: 'I have a dream that one day, this nation will rise up, . . .'. He dedicated his life to this dream, and as we know, tragically died for this dream.

I Dream of a Different School

Sometimes our dreams make sense to us. But sometimes our dreams are disguised, like the famous dream of the Pharaoh which needed Joseph to interpret. Sometimes there is not even a specific dream. In my case, my educational dream began in the sub-conscious, evident only as an unhappy stirring in the mind and heart about the nature of schooling as I had experienced it. From my early years as a teacher, Timbertop, a purpose built residential school, in a remote and rugged part of the Australian 'bush', had captured my imagination and was part of my educational dream, even though I had never seen Timbertop. The thought of it stirred and challenged me. Here was a school that paid more than lip service to residential experiences, not a weekend or a week, but a year! To me this focus on living in a community epitomized the valuing of persons and not just the valuing of minds where the emphasis is on content in education. A Timbertop education recognized the importance of challenge, participation, interaction and involvement. It kept in appropriate proportion those educational tasks whose products are measured by paper and pencil tests.

I can still vividly remember my first camp. It was a church camp and I remember that I was initially reluctant to attend. 'Who are these people who want me to go to camp, where will I sleep at the camp, what will I do?', I asked myself. I was comfortable in my routines. The camp turned out to be fun, the people were interesting and I still think about some of the stories that were told and who told them. Then I was invited to assist with a boys' camp as a junior leader. This was not only fun but it was a major growth-promoting experience. To my surprise I found the adults in this camp were as unsure of themselves as I self-consciously felt myself to be. I was amazed to discover that I had something to offer to other people. Then there was the excitement generated by the personal stories that were told around camp fires, in bed after the lights went out, in the water when the boat had tipped upside down. To my amazement I found that I was entering into relationships only made possible because we were living together and undertaking joint tasks. This was learning that had relevance to me as a growing person, vital learning.

From these early experiences I discovered the educational value of camps, of students and teachers living together for an extended period of time, finding the subject of education in the setting, in the residential community and in the members of that community. As a university student, and later as a teacher, I involved myself as a leader and later as a Director of Camp Bevington, a boys' Christian sailing camp in NSW. It was camps that so attracted my wife and me that we went to Canada where we were leaders in Varsity Christian Fellowship coeducational camps. We would spend our week at work, my wife as a social worker and I as a teacher, and spend the weekends in camps working with students. At that time I wished that I might be able to combine the school teaching and the camps, not have them as separate tasks. My chance came when I returned to Australia. I moved from a Government school to a private school that had boarding students. Subsequently my twenty-six years as a school principal have all been in schools with boarding houses.

As wonderful as the boarding school is, it cannot deliver all that I would like. The boarding school, unless it is exclusively for boarders, plays a subsidiary role to the day school. In a boarding school you cannot have evening or weekend classes because that would exclude the students who are not boarders. Inevitably the curriculum is built around what the 'day' students can do. The result is that the boarding experience is often not a great deal more than a good hostel experience where separate programs with separate staff are run. The boarding house provides accommodation and technical support for an education whose curriculum does not arise from the boarding experience. My goal is to have the residential experiences central to the educational task, to have the substance of education arise from the social setting. This would bring a different focus to education, a more personal one where the learning emphasis is upon personal relationships and community living rather than academic pursuits.

My dream of school as a home, for at least part of the schooling experience, is not an isolated dream. In American literature we find the image for school is the little red school-'house'. Most early Australian schools were in homes. Today Australian schools continue with 'houses', sub-units within the school arranged for pastoral care. A principal welcoming a student might well be heard to say: 'I hope that you will feel at home here.' In our school we have home groups. In educational literature, the words 'home' and 'house' are used as metaphors for schooling. The image projected is of a place where one lives, where there is family, and where relationships are important.

But this is a fantasy of mine. Schools remain artificial contrived settings where the only rooms are classrooms. Here young people compulsorily participate in an adult fabricated curriculum over which students have little control. My memory of my classroom was of a place where I didn't quite belong either socially or academically. Socially it was an artificial environment where we sat in rows facing the front and where we were strongly discouraged from relating to our peers. It was a place where I had no personal authority, my assignment was to do as I was told. This was the teacher's room and not mine. It was a place where I had no personal voice, there were right and wrong answers and the teacher's answers were the right ones. To this day I remember how excited I was by a book that I had read on my initiative, a rare occurrence. When I shared this excitement and achievement with the teacher, he said: 'That is a dreadful book.' There was no explanation as to why it was a bad book. I remember feeling a fool. I thought: 'What kind of person am I that would like a book that was so bad?' A consequence of this interchange was that I did not read another book for quite some time. But these class room experiences were not all bad. It did bring friends, some inspirational teachers, adventure out of class time and subsequently a career. These were good outcomes of significance, but could they have been delivered in a more growth-promoting way? Another aspect of my schooling that still worries me is the lottery nature of it. One vivid memory from that same period was that in year 11, the academic students were divided into two maths classes according to the alphabet. With a surname that begins with L, I was placed in the second class. How lucky I was. Most of our class went on to complete our studies and to pass whereas very few from the other class passed. The difference was not the intelligence of the students but the ability of the two different teachers to control the class. The challenge for students in the other class was to disrupt what that teacher set out to do. The students were not there to learn but to test the teacher. While those students won the classroom battle, they did not succeed at school.

Enter the dream. I wanted to create some more personal and challenging environments for our students. So I went to the school council with my dream for unconventional classrooms. This proposed school was to have different rooms and new spaces; living rooms, kitchens, bedrooms, studies and even a back yard in which to play and study! In this it was to be more like a home than a school. The curriculum would not be contrived. It would arise from the setting, from living together in a challenging environment. This was to be different from any boarding house that I had known. My dream was to build this residential community in Queensland within the tropical rain forest, adjacent to the coral reef amidst seven unique ecological systems. Such a venue would be exciting, challenging and support the academic curriculum goals of the 'day' school. In such a place the focus would be on group living in a stimulating and challenging environment. The setting for this schooling would take the focus off the teacher and place it on the student. It would be in responding to this environment that the students would be seeking the help of adults to make sense of the experience, to solve the real problems that they encounter, and to gain some control over the forces acting upon them. In this way this new enriched setting would help to give more responsibility for learning back to students.

However, the school Council wasn't ready for such a dream. While they liked the idea of school as a home, and they even visited my proposed site, they saw Queensland as too far away, too unprotected, too dangerous. 'No', they said to my dream.

But Was It My Dream?

'I have a dream that one day, this nation will rise up, . . .', said King. And the nation did rise up and there were subsequent changes! The difference between King's dream and mine was that enough of America shared King's dream and not many Council members shared my dream.

It wasn't enough for the principal to have the dream, it had to be a shared dream. Together King and his fellow Americans dreamed and then worked to make it come true. At a later time the Methodist Ladies' College Council was able to dream about home classrooms in a student village in a remote rain forest. When the Council dreamed this, then the village could become a reality. Recently I had reason to rethink this interpretation. Was my dream mine or did it belong to the Methodist Ladies' College community? Did I just dream it for them? Was it my task to hold it until the community was ready for it?

In one sense it does not matter whether it was mine or belonged to the community. The important thing was that it was dreamed and realized. However, in another sense it is important to identify ownership. If it belonged to the community it introduces an interesting idea about what it means to be a leader and how important it is for the leader to be in touch with her/his community. Let me try to explain.

In the Old Testament (*Genesis* 28:10) we read of Jacob who was fleeing from his brother, Esau. He stopped one night and, placing a stone under his head, fell asleep. He dreamed of a staircase to heaven, with angels ascending and descending. Jacob interpreted this to mean that although he was in distress and fleeing for his life, he was yet the object of God's love and care. Jacob was reassured by this dream. His experience and dream were recounted to his children and their children and they too found the reassurance of the presence of a loving and caring God amidst their difficulties. Was this just Jacob's dream or was this the dream of a community? In this sense Jacob was the vehicle for the dream which he dreamed for all his descendants.

Sharing dreams continues even in this scientific period of our human development. For example we dream about ourselves in relation to others within the context of our work. Sometimes we dream of issues and conflicts that are so difficult and tangled that they cannot be voiced and debated publicly. An example of this occurred for me recently. As a result of one of my school decisions, a member of staff dreamed that she saw me, the principal, burying someone in the ground. The interpretation of the dream was clear to me. What she had dreamed was that my decisions had had the effect of making her feel that she no longer had any life, any influence left within the school. It was a very powerful dream and it led to a good discussion between us that would not have been possible otherwise. Previously we had talked only about the decision, nothing about how we were feeling. Now the staff member and I could talk with a different agenda. We also explored the rest of the dream. In this the staff member was packing a suitcase during the burial. When she went to leave, I intervened to stop her leaving. This she interpreted as my wanting her to stay.

As part of my professional development, in order to explore these ideas further, I joined a social dreaming matrix. When I tell people of my participation in social dreaming I always find an attentive, but not always respectful audience. Dreaming is something we all do and probably very few of us understand. We are conscious that others have dreams and that some of these are quite celebrated, such as that of Martin Luther King Jr. Most of us do not disclose our dreams. In some ways we can blame Freud for this as he frightened us about disclosing these dreams. We fear that by revealing our dreams, people will ascertain more about us than we know about ourselves, or even worse, they will learn about the dark side of us that we are trying to pretend does not exist. However, then came Melanie Klein and her followers, particularly Bion, Jaques, and later Menzies Lyth (Lawrence, 1995) who took the focus off the individual and turned our attention to the group. After them the work place, the family and the community became the focus of study and psychoanalysis became a tool of social inquiry not just of individual analysis.

Dreaming Together

The social dreaming matrix was not just a group of people to whom we brought our dreams. A matrix carries the meaning of 'a place out of which something grows'. Thus in the dreaming matrix, our task was 'to associate to one's own and others' dreams, as made available to the matrix, so as to make links and find connections' (*ibid*, p. 7). The experience of the social dreaming matrix is that people in the matrix dream of the matrix and these dreams often precede and anticipate the person's experiences of the matrix. In this sense the dreams are not personal but of the matrix.

The members of the matrix that I joined were Chief Executive Officers (CEOs) from a diverse range of companies, some of whom were school principals. All of us had participated in some previous study of the unconscious. As well as a matrix, we had a Tavistock 'group' in which the focus is on the interaction between members. The program began with a weekend away together in which there was a group and a matrix each day.

A dream is the classic link between the conscious and the unconscious. A night dream is 'a spontaneous symbolic experience lived out in the inner world during sleep. Such dreams are composed of a series of images, actions, thoughts, words and feelings over which we seem to have little or no conscious control' (*ibid*, p. 4).

During my first night at the conference I recorded a dream. My dream was that I had been given a sheet of paper on which were some names of horses that might be good ones on which to place a bet on the Saturday afternoon races. I received the piece of paper with pleasure and thought, yes, it would be fun to do this. While accepting that the advice was good, the source of the information being reliable, I couldn't accept these recommendations without checking. I decided to buy a newspaper so that I could do some research of my own. Unfortunately a number of events intervened and the time passed quickly. The races were half over and I still hadn't bought a newspaper. When I finally did get to a news agency, there was only half a newspaper left. I picked up the newspaper and was contemplating whether I wanted this half of the paper when a little boy came in and said: 'I left part of Dad's newspaper behind.' I gave him the rest of the newspaper. More time passed, the races were over, and no bets had been placed.

I contemplated not presenting this dream to the group. How does horse racing fit into this discussion of work and social dreaming? However, it was the only dream that I had had so I gave it to the group. I was astounded at the response. People immediately associated with different aspects of the dream. One person noted that we (the dream was no longer just mine) were reluctant to take advice, we had to do our own research, we weren't prepared to take action, in this case place a bet, simply on the recommendation of someone else. Implicit in the dream was the ambition, if not the demand, that we must get it right. Mistakes are not to be contemplated. This led the members of the matrix into a discussion of our fear of committing to action unless we had spent a lot of time in careful preparation.

One person commented on the loneliness of our jobs as CEOs. While we have the input of others and are given the benefit of research papers, mostly we work by ourselves and are always held personally accountable for what happens. Another person focused on the race. It represented the fun that we don't have, the adrenalin which we are not allowed to experience and the end that we never reach because there is yet one more task to be undertaken. We live in the 'in between', in a lonely cyberspace of our making. In my case, as a school principal, I saw significance in the little boy. He conveyed the priority given to children, to students, in the school setting. Students properly come first, we stand back. We mark the extra work, stay to answer questions after a class, look for the lost computer, . . . Unless we are very careful (and unfortunately, we know some staff who have succumbed) we can become martyrs. We lose a sense of balance in our life and we are left with no personal space, no newspaper, as it were.

This one seemingly inconsequential dream threw up a number of points. Using this dream that was dreamed by one, others took it into themselves and were able to talk about issues that were personal, immediate and of concern. Through the dream we were able to talk about our organizations and our role in these organizations. From this experience it became clear to me that by exploring the content of members' dreams, the conflicts which sometimes have been too painful to surface in everyday discourse can be understood and resolved through the process of amplification of the dreams. In this sense, social dreaming can have an action research dimension.

Initially I thought that my discovery of social dreaming might be of little use in my role as principal. Imagine going up to a member of staff or a parent and saying: 'Tell me what you dreamed last night.' Yet I have used it successfully in a school setting. Instead of dealing with facts and conjectures, I tried talking about my dreaming and this modelling helped others to talk about their dreams. Imagine the staff meetings when dreams were talked about. Maybe it would do away with the rattling of car keys by people anxious to go home. Everyone would stay in case they missed something interesting!

The Elements of the Home School Dreams

How does this dreaming matrix relate to my home school dream? My belief, with the benefit of matrix experience, is that I was not just dreaming something for the school community but dreaming it while a member of a large dreaming matrix called the Methodist Ladies' College.

The principal's dream was to create a residential community. From the students' experience of living within this community, and from an environmental setting that is intrinsically interesting, the curriculum would arise naturally. The structure of this community should be such as to give responsibility for learning back to students. While there would be challenging academic goals, the focus would be on the growth of persons and of community.

The students' dream was also of a residential community. As students moved from dependent children to independent adults, they dreamt of a place where they could test out their skills of survival. They dreamt of adventure experienced with their friends away from parents, of challenge that they could understand and manage and of a 'place in the sun' that was not boring.

The parents' dream was of a home away from home for their daughters when they were in their more difficult age of 14 to 15 years of age (year 9 at school). At this age their daughters were looking to express their growing maturity in a setting that allowed for some independence of family and interdependence with peers. It was thought that a community setting, remote from the structure and habits of home and local community, would allow students to experience different authority structures, some of which they would have helped establish. At a time when the question of 'Who am I' is dominating their daughter's thinking, a focus on personal identity and relationships in a personally challenging environment would be appropriate.

The teachers dreamed about a curriculum that was not constrained by a time limit of 8.30 am to 3.30 pm, five days a week, and a classroom as a venue for this teaching. A Leunig cartoon[1] captured something of the feeling of that time. It depicted a person in a room looking at a picture on TV of a mountain, while outside the window of that same room could be seen the actual mountain! Implicit was the idea that life was to be experienced and not just observed. The teachers agreed with parents that the best group of students to go to this new home would be the 14 to 15-year-olds as they were the difficult age group in a class situation and because this age group has three more years before they have to face the year 12 external exams. This distance from year 12 gives teachers freedom to modify curriculum without jeopardizing good results in these important exams.

The College Council members dreamed of a remote purpose-built village in a beautiful setting that would give our students growth-promoting experiences. The Council also dreamed of leading the way in education, a dream encapsulated in our mission statement: 'MLC will remain at the forefront of education, both by providing a challenging, enriching and nurturing experience for girls in a Christian environment and by sharing its vision with others.'

We all dreamed of remaking education into a more attractive and personally challenging experience.

One(?) Dream Realized

The result of many people's dreams was Marshmead, a village built on a farm in a remote part of Victoria. The village housed seventy-two students and fifteen staff in nine student houses, five staff houses. As well there were two classrooms, a hall with attached modern group dining room and kitchen and a range of other buildings and sheds. Each student house has four bedrooms, two students to a bedroom, and four students share a bathroom. In each house there is a generous kitchen and a large common area which includes a round[2] dining table, dining and comfortable chairs.

Students

The students believed that their dream was fulfilled. They were given a beautiful site that had access to wilderness areas for walking and camping; recreational water for canoeing, sailing and swimming; space for land activities and a climate to support such activities. Students were delighted to find comfortable modern homes in a rural village setting. Students found that in the village model, in the going out from the village and the returning home, they could experience their dream of independence and community. There was safety because teachers were present to assist students with conflicts, to ensure that the necessities of food etc were provided. There were appropriate adult tasks to undertake. In the Marshmead home there were the daily chores of cooking (the main meal of the day is cooked by the students in their homes), house cleaning, including washing their clothes and linen and group living, including making family decisions about meals and activities.

Students were also given an important responsibility for each other. In this there was a significant departure from the boarding house model. At Marshmead students who were ill were to be left in their home and be cared for by the other members of their home, as would happen in the homes from which the students come. This was a radical departure from what happens in traditional boarding houses where students are extracted from their peers and placed in a 'sick bay', or as it is called at Methodist Ladies' College, a 'health centre'. At Marshmead only a nurse's office was built. It contains all the necessary equipment to deal with emergencies but with only one bed for observation. If a student is seriously ill then the student is transported to hospital, as would happen in a normal family. In the village there are citizenship responsibilities relating to the maintenance of the community. There are the manual chores such as chopping wood for the home fire; cleaning the home and the site; removal of rubbish; cultivating vegetables and herding cows. Then there are other necessary activities such as avoiding mozzies, ticks, leeches, snakes and flies. Marshmead was not made compulsory. Students appreciated that they would be free to choose to attend or not to attend. Surely all of this was an answer to a dream.

So complete is the ownership of Marshmead by students that one girl would not permit her family to stay[3] at Marshmead over a school holiday following her stay. The girl felt that for the family to do this was to trespass into her personal space!

This is how one student[4] experienced Marshmead.

> Marshmead is a place, a place where trees grow and where pastures are green.
> A place where birds sing and cattle and sheep graze in the paddocks.
> Among the rivers and lakes there are animals that called to me.
> Marshmead is so natural and is filled with so much beauty.
> Marshmead is a place where I stayed for a long but short time.
> Where I learned and also taught.
> A place where I smiled.

A place where I cried.

There are houses that surround me.

They are grey and plain but secure and warm and comfortable.

In these houses I can see people.

People who are strangers to me and are individuals to my mind.

Individuals that think in ways that I have never imagined.

People who I admired and also dreaded.

Voices that I heard and learned from.

Voices that talked to me

I have discovered my own individual that was trapped inside of me.

I saw a person who had never been revealed to me before.

A person that impressed me.

A person that thought differently to everyone else.

I wondered why I thought in the present but remembered the past and looked forward to the future.

I thought of why I had imagined and wished for things that were impossible to realize.

All so many questions that filled my mind and were answered at this place, Marshmead.

A place that was special to me.

A place, difficult to forget, but not always remembered.

Principal

The principal was delighted that his dream was fulfilled. Marshmead was more than a second home, it was a challenging site and a developmental community. Being away from civilization, the bush site allows an important detachment from the material and worldly pursuits that so often consume young people. The bush allows a closer relationship with nature, introducing a new perspective to those who have lived in the manufactured environment of a city. The bush setting stimulates thought about one's place in the universe, about time and space and the meaning of life. Marshmead is a place where one is confronted by the God of creation. In such a setting it is possible to 'sponsor the quest for the nature, meaning and purpose of life that underlies not only science, art, and philosophy but also the personal acts of everyday life' (Moffett, 1994, p. xiv). Marshmead encourages this reflection and conversation. When I have dinner with students at Marshmead, often we sit around the dining room table talking for hours, something year 9 boarders at the main school never do. Then there are the long letters to friends and parents, the more formal writing while at Marshmead and the analysis of the experience that will continue for years after. One student wrote: 'I didn't appreciate my parents until I left them. Until then I had taken them for granted.' A student, who before going to Marshmead had considered running away from home, told her parents on her return from Marshmead of this but added: 'After being away and thinking of what I did, I wonder why you did not run away from me!'

Teachers

Teachers were delighted that their dream was fulfilled. Marshmead could provide for the curriculum goals of the school while remaining largely student directed. Meals do not appear routinely, clothes have to be washed, the day has to be organized, homework managed and community chores completed. Student initiative, student responsibility and student independence from staff and interdependence with peers is required. The unexpected arrival of rain can see a student excuse herself from the activity in which she is involved in order to bring in the household washing! This is a curriculum that has neither bells nor Belles. Staff at Marshmead set up structures; work with students to define standards such as cleanliness and balance in meals; support students as they resolve conflicts; provide teaching in skills and academic work — and are always available to the students.

Marshmead fulfils part of the dream about learning. Learning is not something that only occurs in schools, at special times. Rather, learning can take place anywhere. It could be while sitting on a log across a stream, or walking through a rain forest, or typing on a computer, or paddling across a lake, or looking after a sick friend, hand feeding calves or talking to a 'local'. Learning can take place at any time of the day or night, any day of the week. Learning knows no timetable. The Marshmead experience is a seven-day week, twenty-four-hour day and an eight-week program.

Marshmead has a curriculum statement which is devised around four themes: 'Marshmead, a matter of life' which centres around the student's social life; 'Marshmead matters' focuses on the farm and on energy-efficient living; 'Marshmead, beyond the boundaries' is about ecosystems; and 'Marshmead pursuits' includes leisure and life skills. The curriculum for these four themes is taken from current studies in years 7 to 10. This has meant significant rearrangement of what is taught in those years.

Parents

Parents were delighted that their dream was fulfilled. Parents found Marshmead to be a safe comfortable site, relatively isolated to avoid unwanted visitors, and educationally significant. They found the eight weeks gave their daughters and themselves some helpful independence from each other. One parent told of how her daughter cried for days before she left for Marshmead and she (Mum) cried for days after her daughter had left! Mum and daughter are now happily reunited and both agree that eight weeks, in retrospect, is not long enough. Parents have been delighted to find that there has been significant learning transferred back as new understandings and skills into the parental home.

The Council

The Council found their dream answered. Marshmead provided a model environment that would deliver the educational goals and show leadership in education.

The village was sympathetic to the environment. The houses face north and are of energy-efficient design, split level with mud brick feature/energy walls. The site is energy-efficient and encourages the use of renewable energy sources including wind, sun, trees and water.

New Dreams

One of the difficult tasks for a principal who has had a dream that has been realized is to recognize that others may start with the product of your dream and dream a new dream. Marshmead does not belong to the dreamer and others will dream new dreams for Marshmead. What will Marshmead become? This is why it is important for leaders to recognize that you dream for your community, that you are part of a large social dreaming matrix and not a lone individual, as much as it may feel that way sometimes.

It has been hard for me to walk away from Marshmead as it has so much of me in it. Yet it also has lots belonging to others. As principals our privilege is to dream but we cannot own the outcome. In many ways this is like the children that we conceive. We can bring them into life but we cannot own them.

Methodist Ladies' College exists today because its founders dared to dream. They 'dreamed of a school in the far-off years, a school that should lighten the world's dark days, . . .' and because they had 'faith in the school which their dreams had made'.[5] Let the dreaming continue!

Dreams As Revelation

The action research consultancy originating from the Tavistock tradition is grounded in revelation rather than in salvation. Salvation has the idea of a rescue fantasy, saving a person or the organization from its problems. In contrast, revelation is centred on the idea that the clients can take personal responsibility and authority to disentangle and understand the nature of realities for themselves (Lawrence, 1995, p. 4).

One of the occupational hazards of leadership is that you think that you must save people, fix problems and do whatever has to be done. People come to ask your advice, require your decisions, and you unconsciously move into salvation mode. What is worse is that when we cannot wave a magic wand and thus save these people we feel inadequate. An example of a request for salvation happened as I was writing this chapter. A parent of a year 12 student phoned. She informed me that three of her daughter's year 12 teachers would not be completing the year with her daughter. These teachers were either leaving the school or taking special leave. She wanted her daughter saved from this predicament. Of course I could not save her from this. There were good reasons why all three staff were leaving. The issue was 'how do we cope with a situation that could not be changed?' Yes, I admitted that the departure of teachers was not a desirable event. The parent was not interested in listening to how we could minimize the impact of this event on her daughter. She wanted the situation changed. Her daughter had been at the school for seven years and this should not happen to her. The parent was paying fees so I should do something about this. Not just this parent but all of us often are looking for salvation rather than some sort of revelation as to how we might act; where we might go; what we might do; how we might again take authority for ourselves.

Dreams can provide understanding that may help us to identify other ways of acting. The Pharaoh's dream of an imminent drought was about revelation, and not about salvation. The Pharaoh was left to take action. In our dreaming matrix of CEOs we all experienced some revelation through the dream of one of our members. The member talked about a person being in a pool of water and apparently drowning. She didn't want to go down to save him. However, she did go to him, leaned over the water and reached out to him. She wondered whether there was anyone there to support her. Having grasped him she then decided that she didn't want to drown with him, so she let him go. Using this dream, group members were able to associate to this dream. They talked about their work places, about having to make decisions that affect the lives of others, about their vulnerability as leaders at the hands of others and the loneliness in the role that they feel when they are left with the final decisions and the accountability for these decisions. Suddenly the dream was not a tragic story in someone else's dream but rather a personal experience awakened by another's dream.

Empowered To Speak

While dreams may be vague and not the things science is made of, they are important. They can help us to stay in touch with ourselves. They may help us to create a better future. They can provide a reference point from which to react and to make use of the dreams of others. Barth (1991) encourages us as follows:

> I travelled a thousand miles to find a vision, I came to the citadel of learning, for surely Harvard would have the vision I needed. I asked and probed and thought and reflected. I questioned and looked from person to person.
>
> I found visions. Many of them. They came in all sorts of shapes and sizes. They were large ones and modest ones. They were complex ones and simple ones. They all seem to fit — yet none of them fit me. Why?
>
> Then I remembered that I once had a vision — a vision that was my very own. Where had it gone? What had I done with it? So I started searching those long dark corridors of past years.
>
> I found my vision. Rusty, dirty from lack of care — but still there. It was my vision, a vision not exactly like anyone else's. With the power to carry me forward, to shine light on the path of the future — for me and for those with whom I might share my vision.
>
> And I learned an important lesson. I learned that each of us must have a vision. It must be uniquely ours. For until we have a vision to share, we can't understand anyone else's. I learned I must keep my vision polished brightly through

daily attention, or I will lose it again. That it can act as a guiding beacon only as long as I hold it in front on me.

And I discovered that I can look to myself. That I am rich in resources and thoughts and ideas. That the future, my future, lies not there but inside me. (pp. 158–9)

Charles Handy (1994) encourages us to take authority for ourselves. 'We cannot wait for great visions from great people, for they are in short supply at the end of history. It is up to us to light our own small fires in the darkness' (p. 271).

Postscript

I end this chapter with a recent dream.

My wife and I were at a party where we had been standing around chatting, eating 'finger food' and drinking wine. In the middle of a conversation I suddenly became aware that I had something solid in my mouth. At my age this usually means a broken tooth. When I extracted the troubling item from my mouth I discovered that it was a piece of blue shattered glass. To my surprise I found another piece of glass in my mouth and yet one more. 'Where did this glass come from?' I asked myself. Then I saw the answer. The blue wine glass, from which I had been drinking, had a gap in the rim that looked as though a bite had been taken out of it.

I was very concerned that maybe I had swallowed some of this glass. The person to whom I was talking said: 'Don't worry, the glass will pass through you.' I wasn't convinced about this and was becoming more agitated. My friend, responding to my concerns, suggested that I might swallow a large leaf that he had collected. He advised me that when the leaf is in the stomach it will wrap around the glass and then the glass will pass safely through me.

I shared this dream with other CEOs in my dreaming matrix. One of the members was quick to reply: 'This time you have bitten off more than you can chew.' Yes, I thought, particularly in attempting to write a book while being a school principal at the same time.

While I was contemplating this further, another member of the group offered this comment: 'Perhaps you have bitten off what you don't want to chew.' As I thought about this later comment, I thought of the reader of this book and hoped that this dream wasn't a statement about you.

Notes

1 Leunig, a social comment cartoonist, is published in the *Melbourne Age* newspaper on a daily basis.
2 The round table is symbolic as well as functional.
3 Parents are allowed to hire houses over school holiday periods.
4 Tina Tran was a student at Marshmead in its first year of operation.
5 From a school song that is sung today in student assemblies.

Chapter 10

The Big Top Principal

The old brown hen and the old blue sky,
Between the two we live and die –
The broken cartwheel on the hill.
(Wallace Stevens, 1984, *Continual Conversation With A Silent Man*)

I remember relating with enthusiasm and vigour to an interaction that had happened in a staff meeting. The person to whom I was speaking said: 'You have never been able to resist the sawdust!' At the time we laughed at that circus image. I have thought a lot about that image since and recognize that there are a lot of similarities between schools and circuses. So in this chapter I would like to explore the idea of the circus metaphor with a view not only to providing an opportunity to laugh with and at those of us in the school business, but also to obtain some educational insights. Using a new metaphor of circus we will explore older unconscious metaphors that constrain our thinking.

Framing Rings

The circus metaphor provides a colourful, young-person-focused framing 'ring' for our exploration of schooling. The metaphor facilitates our looking through our experiences and habits using a different reference frame, it allows and even encourages us to think through and question the mental models that we hold in our minds about schooling. Those mental pictures or images that we carry make up the mental models which influence our action. Often these mental models involve deeply in-grained assumptions or powerful generalizations that we have built up over time from our life experiences or we have inherited from others. In the case of education, one of the mental models that our community carries is that schooling and learning for young people are synonymous. Other strongly held mental models, ones that the community pays a lot of money to support, include a belief: in the need for class-rooms; in teachers at the front of these classrooms teaching; that more schooling is always better; that the outcome of schooling can be measured by a number out of 100; that schooling is a serious business not to be confused with circuses.

It is unfortunately true that some inspired and appropriate learning practices are not adopted because they conflict with what Senge (1992) calls 'powerful, tacit mental models' that we and society hold in our heads. It is important to 'unearth our internal pictures of the world, to bring them to the surface and hold them rigorously to scrutiny' (p. 9). It is only then that we can discover the shortcomings in our present ways of seeing schooling or, for that matter, the shortcomings in all that we attempt to do. In undertaking such an exercise as this we may be able to dislodge some of these outmoded mental models and introduce some new more appropriate archetypes. Then we can move on to develop better practices which, in turn, will allow us as a learning community to enter the next century more confidently.

The Circus

As a child with no TV and only rare visits to films, the circus coming to town was a big event for me. There would be a grand parade through the streets to watch. There would be the clowns in front, animals in cages interspersed with glamorous folk on horseback, the stilt walkers up and down the edges and then the ringmaster with pride of place at the end. Next for me came the visits to the circus grounds during the day to walk amongst the tents and caravans to see and smell the animals, to spy on the circus people and wonder about their seemingly romantic adventurous life. Sometimes this was all that I managed, the suggestion of an event through the sights, sounds and smells but not the event itself.

Children and young people have always been drawn to circuses. The circus has enriched and fed childhood fantasy. In my day there were the stunts by people defying the rage of wild animals. Today the circus has lost these wild animals and so the danger element has to be associated directly with human exploits. 'Wallendas, a famous circus family, developed the most spectacular highwire act in history. Seven of them stood on each other's shoulders, then walked along the wire. Four members of the act were killed and one was paralysed in falls from the high wire during the 1960s and 1970s' (*The World Book Encyclopaedia*, 1994, p. 13).

In my youth I did not understood that the word 'circus' referred to the shape of the performance area. Nor did I realize that the circus had its origins in Roman antiquity. In ancient Rome a fixed circular outdoor arena surrounded by seats, known as the amphitheatre, provided the space where chariot races, athletic contests and combats with wild beasts occurred. These were brutal affairs that to the locals were spectacular and exciting.

How important is the shape? Do we unconsciously connect with it? 'The circle, the essence of the circus experience, has been frequently described as a primordial symbol. Children establish the circle of space around them as soon as they are able to move' (Ramsland, 1993, p. 4). If the shape is significant, why do we persist in building our schools, and more importantly the learning spaces, in rectangular shapes?

Wild Animals Banned

The wild animals that were a feature of my circus-going days — lions, tigers and bears — are now banned from most circuses. The animal liberationists have properly argued that the inclusion of these acts is cruel. So in the modern day circus, such as Circus Oz, the only animals allowed to perform are humans. Presumably humans in such settings can choose to participate or not to participate! For humans the whips have been banned too.

Schools try to ban wild animals too. We have an image of the acceptable student, one who is eager to learn, industrious, cooperative, delivers work in on time and achieves well in examinations and other assessments. On the sporting field we are looking for students who train hard and always put the team first. In the orchestra or the choir we are expecting discipline as well as talent from our students. Even in dress we expect students to conform to the dress rules. What place is there in schools for the wild, the restless, the exuberant, the difficult and the bored? Would we like to ban all wild animals from schools?

However, unlike the circus, I think there is a case for creating spaces for wild animals in schools. Schools must not be allowed to be factories which turn out customized products. Schools ought to be communities where variety and colour are prized and even celebrated. The wild animal, in this sense, is valuable because that student is challenging existing norms, suggesting alternative ways of behaving and adding life to an institution. It is quite amazing how many great leaders had undistinguished and even aborted school careers!

The inclusion of wild animals into the circus was meant to convey the mythological struggle for mastery by humans over wild beasts and the natural environment. Maybe the time has come to acknowledge that life is not as simple as this. The goal is not to dominate but to live together, to learn from each other. We should not be killing off the wild students but taking them into our community so that we might learn from them.

It is also worth noting that the animal after taming is no longer a true representative of that class of animals. Can you compare a tiger in the wild with one who has been domesticated in a circus? While I could not go so far as to suggest that the animal has been demolished, the spirit that characterized that animal has been 'tamed'.

Big Top

The focus of the circus of my childhood was the large canvas tent, the Big Top. It was in this Big Top that all the action took place: the daring deeds of the trapeze artists, the antics of the clowns, the skills of the horseback riders and, in those days, the performance of the trained animals. I can still remember the smell of the sawdust, the hard wooden seats we sat on, the colourful costumes, the music, the ring master and the excitement that the circus people and events generated. For a young city boy to enter this Big Top was more than an adventure; it was the stuff of fantasies.

The Big Top isn't the exclusive property of the circus. When I was directing a boys' camp, we used a large canvas Big Top. I remember the fun and tensions amongst staff as we tried, with no expertise but lots of enthusiasm, to erect this huge tent. That Big Top provided economical protection from the rain and sun but it was more than that. The Big Top made a space in which we created community, it made a place in which to perform and a place in which to have fun.

When I arrived at Methodist Ladies' College Melbourne in 1979 I found that one of the principals before me had also erected, not a canvas tent, but a huge assembly hall to seat 1100 students and staff. This had been described as his classroom. At the time of arrival I didn't think this was such a strange idea. I was used to big assemblies. Although not always a good performer, I did enjoy, mostly, my time in this Big Top. Later I began to question whether this was an appropriate place for meeting and for principal instruction. There was a high stage on which I, and others, performed and rows of terraced seats in front of this stage where the students sat and listened. It was too impersonal; it emphasized one-way communication and it expected a passive student body. In short it represented all that we said that we did not believe in philosophically. So, as a staff, we scaled down the number and duration of the assemblies and emphasized small interactive group meetings between students and their home-group teacher/tutor/form teacher/class teacher. We retained the hall for big events and theatre.

In the boys' camp Big Top we had a wooden box which we called the Bull[1] Box. At the end of the day's events people were invited to sit on this Bull Box and tell the stories of the day. I often wonder why I haven't continued that practice in schools for teachers. Have schools become too serious? The Bull Box has great possibilities not only for releasing energy but also encouraging the story teller in us all. The closest that I came to this was in my early years as a principal in a small school when our private home could accommodate all the teachers. In that school, after the parent teacher nights, we invited all the teachers home. For many teachers these parent teacher nights were difficult as some parents were not easy to deal with. So when the teachers came home, I gave them both the equivalent of the Bull Box and the audience so that they could tell stories about the worst and best parents that they had met that night.

In a recent in-service for senior staff, the consultant that was working with us invited us to develop a story. The introduction was given to us: 'Once upon a time the principal and his senior management team, together with a consultant, decided to develop a learning organization and . . .' We worked in groups of three. One group wrote poetry, another group a play and our group developed the metaphor of the jazz band. It was fun doing this and in the process we were able to explore the idea of the learning organization. Collaboration, creativity, insight, sharing, visioning, backcasting and evaluation were outcomes of this task. Why don't we do more story writing and story telling in our learning organizations?

There is something special about those big tents with sawdust floors. Have we lost something in our modern day, carpeted, rectangular classrooms? Have our learning spaces become too restrictive, prescriptive and boring? Currently we are retro-fitting an old classroom block. We are taking out most of the classrooms and replacing them with learning spaces of different sizes and shapes. I have asked the architect if we can have a decor that is more conducive to fantasy, to fun and to multipurpose use.

Perhaps it is time for us to think of teachers and principals as set designers. We are not mere functionaries, process operators, in factory type spaces provided by others. Instead we need to be proactive in designing our setting for the imaginative schooling that is designed for today. In teacher training we need new courses that reflect this larger role; clowning workshops, set designing, tightrope walking.

Riding Two Horses

Riding one horse is difficult enough for most people, but if you go to the circus you find people who can ride two horses at once — one foot on one saddle and the other foot on the other saddle. This is an interesting image of the challenge of school life today. School principals must be able to look over the horizon and see the future. This is to ride one horse. At the same time principals must deal with today's issues and problems, that is to ride a different horse. It is not a question of choosing one feat but of doing both simultaneously.

There are many times when the principal is expected to ride two horses. There are also times when the principal wants to be able to ride two horses, one as principal and one as a real person. I am reminded of an incident at my present school where I believe I had been tricked by a teachers' union representative. I had allowed a meeting to occur and gone along innocently believing that the meeting was about new work practices. As the meeting proceeded and the story unfolded I discovered that the meeting was about the untrustworthiness of employers, school principals. I became angrier and angrier as I listened to the stories of bad principals. I do not doubt that they exist, but I was not the one that he was describing. If I was responsible for paying less than the award, then tell me about it. But do not come into our school staff room and create fear about the future based on tales from the badlands. A good future is built upon trust, not on fear. Finally, when the speaker asked for questions or comments, I waited what seemed like an eternity to me, but staff felt was probably ten seconds, before I rose to my feet to speak with some emotion against what had just been said. Many staff regard my emotional outburst as one of my big mistakes. Staff felt that I didn't have a right to a personal opinion or emotion, that I had always to be in my role as the principal. I admit that it was not the proclamation of a statesman. I was insulted and I let it be known that I was too. In subsequent discussions with staff, in defence of my behaviour, I argued that blood ran in my veins just as it did in theirs. Today I continue to claim the right to be a person as well as a principal, to ride two horses.

The Sawdust

Sitting in my office and attending to all the routine and not so routine matters of correspondence, phone calls and reports generates little excitement although it is an important part of my task. The thrill comes in the interaction with people and their ideas and in the performance opportunities. Some principals love to 'escape' into the classroom in order to enjoy the interaction with students. They quickly move into performance role, sometimes as the ring or band leader, the wild animal tamer, the juggler or even as the clown. While I continue to enjoy the student interaction which gives me energy, it is the staff meetings that attract me. It is the challenge, the meeting of minds and, I confess, the opportunity for performance. A staff meeting to me is an event, not just a routine episode in a communication dialogue. Having said that it is meant to be a special affair, I am only too aware that some of my staff meetings have been failures. They have been flat, boring, uninteresting and this was evident as staff wanted to be somewhere else. Other sawdust opportunities include meeting with parents, the press and council meetings. I am a people person and I think most people who enter the teaching profession delight in people too.

It is not just the sawdust event that produces emotion, the preparation for the event makes the adrenaline flow. Just to contemplate the venue can create anxiety. I have been in some terrifyingly large venues; one audience was in excess of 10,000. Preparing for the happening requires not only a knowledge of content but, just as importantly, of audience. Where possible before going on to the stage I try to talk to some of the audience. This anchors me with my audience.

It helps my personal performance if my co-performers are exciting and different. It is not much of a circus if it has only one event. I love our school speech nights where we have a mixture of drama, gymnastics, singing and speech, all of performance quality. The night then is a gala event. It provides opportunities for lots of people to participate and each performance enhances the others.

Death Defying Feats

All circus events appear to be dangerous. One of these dangerous acts is that of the tightrope. Usually the tightrope is high and so there is a significant element of danger. The person who walks the tightrope has majors in both faith and balancing.

Not much that happens at schools is without danger. From the time of arrival at school to the time the student leaves, responsibility of care is upon the staff through to the principal. There are the excursions, students travelling on buses, trams and trains — could there be an accident? There is the sporting program — flying balls, javelins and dangerous tricks such as you might see in the gymnastics program. There is the danger of wrong advice in relation to careers or personal matters. How many of the personal stories that you hear from students can you report and what must you hold and what danger is there in either action? If students break significant rules, do they stay in the school or are they to be expelled and what are the consequences for those students, for the remaining students and for the community?

Principals walk tightropes each day. This needs skill and confidence. Unfortunately some principals lose the confidence or the skills to make the walk. When this happens, then it is time for that person to leave the profession. To purge the school task so that all risks are removed is to fail to engage with what is, by its very nature, a risky task.

The Invisible Act

This is not an event that normally occurs in the Big Top. The invisible act is usually a feature of the side shows associated with the circus. In these performances you are invited to see something that isn't there. I can remember attending many outrageous acts. One involved a person lying down in a box, then the assistant took a saw and cut through the centre of that box. Another involved a person who could catch a speeding bullet in her mouth and there was always the magician who could make live birds appear from a hat.

There are some direct parallels to these acts in schools. I know one principal who spends a lot of time outside the school and he claims that he leaves a cardboard replica of himself sitting in his office chair. In a large school that has so many activities and so many associated commitments, I can find myself so often away from the office and sometimes the school, at required activities. I could be at a sports match, a musical event, a drama production, meetings of council, staff, parents or other principals, conferences, in architects' offices, visiting staff in hospital, representing the school at public occasions. People expect you to be at all these events but they also expect you to work, to plan, to answer their correspondence. This is where principals have to perform their magic. The task is to project a present image of themselves but not always be there in person. The goal is to be supporting, but not always present.

The necessary participation by principals in so many events does raise the question as to what is the real work of a school principal. Is the principal, like the school emblem, to be trotted out on all public occasions? Some staff would feel that an event is devalued if the principal is not there to see and participate in that event. If a principal puts attendance ahead of planning, the real task of leadership will be unattended. In reality it is probably not an 'either I do this or I do that' as much as a priority for one action ahead, but not at the expense, of the other.

Spotlights

The lighting of events is important. The lights need to be bright, can be coloured, and they need to be focused. Spotlights allow us to see the detail and colour. Spotlights focus upon our drama students as they perform their plays and upon our musicians whether as individual performers or as part of an orchestra or choir. There are virtual spotlights on our academic students as they impatiently wait for their examination results which will determine their future, whether they will achieve entry to the university course of their selection. The media can direct welcome and unwelcome spotlights upon the school. A school in a neighbouring city recently was front page news. The newspaper spotlighted this school with a story of how drugs had been found at that school and five students had been expelled as a result. In general, it is better to assume that if something goes wrong, then someone will have a spotlight on it and the principal should be prepared for this so that s/he can turn this to the school's best advantage.

Let us not be afraid of the spotlight. As leaders we have not just an opportunity but a responsibility to speak both within our communities and to society. Kress (1996) argues:

> ... why should we believe that we have no right, no duty, no responsibility in shaping that future? Others have no hesitation, no qualms, no second thoughts. The gurus of Fast Capitalism ... feel free to tell us what our future is; politicians have no reluctance; moralists of all persuasions are only too eager to push us in their direction; business men and women have their answers ready. In a period of intense change we have a duty to be involved in design; the design of socialities; of forms of economic life; of ideas of pleasure and of value systems. ... A deliberate move away from past agendas, a move beyond critique, a move to a notion of competence in design, for individuals seen as constantly innovative and creative, that for me is a productive notion ... (p. 19)

Series Of Acts

When you go to the circus there seems to be no particular coherence about the program. One event follows another and while the next is being set up the clowns will come out and entertain you.

This lack of coherence is also found within the school in the curriculum that we give students. They study discrete curriculum areas such as geography, history, maths, science, literature, languages, health, art and music. My experience is that these subject departments are regularly contending with each other for more time in the curriculum, for status and for more students. I have heard these departments described as the fiefdoms of the organization. These fiefdoms have 'turf' to protect or even to extend. They want their subject to be in the core curriculum, where students are required to attend, rather than in the elective program, where students might choose not to attend. This desire for core status is motivated firstly by a belief that teachers have in the importance of their subject and secondly by a fear that if there are no students choosing their subject, they could become unemployed.

Coherence in today's curriculum is strangely defined by the final examination where you must have some of this and some of that in order to graduate. Coherence is not necessarily achieved by an integration of knowledge gained while studying at school. I hope the future will see the studying of themes; the resolution of problems; adding to existing knowledge; learning tasks that cross existing subject boundaries; all of this driving future curriculum development. There is no reason to believe that an integrated curriculum is any less rigorous a study than the existing discrete curriculum challenges. Such an integrated curriculum should be driven by what students want to know as well as what teachers think that they should know. It could confront students with the big questions about their own lives within their learning, and enable them to make their learning personally meaningful. As Kress points out:

> A curriculum is a design for the future. In the knowledges which it offers, and in the organisations and principles of the construction of those knowledges, it makes

available to students one set of means whereby they can form themselves as human subjects. (*ibid*, 16)

But education is not an education for the future. Dewey, and many after him, have argued that:

education as preparation for adult life denied the inherent ebullience and curiosity children brought with them to school, and removed the focus from students' present interests and abilities to some more abstract notion of what they wish to do in future years. Dewey urged that education be viewed as a 'process of living and not a preparation for future living'. (Brooks and Brooks, 1993, p. 9)

A lack of coherence is also evident in the fragmentation of the school day. Imagine trying to work in an office where you had to pack up what you are doing and change both desks and tasks every forty-five minutes regardless of your readiness for these changes! In addition there is the fragmentation of the working day into school work and homework. Is school only between 8.30 am and 3.30 pm? Why do we make sport and music, for example, occur 'out of hours'? Isn't the task to be a learner and shouldn't this happen at any time of the day or night, holidays or workdays in diverse settings?

There is also the view that one can undertake the learning for the future while at school. This is 'just in case' learning. What is needed is 'just in time' learning, learning that occurs when you appreciate a need for this learning. In order to read the world, students will need to learn certain languages: written; visual; mathematical; scientific; spiritual and social. This is necessary learning. It does not have to happen all at once. Students to fully appreciate the value of these languages need to see their relevance and be able to integrate them into their lives. But do they need a prescribed curriculum of non-integrated bits with which they have trouble engaging themselves intellectually or in any other way? Why cannot all this follow from student chosen themes?

Senge (1992) believes that much of what happens today is focused on the parts, what he calls elemental thinking, or is attempting to so simplify what is a complex whole in order to obtain simple solutions, what he calls reductionism. He exhorts us to look at the interrelationships, see the patterns and not be caught up in static 'snapshots' that do not give the dynamic whole. He writes:

organizations break down, despite individual brilliance and innovative products, because they are unable to pull their diverse functions and talents into a productive whole.... system thinking ... is the conceptual cornerstone that underlies ... (it is) concerned with a shift of mind from seeing parts to seeing wholes, from seeing people as helpless reactors to seeing them as active participants in shaping their reality, from reacting to the present to creating the future. (p. 69)

A philosopher who is focused on reasoning wants us to know and experience empathy. 'Reason without emotion is impotent; but equally, emotion without reason has led to some of the worst horrors our history has known' (Singer, 1996, p. 296).

Knowledge needs to be personally mediated, it needs to be linked at a personal level to our experiences and to our emotions and passions. For this reason student choice as well as adult guidance is so important. Life themes, issues that are relevant to students are more important than reductionist defined fields of study.

There is another arbitrary adult rule by which we seem to work. Why are student classes organized according to age? Once again we are dealing with 'bits'. Why can't there be more flexibility so that classes centre around learning tasks? It is agreed that keeping young people with peers of their own age is important, but surely not to be slavishly implemented. The goal is to match students and programs.

From a series of acts to a coherent whole, but how is this to be achieved?

The Critics

Every show that opens needs good critical reviews. If the critics like the show, they will encourage others to attend that show. Schools too are dependent upon the critics' assessments. We need good publicity to assure full enrolments. We need full enrolments to ensure that we can deliver the programs we have in mind.

Our most important critics are parents and students. If they understand and are committed to what we are doing, then we are well on the way to ensuring a continued existence for the school. In today's society, we need to do more than that. We need to project the image of a good and successful school to the wider community. We need to have people who will never use our school believing in the work of our school. This means that a principal will need to spend a significant amount of time being available to the wider society, and the media in particular. When they present themselves the principal needs to take opportunities to promote the school and its policies. I've had important issues I wanted to place in the media but failed because, at that time, the media was not interested. The media, and society in general, will determine when a story will run. Principals have to be there when they are phoned, be willing to speak on a range of issues and need to have something to say.

There are some principals who so fear the critics that they will not allow the media into their schools and will not talk to the media themselves. They have become paralyzed by the critics. While this is a little better than those who do not hear the criticisms of their schools, it remains counter productive. The media like to create a story and the non-compliance of principals helps them to do this. On the other hand the principal's participation allows the story to be told, a story that might not be heard without the media's help. My experience of the media has been good. They have helped me to get my message to a larger community. But it has to be a win/win situation, the media do not exist just to promote the school. The media has to receive something that it believes to be newsworthy and we have to provide a positive message about our community.

My best media story relates to computers. When we required students in grade five to have their own laptop computer in 1990, this was controversial. There was naturally some concern by parents and some parents fought against the introduction of compulsory computing very hard. One incident remains vividly etched in my mind. One parent thought that, by going to the press and giving a negative story, this would kill this crazy idea. Unfortunately for that parent the journalist phoned the school to hear our view. The journalist listened to our story, liked it better than the one she had originally been given, and ran a story that congratulated the school on the introduction of personal computing.

The Clowns

How serious must a principal appear? A fellow principal wrote to me:

> It's interesting that these days we don't seem to expect our politicians to be leaders, but rather we are resigned to them being just politicians. In the same sort of way, society does not seem to demand of its school principals that they be people, but that they be merely school principals. To be honest, I'm not sure I'm totally comfortable with the dehumanised image of headship — the humourless grey-suited dusty bureaucrat guarded from the reality of life by owlish secretaries and reserved car parking spaces — it is something that doesn't sit well with me. I think it's important that our community is reminded that we also like to laugh, love and barrack for Hawthorn[2].

Can the community enjoy a principal who clowns? I have ridden on a Harley Davidson into and around a school hall where there was a staff social function in progress. I add, in self defence, the theme of the social event was 'Happy days' and leathers were in fashion! I know a principal who has ridden onto the stage of the assembly hall on a white horse and from that position of height talked to the students about leadership. The clown, the performer in us, can have an important role within the community. Principals need to be able to laugh at themselves, make fun of themselves, be human as well as be serious. I like to be able to dress in different clothes for the different occasions in the life of the community. The bathers for the swimming carnival, the academic gown for speech days, a character's clothes in a drama performance, power dressing in a pin striped suit for important occasions. There are times when my role would be to entertain, other times when I will be encouraging, giving confidence and courage and there will be times when I can have tears and share these with the community.

There is a sense in which the principal, like the clown, appears between acts. The principal is the 'filler' act, a link between the star performers, providing the commentary on the performance, projecting the mood for the total event and supplying the audience with the opportunity to stop holding their breath and get their collective adrenaline under control. The principal is also the *agent provocateur* of both the audience and the performers.

Circus Band

The band is an important part of the circus. It plays throughout the show. It helps manage the individual acts by introducing them and keeping them on time. It also helps manage the audience by playing faster or slower, or by changing moods and changing tunes. Without our knowing it we are caught in its melodic web, feeling danger, excitement or whatever the band wills.

In a similar way, the principal has to have the whole picture in mind. The principal is not an individual act. The principal chooses the tempo, the loudness, the tunes and may improvize with these. The idea of the principal calling the tune does not mean that the principal is the most important person. The music by itself is not going to draw the crowds. The drum roll only makes an emotional impact when it is associated with people risking their lives in some death defying event such as on the trapeze. It is likely that people attend the circus for a number of reasons and they could be to witness particular acts, not to hear the band. Similarly it is the good teaching, the special programs, the emphasis on computing or some other unique quality of the school and not because of the principal, that students enrol in a school.

The Ringmaster

When I told a friend that I was playing with this circus metaphor, I received a letter. Suggesting that the role in the circus that most resembles the role of principal in a school is ringmaster. The friend does not wish to be identified and I cannot take credit for this evocative picture. This is what I received:

> The ringmaster had to be an imposing figure (of a man!). He wore tails and a top hat to add to the impression of importance. Under the white 'dicky' shirt was a grubby singlet, no doubt, but we did not see it. He also carried a whip and used it for show and to gain attention. He made the announcements, did the publicity and was the public voice of the circus. He was often also the patriarch — too old for the trapeze, too scarred to tame lions, too clever to eat fire for a living and not yet sad enough to be a clown. Yet, I suspect, the best ringmasters understood what it was like to be all of those performers and had probably done a bit of everything themselves at some time.
>
> Of all the circus performers, the ringmaster is the most forgettable. The focus is on the glamour girls on horses, the daring trapeze artists, the fearless death-defyers and the hilarious clowns. While acting important, the ringmaster ends up being the last person to be remembered. Centre stage — even with a spotlight — is not where the most memorable action occurs!
>
> The ringmaster builds suspense, exaggerates the skill, brilliance and daring of the acts that are to follow, and then leads the audience in applause. He keeps talking when the elephants are being difficult, or his wife is doing a quick change from her fortune-teller costume to her sequinned tutu for her high wire act. And at the end he encourages us to go home so they can all pack up and go to bed in their caravans. And he reminds us to tell all our friends about the circus so that they can have a full house for the next night too.
>
> Of all the performers, the ringmaster is most like the clown. He is the ultimate 'straight man', the obvious butt of all the jokes and the one most easily mocked for his performances. Did you ever have the impression that without the red nose and the moppy wig there was a remarkable similarity between the ringmaster and the clown? Did you suspect, as I did, that they were in fact one and the same person?

Stars, Established and Beginning

At any particular time, a circus will have a star or stars for which it is famous. These stars are promoted in all advertising media. The fame of these stars is also the fame of the circus. At the same time the circus is looking for new stars. Often they have had to 'grow' new stars and circus people have 'adopted' children with this in mind. 'Young blood kept the travelling circus alive and kicking. Aboriginal children were easily obtained from families living in degraded circumstances . . .' (Ramsland and St Leon, 1993, p. 25).

Similarly schools can grow and decline according to their star performers who may be individuals, programs or a combination of these. A school can be riding high with full enrolments and a good status within the community. But then something can go wrong, the program is no longer valued, a star performer leaves, the community is wanting different acts.

Charles Handy (1994) reminds us that you don't ride out a success wave. Rather his advice is that to ensure a successful future, you need to catch a new wave that is already forming. Handy's actual metaphor is not that of a wave but of a curve, a Sigmoid Curve, which looks remarkably like an 's' on its side. He claims that the curve sums up the story of life itself. We start life slowly, experimentally and falteringly, we wax and then we wane. He instances the life stories of the British Empire and of the Russian Empire which had their times of greatness and then fell from power. Handy sees this repeated in the life cycle of a product, one moment being necessary and the next replaced by another product. He sees this wave pattern in the stories of the rise and fall of many corporations. So it is in the life cycle of schools.

Handy's belief is that the right place to start the second curve is before the first one peaks. At that time there are resources and energy to get through the initial exploration and floundering associated with the commencement of the second curve as it dips downward. If you wait until after the first curve dips, or to use my metaphor, until the first wave breaks, you are then struggling with the lost credibility associated with the first wave collapsing and consequently it is difficult to mobilise resources for the second wave (*ibid*, p. 50). Although I don't subscribe to the idea that we should do what business tells us, I do believe in reading the business literature, listening to the advice of business people and then attempting to interpret these insights within the educational setting.

So what is this next wave that schools must catch? The next wave in technology is not multimedia — that is already here. I see the next wave as being the incorporation of the laptop computers into the curriculum. The old curriculum was built around the technology of pen and paper. The present curriculum is being built around electrons and software as well as around texts, paper and pencil. So this is where schools need to be placing their resources.

The End of Circuses

The question has to be asked: Will circuses survive in today's technological world? If they are to survive, they will have to change dramatically. The loss of the wild animals was only the first challenge. A potential circus audience today is much more sophisticated and the circus, to survive, has to adapt to their new environment. 'When the rate of change outside exceeds the rate of change inside, the end is in sight' (Davis and Botkin, 1994, p. 109).

Similarly will schools survive the changes that are happening around them? This is a reasonable question as already people are beginning to learn more outside schools than in. 'Since personal computers hit the market in 1981 . . . more than 60 million people have learnt to operate them . . . most of those 60 million people learned computing . . . outside of school' (*ibid*, p. 32). Businesses are already thinking of their customers as learners and this gives them a new role as educators. While their motives are commercial, that does not necessarily make them poor educators. Business will be driven by competition and will see opportunities in the unmet needs to be found in the market place. Suppliers such as publishing and entertainment industries could potentially make more money selling direct into the home. Similarly distributors such as phone and cable companies can see wonderfully lucrative opportunities selling education directly, without having to go through schools. This has been described as 'L'earning'! (*ibid*, p. 84). Businesses are not just seeing earning power from sales. They realize that their competitive edge is their educated employee. Employee education, which is not to be dismissed as just training, is an education that is critical for the success of the business and employee education is consequently one of the fastest growing learning segments in our society.

Corporations are setting up high quality institutions, including universities, in which to teach their employees, so that both staff and the corporations will do their job well and succeed. McDonald's Hamburger University concentrates on preparing and serving food for the world and has high-class facilities for simultaneous translation into eighteen languages. The Holiday Inn University campus was initially established near Memphis, Tennessee in 1972. Now with their business more outside the US, they have opened a university in China where their business is expanding rapidly. Other corporations have similar institutions: American Express Quality University, Apple University, Disney University, Dow Chemicals Midland Learning Centre, Eastman Kodak, First of America Bank's Quality Service University, Mastercard University, Motorola University . . . The critics of these corporate universities point to the lack of attention in these institutions to philosophy and academic learning. However there are also critics of traditional universities, referring to them as 'vocational' with few graduates in philosophy and 'higher learning' (*ibid*, pp. 98–101).

As schools and institutes of higher learning lose their monopoly over education, they will become less and less relevant to the community and their funding will be in jeopardy. Papert has asserted that while learning is a natural process, schooling as we are providing it today, fixed curriculum, standardized tests, 'is not a natural act' (Papert, 1993, p. 55). Students are nowhere as hesitant as their schools in taking up this new learning delivered through technology. As customers, outside school, young people are competent, and focused on Nintendo and other sophisticated computer learning games. They regularly use CD players, camcorders and computers. They are not waiting for their schools to catch up. If education is redefined and the private sector becomes responsible for bigger segments of it, more will take place outside school classrooms. It will be mediated more by technology than by instructors. 'It will be available on an as-needed basis, in real time, and tailored to the learners' particular requirements' (Davis and Botkin, 1994, p. 124).

Are we happy with such a future? Will it deliver a holistic education, one that relates to the ethical, rational and spiritual issues as well as providing for employment and entertainment? Is this the bright new millennium or a grim apocalypse?

Strategic Intent

> The travelling circus is an interesting facet of Australia's past . . . A significant, well-regarded form of popular entertainment by the second half of the nineteenth century . . . It has lingered on in a leaner economic form until the present day . . . (Ramsland and St Leon, 1993, p. vii)

Could schools have a similar fate? What can be done about this? We need to be proactive, thinking strategically[3] to ensure the future as well as the present, not just for schools, but for the young people who might benefit. Mintzberg in 1987 was responsible for identifying strategy as a process that is shaped as much by the people in the organization, in our case teachers and students who can respond or create unexpected opportunities, as by the strategic intentions of those at the top. The strategy development process is therefore interactive rather than sequential. No circus director, school principal or school council alone defines the outcome; many have a part in its definition.

It is interesting and relevant to view this strategic planning from an historical point. In the mid-60s competition was relatively minimal as schools concentrated on their own wedge of an expanding pie. But in the late 60s the economic pie stopped growing. At that time the moves and countermoves of adversaries had to be reckoned with and parried. The result was an increasingly complex and potentially infinite regress of responses. Strategy was transformed into a competitive process. 'What are our neighbours doing?' became a vital and relevant question.

Today this does not work. Unfortunately it is not as simple as looking at our competitors. The circus environment bears testimony to this. To have copied a successful circus in the 1980s would not have delivered a successful circus in the 1990s when nearly all circuses vanished. Similarly the world outside schools has not remained stationary. The strategically relevant variables keep changing; the goal posts do not remain stationary. It is difficult to decide whether we are moving towards a global economy as some have predicted or are moving to smaller units, smaller even than national state units such as Crimea, Serbia. Worse, are we moving towards both situations simultaneously? In the light of such geopolitical discontinuities as the disintegration of the former Soviet Empire, where do we go?

Today the rate at which environmental data is changing is faster than the rate at which we can capture, process and act upon it. Events are happening that were impossible to predict. Thus a case can be made for lone individuals acting opportunistically in isolation to be given some freedom. This process the literature describes as 'intra-preneurship'. This is not to give up the planning model. Whatever happens needs to be consistent with our total vision for the school. A unity and coherence to all that is attempted is important. I have supported this intrapreneurship because it allows leverage of the unique talents and diverse initiatives of our professional and committed staff for the benefit of our students and college.

For a circus or school to survive, the rate of change in the external environment needs to be matched by changes in its internal functioning.

Notes

1   Australian slang for 'tall' story.
2   Hawthorn is the local football team.
3   I found an article by Max Boisot invaluable in helping me to understand the concept of strategic intent.

Chapter 11

The Journeying Principal

Once a jolly swagman camped by a bill-a-bong
Under the shade of a coolibah tree
and he sang as he watched and waited till his billy boiled
who'll come a waltzing Matilda with me.
(*Waltzing Matilda*, an Australian song)

Coming Out

When I have told friends that I am writing a book, the inevitable question is: 'What is it about?' I have been giving different answers depending upon what stage of the book I was at and these were basically factual answers summarizing content. Then suddenly I found that my answers changed and that I was interpreting my writing as 'my coming out', as a self-revelation that I had not previously been willing to make. What started in my writing as a relatively academic treatment of management and education in 'The Stumble Principal' became more personal with 'The Paranoid Principal'. In that chapter I managed to get in touch with my loneliness and, what is more, to talk about it publicly. By that stage I was identifying my feelings and was encouraged by the reading of *The Alchemist* to believe that feelings and intuition were respectable, and then to dare to write about them. Because the writing of 'The Alchemist Principal' coincided with my decision to leave my present job, there were plenty of feelings to explore and this I tried to do honestly. I was assisted by the honest reactions of my friends, and some of their comments I have included.

The words 'self-exposure' have definite negative overtones. One knows the consequences of physical self-exposure. But what are the consequences for personal self-exposure? I remember reading *The Naked Civil Servant*. I am not expecting the same horrors as Crisp experienced as his self-revelation was in a different and more Victorian generation. I will have to wait and see whether it is permissible for there to be an inner, as well as an outer, principal in this generation.

Fear of self-revelation is part of my personal history. I remember that as a new teacher in a rough working class school, I worked hard to leave little of myself visible to my students. I did not want to be vulnerable. I was there to teach them maths and teach maths I would. I think that I even managed to hide the fact that I was a first-year-out teacher. When I went to Canada to teach, the students helped me to begin my professional coming out. The personal dialogues, instead of hindering the teaching, actually facilitated the process. At that time I was not pushing unwilling students to attempt death-defying feats. Nor was I serving my masters, cap in hand. Instead I was beginning to work with, learn with and share in the learning process with my students. While a beginning had been made, it was not until I came to Methodist Ladies' College that I began to understand and appreciate the concept of a learning community. Was it significant that it was a girls' school in which there was a female ethos? There were networks, personal dialogues and an expectation of caring. In some strange way I was at home and, importantly, I had been chosen for this job. The result was that I could address the issues of collaboration and structures without being entangled in discussions of authority and hierarchy.

The fear of self-disclosure continues with me. As I was looking through material I found this quote gathered when I was in the US. This statement must have meant enough to me for me to have collected it and, more importantly, to have been able to find it again.

> We learn in school to conceal our own ignorance and confusion and this not only inhibits us from exploring the very moves that would be crowned with success but saps our self confidence. With no fund of shared experience of screwing up, we are apt to harbour wildly unrealistic fantasies about the intellectual prowess, the clarity and rigour of our teachers and peers. This Victorian prudishness about our cognitive disabilities is built right into the fundamental structure of school and it spawns a host of secondary effects, all debilitating . . . The current systems are so toxic for so many children that we risk little by taking the leap. (Dennett, 1993, p. 46)

Instead of crippling taboos against self-exposure, personal revelation could provide us with a way forward in times when there are no correct answers, only new answers. As we stumble forward, honest and open dialogue can enable sharing, caring and modelling. It could promote an interactive constructive professional dialogue between people rather than the one-way raconteur conversations between talkers and listeners, or worse, between talkers and talkers. I am frustrated with shallow impersonal conversations where the other person has to tell me how great their school is and, by implication, how great they are. What is worse, I know that I do it too! For a conversation to have depth for me there needs to be some content and context, successes as well as failures, and something of the person in it.

Yeats on Courage

I was discussing this 'coming out' with a member of the Methodist Ladies' College English faculty and she gave me *The Courage of the Artist*, in this case about Lionel Johnson. While I do not see myself in the same category as Tennyson, Yeats or Johnson, I do like the sentiment expressed. There needs to be a congruence between who we are and what we write or do. Furthermore for those who read our writings or our deeds, to know who we are and what we think helps them make sense of what we express. W.B. Yeats writes:

I am speaking of him very candidly; probably he would not (wish) to be spoken of in this way, but I would wish to be spoken of with just such candour when I am dead. I have no sympathy with the mid-Victorian thought to which Tennyson gave his support, that a poet's life concerns nobody but himself. A poet is by the very nature of things a man who lives with entire sincerity, or rather, the better his poetry the more sincere his life. His life is an experiment in living and those that come after have a right to know it. Above all it is necessary that the lyric poet's life should be known, that we should understand that his poetry is no rootless flower but the speech of a man, (that it is no little thing) to achieve anything in any art, to stand alone perhaps for many years, to go a path no other man has gone, to accept one's own thought when the thought of others has the authority of the world behind it, . . . to give one's life as well as one's words which are so much nearer to one's soul to the criticism of the world . . . Why should we honour those that die upon the field of battle, a man may show as reckless a courage in entering into the abyss of himself.[1] (Ellmann and Feidelson, 1965, pp. 5–6)

When The Sun Rose

As with all my journeying, I find it easier to set out than to travel. I believe that I should be honest about this but it is hard to do that when I do not always know what I am feeling or thinking. I get caught up in the clichés and the existing thought patterns of today. How am I to break free? Where do I find the sunshine? How can I fulfil my chosen destury?

As I write this I am reminded of my experience of flying from Los Angeles to London. In the midst of this flight I wrote;

> I am not enjoying flying this morning. I cannot sleep, I am uncomfortable and I know that when I arrive in London my personal time clock will take days to acclimatize. Before I left Australia, I had imagined the freedom of the flight — as the plane takes off I would leave all my worries behind. I felt this freedom when I left Australia. Today that is not my experience, not being able to sleep despite the fact that I have been awake for about twenty-two hours. There is nothing else to do but to watch a silly movie named *Gypsy Rose Lee*, which is about someone else's fantasies and dreams, and try to sleep. . . . Now the sun is coming up over the cotton wool clouds, a beautiful soft coloured light is entering the cabin. It is as beautiful as I had imagined it would be when I was back in Melbourne. Then each morning, before the sun had risen, I had got up to go swimming and had thought of this moment. It is beautiful this morning but it no longer emotionally moves me like it did when I first travelled thirty years before. I am tired, is that all that is different? . . . The sun is now up and its warmth is in the cabin. My thoughts are now turning to walking through London, of theatre, of the shortness of life and the need to spend it well. I am thinking of the flat that is waiting for us where we will be able to unpack the suitcases, cook simple food and achieve a little normality. I can feel the excitement growing, tiredness is no longer my dominant thought. The night and its blackness is passing.

In a few short hours I had made a transition from blackness to light. In many ways this is also how I experience leadership. Setting out and arriving are good but in between are some really bad moments. Why do we leaders only tell about the good moments, the destinations achieved? Why do we leave out the periods of despair? Are we afraid to tell these? Wouldn't it be more beneficial to the new traveller to know of the downside of the journey?

So in this chapter I want to convey something of the inner journey and not just regale you with tall stories of mountains conquered. Furthermore, I know that when I read this in print, I will want to withdraw the book for correction. Truth is disclosed in some evolutionary way. I do not have it and I will never have it other than in a partial way. This writing will not be perfect and that is all the more reason to try to put the writing in the context of both a journey and a growing, changing person.

Self As Institution

I have learned to distinguish between being personal, something which I have been espousing, and personalizing everything. This was one of my most traumatic learning experiences. It occurred in my early years as a principal of a small struggling country independent school[2] which was in competition for survival with a neighbouring independent school. It was clear that only one school would survive. At that time I identified too closely with my school. Its successes were my successes, its failures were mine too. Criticisms of 'my school' were taken personally, as criticisms of me. With this mind set it became very hard to have a private separate life. In a small town where everything is political, I was reluctant to make political comments lest they reflected badly on the school. My personal failure was that I had no sense of myself as separate from the institution.

Whether we had won or lost the competition for students, the result for me probably would have been the same. We did survive and eventually took over the other school, accommodating those of that student community who wanted to be in our school. The result was effectively an amalgamated school. To go with this mind set of ownership into the new, amalgamated school was even more difficult. In the new school were many who previously had not chosen us and now they were part of our family. Not surprisingly they didn't like all that we did and this now they expressed from within. Whether as a result of this stress, or quite independently, I had a brain haemorrhage at that time. In the convalescent period I determined that never again would I 'own' a school. The school would be a place in which I would work and work very hard but it would never be part of my psyche again. I was determined to have a sense of self which would be separate from the institution.

Journeying

The literary device of the metaphor is an important way in which we can make sense of the world that we experience. It provides a powerful way of linking the abstract with the known world of our experiences, linking the simple with the complex and linking the familiar with the unfamiliar. The metaphor enables us to know and to have some control over our environment. For me journeying is one such powerful metaphor.

The journeying has a number of recognizable parts. First one chooses a destination, plans the details including how to travel, with whom and with what luggage. With this done and the appropriate paper work completed, one sets out confidently expecting to arrive safely and achieve one's objects. But it rarely works out this way. We never know all the facts and so the preparation is never complete. While outwardly confident, we do fear the worst particularly as we get older and we have accumulated some bad experiences. Then the goal is achieved and we return triumphant wondering why we had been fearful. If you are like me you will then immediately plan the next trip thinking of the successes of the last one and not remembering the horrors until you begin the next trip. At that time the fears come flooding back.

To travel metaphorically one does not have to leave one's school. The travel might be a learning adventure, to research some topic of interest and relevance. Or the travel might be through some traumatic experience. As I write, a school community in which children were killed in an accident when a cliff collapsed is in the midst of such a fearful travel.

I have been fortunate to have had some overseas travel as part of my role as principal. One such journey took me to Indonesia, a near and important neighbour. But Indonesia poses some challenges for which one prepares as best one can, injections, reading and equipment. The travel is a privilege and mostly a joy. The goal in this instance was important to the school. I was to travel alone and this travel was to occur in the midst of a busy term. This is how I recorded a part of this travel after arrival at my destination.

> Travel began the night before departure with packing, trying to think about all the things that had to be included. One day I will be packed a day in advance! But I may have to wait until retirement when I will not have last minute tasks at school which will have priority.
>
> Then there was the early morning rise at 4.10 am to be on a plane at 6.00 am. How hard it was to get up so early when I knew that so much time would be wasted changing planes and waiting in airports. The first change of plane was in Sydney. There I had also to change terminals, frustrating because I was in work mode and so a good novel did not distract me from my predicament. The flight across Australia to Jakarta had been a delight, sitting comfortably working on the computer with food and wine served. The arrival in Jakarta was at the international airport. I expected to be sitting in the airport for three hours. Unfortunately my next plane had been delayed for three additional hours. The result was six hours in the middle of nowhere. I could not even find a power point to plug in my computer — the three batteries that I carried had all been used up in the flight from Australia. This six hours was not easily accommodated. As well I had a slight headache — was it the tension of travel or perhaps was it the red wine on the plane? To add to the discomfort, the Jakarta temperature was 32°C with 95 per cent humidity and no air conditioned lounge into which to escape.

In Jakarta I had to move to the local airport. There were plenty of people touting various rides but I chose to go on the community bus. When I made that decision I had been worried that I might not know where to leave the bus. That did not pose a problem. The bus driver accepted my money and instead of taking 500 rupees he took 2500. Not a bad payment for him. When he offered to carry my bag off the bus, I agreed since I had really paid him well! This experience, however, had left me with some anxiety. Would there be more like him in Indonesia or were most people honest?

Finally the local plane arrives and I depart on it. Now begins my preoccupation with food. I wasn't sure whether to eat the strange cold food and consume the drink that was provided from a jug, not from the plastic bottle that I had hoped to see. Everyone else was eating and drinking and so I did too.

The arrival in Padang was smooth, but late at night. A taxi seemed appropriate and I noticed that the taxi had neither a seat belt nor a meter. How much would I have to pay for this taxi fare? Would he take me to the right hotel? Now I had new worries. When we had travelled in the taxi for over twenty minutes, and I had thought Padang was a small city, I was anxious again. I wondered if I had given him the right information. Since we spoke different languages, speaking was impossible. Finally we arrived at my hotel where I was delighted to see that the person receiving the taxi spoke English.

The bed in the hotel was welcome — it was nearly twenty hours since I had risen that morning.

The next morning brought the problem of food again, what to eat. It is amazing how big a problem this is, at least initially when I arrive. By the time that I leave the country I will have forgotten the food worries but in the early stages it is always traumatic. I did not want to spend my time in a foreign country sick. I decide on watermelon juice and tried to tell the waiter that I want no additional ice or water. I am not convinced the waiter understood. Local cooked food is best and so that was what I choose. And then there was the question of coffee. This was the only time when I hoped that the coffee had been brewing for ages; that way the water would be safe!

Wimpish isn't it? I am embarrassed to be writing this. Yet it is the account of what I wrote on arrival in Padang. Furthermore I made a second trip to a different place in Indonesia and had similar worries. With further opportunities I will travel again, and worry, but perhaps a little less each time because my experience and skills are increasing in this type of travel.

A Psychoanalytic Perspective

Throughout this book there has been an attempt to look at leadership from a personal perspective. Some of the fears, dreams, beliefs, fantasies and aspirations have been discussed. It is amazing, given the extensive literature on leadership, that little appears to have been written from the psychoanalytic perspective. In fact little seems to have been written about the emotions of those leading schools. Why is this? In setting out to write about the inner principal I have worries like those I had when I travelled to Indonesia because this, too, is new territory for me.

The psychoanalytic approach builds upon the early work of Freud. The researchers who followed Freud saw leadership

> as a result of the personal dispositions, qualities, and attributes of the individual occupying a position of authority. Leadership is that part of executive action that may be directly attributed to the inner life of the leader, to her personal vision, her ways of being and acting, her deep rooted beliefs, her imagination and her fantasies . . . (Lapierre, 1991, pp. 70–1)

These observations about the inner qualities that define people and their actions are not new. They go back to Socrates and Plato who had taught us about the importance of self-knowledge and how this knowledge could illuminate our thought and direct our action.

It is not suggested that the psychoanalytic approach to leadership gives the full picture. It does not address all the external issues, the relationships with others, but it does give a new and important focus on the leader as a person. Is the leader a risk taker or does s/he always play safe? In terms of leadership, what are the consequences of the deep-seated elements of the leader's personality?

This Journey

With the destination of an enlightened community situated on a far shore, I have set out on a beginning voyage of learning discovery. The waters for me have not been charted and, if they have, I did not find the maps in the educational libraries. The seas have sometimes been tumultuous and I wondered whether the institutional boat would stay afloat and, if it did, would I avoid the sickness of the sea? Sometimes I was becalmed for long periods not knowing what to write. But then the wind of inspiration came, mostly slowly but sometimes rushing. The winds have blown sometimes from unexpected quarters but the sails have held the wind and with my rudder of experience, the boat has managed to stay on course. There have been some wonderful ports on the way where I have been able to dock, exchange the tales of travel and replenish stores for further journeying. Although I could not see the lighthouse, I have felt its presence and been guided by it.

In this book of travels you are not only invited to share in these travels but to add to them with your tales. Find that Bull Box[3] which I am sure is close at hand. Add not only to your knowledge but also to ours through your sharing. Identify your dream and work towards its fulfilment. Be energized by the uncertainties, mysteries and doubts. In the midst of your leadership write of your experiences to help us weary but excited fellow travellers. Perhaps you may be able to fill in the gaps and write the unwritten stories about 'The humpty dumpty principal'; 'The moral turpitude principal'; 'The lazy principal'; 'The zealot principal'; 'The proper principal'; 'The pre-emptory principal'; 'The humble principal'; or other principals. Together with Mary Mason I am planning a sequel on 'The no-walls principal'. 'Who'll come a waltzing Matilda with me?'

Finally

Most attempts at reform have come from the outside, people wishing to impose curriculum and benchmarks. This book assumes that schools can transform themselves. Better schools will eventuate when those in the schools, particularly the principal, become not only more aware of their community and its requirements but also more aware of what is happening within themselves. A sensitive, thoughtful, proactive leadership might yet deliver the quality outcomes that the community desires from schooling.

In this book I have been principally concerned with the person of the leader, with her/his personality and with her/his dreams. I have explored leadership in terms of the 'personal inner theatre of the leader', in terms of the 'original vision, of personal qualities that derive their strength from an inner complexity (whether tumultuous, conflicted, or harmonious) . . .' (*ibid*, p. 71).

Within any organization there are many who lead and, through the complex interactions of these people, leadership occurs. More than one person needs to be studied in order to obtain a picture of the unconscious dynamic of that organization. The designated leader, the principal, is an important person to study in depth. That person is in a unique position as Chief Executive Officer of the school. That person by virtue of the role has access to more information, has more influence and has authority over the allocation of resources on a day-to-day basis.

Notes

1 An unpublished speech (1907).
2 This school is now the successful Kinross Wolaroi School in Orange.
3 See page 131 for a description of the Bull Box.

Chapter 12

The Frog Prince'pal

... education is as yet something more envisioned than practised. (Goodlad, 1984, p. 361)

Transformation

The Frog Prince'pal is a description of one principal's dream of a transformed school that might become a reality in the future. This principal wants to establish a school that assists all students, not just the top 10 per cent, to graduate with a knowledge of self and others, a capacity and desire to shape her/his environment and an enhanced self-esteem. This school will be a place where all students learn, rather than a place where many fail. This is not a vote for mediocrity and the lowest common denominator. Rather it is an assertion that grading and sorting students for the best university faculties, which has become a major preoccupation of schools today, has hijacked the purpose of schooling. This emphasis on finding the very best and being able to discriminate among the top students has driven the curriculum and focused the mind of all associated with schools on a narrow band of schooling outcomes. Students who do not make it into the elite category leave school feeling they are failures. Subsequently they do not perform well either as individuals or as members of society and this has contributed to the breakdown of our present society. Any school leaver who is going to cope in what is basically a hostile society needs a 'secure understanding of self, others and an awareness of one's place in the universe' (Thwaites, Wysock-Wright, 1983, p. 20).

The reader may well question why, in this chapter, there is a reference to a fairy tale in which a frog is magically transformed into a charming prince. Is such a thought contrary to the thesis of 'The Cinderella Principal'? I think not. The frog could represent the school waiting to be released from a more primitive form. This release will come when someone addresses appropriately the frog's condition. This will not be by a kiss but it will be a tender and affectionate personal act. The prince could represent the confident and endowed youth of tomorrow who will be our future.

Yearning

Although what follows is written by one who is discontented with what is being achieved by schools, this is not to be read as a criticism of those in the schools who do a great job, given the external constraints within which they have to work. They are mostly dedicated professionals and their achievements need to be celebrated. The discontent follows, rather, from how the task of schools is conceived and from the opportunities consequently forgone.

Our generation has been brought up with schools, classrooms and teachers and so we tend to see them continuing into the future. But is this likely? Consider the following critical views of schooling, firstly by Papert (1993) and then by Moffett (1994):

> This book (*The Children's Machine*) is informed and shaped by the belief that strong feelings of dissatisfaction within society at large are rapidly making it impossible to save education, as we know it, by continuing to tinker around the edges. (p. 6)

> A few decades from now people will regard the schooling of today with revulsion, as astonishingly primitive, in the same way we deplore the eighteenth-century treatment of the mentally ill. Our successors will not be able to understand how citizens dedicated to personal liberty and democracy could have placed learning on a compulsory basis, such that citizens had to report to certain buildings every working day of their youth in order to be bossed about by agents of the state. (p. 5)

If schools are to continue into the future, then they will need to change. Schools could be centres of more natural learning with curriculum that is less contrived. Schools as institutions need to be more congruent with human nature providing for people's higher order needs, self-respect and self-actualization (Senge, 1992, p. 140). The schools could be more differentiated from each other than the look-alikes that we know and have known for more than 100 years and integrated into a network of other institutions such as homes and work places. They should be using current technology to achieve their purposes and be providing significant residential experiences for every student. All of this could be achieved without additional resource allocation, but it would mean going without some of what we have now such as school buildings, classrooms and 'teachers'.

Teaching too needs to change. It has become a technical task of imparting knowledge although teachers have tended to resist this utilitarian view of their role by bringing into the classroom warm, natural, human relationships (Papert, 1993, p. 55)

I approach this chapter as a yearner and learner, as a school principal and as a concerned community member. I want to understand the business of schooling that I am in. I am prepared to put in time to research and to risk the consequences of speaking out against established traditions. I need to be joined by others in this search and look forward to debating their conclusions. An informed dialogue is sought. Schools do not belong to individuals, the teaching profession or other select groups. They are instruments of a society, conceived and provided to enable that society and its members to manage the complexity of living in 1997 and beyond. Our answers must provide for the opposing views and tensions as to whether education is to achieve intrinsic or extrinsic goals, the conflicting traditions and values of East and West in our community, economic imperatives and personal preferences.

A Personal View

In the face of such tensions, ambiguities and uncertainties, I have gone back to my educational beginnings, to Martin Buber and to R.S. Peters and to assumptions derived from my Christian faith to find some core values. This in turn has forced me to reflect deeply on my experience, to search for what I value, and has encouraged me to speak out for what I believe.

Education, as I would like to see it transformed, requires a person's participation and interaction with other people and objects. The conceptual basis for these relationships between people and with the object world I have taken from Martin Buber[1] and his 'I-It' and 'I-Thou' analysis. His thesis is that our humanity is in the mystical 'between' generated in the 'I-Thou' relationship and has derived from our relationship with the greatest and most worthy other — God. Schools are not about inert knowledge but about the growth of people, the extension of their intellectual, social and cultural capacities, and also about the growth and maturity of a society in which people can live and grow and find meaning in their lives.

The competent individual and the good society are not passive recipients of what comes their way. Both are proactive, asserting their responsibilities and working to create a better future. Given that our society is not stable and that our society has substantial deficiencies, education too needs to be proactive in repairing the deficiencies. In schools, as in society itself, this is a time for bold imaginings, when a future must be chosen through open dialogue and a consideration of intelligent alternatives. Teachers, students and principals have a major part to play in this process. Schools could be places of significance where culture and knowledge are communicated and, importantly, places where community could be generated and where people could grow. Schools need to be safe environments to foster that growth as well as honest, open communities that struggle with the chaotic and continually changing world. The goal is both to empower students and to build tomorrow's society. Crichton's book, *Jurassic Park*, reminds readers of the importance of keeping the big picture in mind. The expert professionals of Jurassic Park exceeded the skill and knowledge of their peers, the administrators achieved their given primary goal, but that was not enough when the future of society was threatened.

Having forcefully asserted that respect for all persons is important, I do not wish it to be pursued with a cavalier disregard for quality of experiences. All students need intellectual skills, cultural knowledge and a perspective from which to make sense of their environment.

> Whitehead very wisely put the matter in perspective when he argued that individuals have to pass from the stage of romance, when their interest is awakened, to a stage of precision when their interest is disciplined. (Peters, 1966, p. 57)

In my preferred society people will think, and take responsibility, for themselves while at the same time demonstrating respect for others. In developing a model of a future school that will prepare young people for that society, the school's social role of nurturing the growth of mature, independent, cooperating people needs to be given priority. Such a view is not only consistent with the appropriate respect for a human person but also consistent with the 'business' view of the world. A successful business places its hopes on small work units which are independent and accountable, not on massive organization in which hierarchical structures can hide responsibility and not deliver outcomes.

The realities of our pluralist and divided society must be kept in mind. Teachers who frequented an education book shop in Melbourne were described by the staff of that book shop as being anxious, apathetic or angry.[2] The war of the Balkans spills over into fights in Melbourne streets. Many members of Christian churches view the role of women differently from many Moslem believers. More than 8 per cent of our population are without jobs and some of these unemployed people may never in their lifetime obtain work. Today's schools need to prepare students for the complexities and tensions of life in such a society. This is a strength of western society, a productive resource rather than a problem. The three Rs may have been a good description of the basics in earlier times but they are not sufficient to equip our young people today.

The Curriculum

In schools there are important skills, necessary knowledge and important activities that need to be taught. In Australia a committee chaired by Mayer was funded to identify a list of 'key competencies'. They identified seven:

1 Collecting, analyzing and organizing information.
2 Communicating ideas and information.
3 Planning and organizing activities.
4 Working with others and in teams.
5 Using mathematical ideas and techniques.
6 Solving problems.
7 Using technology.

This is a rather dull view of education, emphasizing a technical view of the task of educators. Where is the mention of cultural knowledge, of value statements other than economic and technical, and where is the mention of social setting, of key intellectual issues, of formulating insightful questions, of the relevance of different questions, of creative thinking, of looking for underlying patterns or of understanding?

Instead of this recipe of tasks, we need an inclusive framework for education, one that takes us from consciousness through culture to the cosmos itself.

> The ultimate systemic thinking is cosmological, metaphysical. . . . (An) education system would most sensibly sponsor the quest for the nature, meaning and purpose of life that underlies not only science, art, and philosophy but also the personal acts of everyday life. . . . Within this cosmic framework, not politics and economics, but culture and consciousness should provide the dual focus for a new sort of education. (Moffett, 1994, p. xiv)

In Perspective

Through successive periods in our recent history, responsibility for education has moved from one institution to another. These changes have been reflected in the major buildings of the period. In early Australia the churches dominated the landscape and in regional towns such as Bendigo this can yet be seen. Then came the public buildings, the town halls, parliament buildings and post offices. These were imposing edifices for their day, built to last from quarried stone and marble. Today the landscape of cities is dominated by commercial buildings reaching to the sky, making their statements as to where power now resides. These buildings are not meant to last forever and we watch as large buildings are demolished to make way for bigger and better ones.

Reflecting these changes in the landscape are the educational changes. In early America and Australia, the church controlled much of the education. 'Harvard's stated purpose, for example, was instruction to "know God and Jesus Christ"' (Davis and Botkin, 1994, p. 24). The values that this church-sponsored education espoused were humbleness, faith and obedience, to live according to God's will. To forge a union of the competing religious groups, a separation of church and state followed. The change from church to state was propelled chiefly by political rather than economic motives. Taxation provided free, compulsory and secular education. The language of the schools was to be that of daily life, not the Latin of the church. National unity and dominance was to be a major goal. Thus when Sputnik appeared in US skies in 1957, there was a national cry to improve education, not for intrinsic reasons, but for the security of the country and for national pride. The problem of racial integration in the US was to be solved in the schools by bussing students from home to schools not in their neighbourhood. Political forces were mandating reform, sometimes responding to concerns about national defence. Teaching in government schools was a public service rather than a service to God. Enter the large and powerful corporations with their dominating buildings and powerful purses. Now enterprise is beginning to become the educator. As people begin to learn more outside of schools than in, schools begin to become less and less relevant to the community's lives. New methods for delivering education are being developed by business and these are consistent with their values of competition, customer needs and service. Business will compete to fulfil the unmet needs in the market place. It will educate minorities but more for its own good, not out of social considerations. 'Since the teaching of moral values has long been the province of the church, church educators are often surprised to discover that corporations devote more time to values education than public schools do' (*ibid*, p. 38).

In a learning system dominated by business, a key question will be whether its values and practices — such as the need to integrate a work force increasingly diversified by race, gender and national origin — will lead to greater success than the government has had in its attempts to legally enforce integration. (*ibid*, p. 36)

In 1996 we are lectured on the merits of competition and urged to emphasize vocational (relevant) education. At a conference I recently attended, the Business Council of Australia president was urging us educators forward to greater effort so that Australia could regain its lost status as a country in the top ten. How is this to be measured? By measuring the average per capita income. There is no hope for Australia if this is how greatness is to be measured!

But the story does not end here. Perhaps there is yet one more change to occur and this is already apparent. The corporations are having to downsize, to outsource. The home is becoming a place from which to work. The individual no longer needs the resources previously only obtainable in large corporations. Are we about to see a resurgence in the power of one? How will these people be educated? Moffett (1994) argues:

The very concept of schools, classes, courses, exams, and curriculum is super-seded. Subjects and methods are reorganised around individual learners forging their personal curricula in interaction with others doing the same across a whole spectrum of learning sites, situations, and technologies. This is what I am calling the universal schoolhouse. (p. xvi)

Walls Crumbling

The most obvious difference between education in the future and now is likely to be in the use of technology. Simulation devices, virtual reality, interactive video and personal computers will be ubiquitous. One school, Methodist Ladies' College, by 1994 had already made personal computing a reality[3] — every student with her private laptop computer with its knowledge space, powerful programs and access to the world through Internet. The future of these students is not constrained by the walls of a classroom, by the people in the classroom or by the culture in which they reside. Their learning does not have to take place at school and, even while at school, their learning may be sourced outside this school.

If we consider only the technical Mayer competencies, it is clear that the learning could be divided into two groups — that which can be best achieved within a specifically constructed physical community such as a school and that which can be achieved by the individual learner working apart from such a community but not necessarily alone.

Consider, firstly, what the individual learner can achieve away from the institution. This would include most of the knowledge content of the curriculum. A person at home, in hospital, on holidays, in a car, in a library, at a friend's home, or a person in a community group, a work group or a holiday group, or joined to others across the world by Internet, can write essays, research data, learn and use mathematical ideas and techniques, discover much of the content of geography and history, learn the rudiments of a language, manage technology, ask and be asked important questions, be intellectually engaged, find role models, gain a world perspective, be enterprising, be imaginative and creative, and gain self-respect and confidence through these processes. *The Times Educational Supplement* (17 December 1993) carried an article 'Far Flung and Friendly' by Mike Holderness which extolled the virtues of the fax in distance learning.

> For some students, it's almost the first time that they've been able to feel there's one person dealing exclusively with them. . . . The fax, often perceived as the most impersonal of media, allows some children more personal and trusting communication than they have been able to achieve with a teacher in person.

As well as the fax, there are telephones, TV, electronic mail and other computer driven assistance to support the separated learner.

In a school, all of the above can be achieved, but would it be achieved effectively, efficiently and economically? So significant is the learning that can take place away from a school, some have questioned the value of providing new schools and some have speculated what existing schools may become. They suggest modifying existing school buildings into home residential units with sporting and cultural facilities as part of the complex!

Day and Night School

Without wanting to participate in an economic rationalist dialogue, I suggest that schools will need to provide something that cannot otherwise be provided if they are to continue to exist. Schools are expensive and, in general, are paid for from a tight taxpayer's purse which has also to provide for health, defence, roads, etc. So it is important to identify what extra dimensions schools as places could bring to the learning process. In the social setting of a school it is possible to attend to relationships (relating to others with respect and empathy), to personal communication (listening skills and sensitivity as well as speaking), to working in teams (the challenge of living in a fragile democracy), to mentoring, to leadership, to values. The unique contribution of a school no longer resides in the provision of basic educational knowledge but in the experiences not possible if one were not present in a group setting such as a school. These experiences include the process of engaging intellectually and personally with significant others — teachers and peers — and in the study of the school as a microcosm of the society that exists and might exist.

If this is to be the emphasis in schools then it is appropriate to consider the relevance of an extended day that could include a residential component. We know of the educational value of camps, of students and teachers living together for an extended period of time, finding the subject of education in the setting and in the community life. Camps can provide experiences not possible in a day school that begins at 8.30 am and finishes at 3.30 pm but their short duration of usually less than one week, their single focus and their restricted facilities limit their value. Another option is an extended residential school experience which potentially can offer even more than a camp and more than a day school.

The best known extended residential experiences in Australia are military camps, such as were provided and made compulsory in the late 1950s, and boarding schools. There are today many who continue to extol the virtues of the army to put some discipline into young people's lives through a compulsory military camp. To me, the idea is abhorrent. Military discipline is necessary in war, indeed it is difficult to imagine an army without it! In peace the hierarchical structure and rigid external controls do not lead to the development of independent ('We will all run ten kms today'), questioning ('Do as you are told!') and respectful ('Shoot the enemy!') members of a society.

Today there are many who see a boarding school experience as important. While some boarding houses have been run like military institutions, most have been more like a hostel and some even like a home away from home. Unfortunately most existing boarding schools have been intellectually separated from the day schools to which they are attached. The activities of the boarding house and the school are not usually related in any significant educational way. This separation is a relatively new phenomenon. Only in recent years has the boarding house played such a minor role as an adjunct to the day school. Before that, the boarding house and school were integrated, and together were the focus of the educational activity. History shows that in most societies, whether primitive, ancient or modern, use has been made of some form of boarding as a means of transmitting 'mysteries' as in the training of warriors and religious elites. The more embracing and sustained the experience of the boarding school, the more it facilitated the 'communication of values, norms and cultural patterns' (Lambert, 1975, p. 10).

Boarding schools have not been subjected to the same scrutiny as day schools. Consequently they have changed little from their early beginnings in the nineteenth century British public schools despite the fact that their purposes now are different. The British public schools were established to support the changing national needs brought about by the advent of the empire, giving high priority to outcomes such as 'manliness' and 'leadership'. In Australia the boarding schools were adopted for more middle class reasons and to address the problem of small populations in remote regions that could not support schools.

The establishment of Marshmead[4], described more fully in chapter 10, ushered in a different form of school experience. In this case the residential experience is the basis of the educational study, not simply an adjunct hostel experience. Students in year 9 are offered an eight-week residential program (one school term) in a stimulating ecologically significant environment. The curriculum is taken from the community life which the students experience and the environmental setting of their new home. The paradigm chosen for Marshmead was a comfortable home in a village. In the home setting, in the village community and in going out from the village and returning home students are to achieve a growth in personal, community and world knowledge. In such a setting, away from the parental home, a young person's fantasy of self-reliance can be lived out.

Other purpose-built communities have been established. Religious communities bring the challenge of spirituality more effectively in a residential setting by integrating it into daily living. The Australian Institute of Sport provides accommodation so that no time is lost in travel, sport has a twenty-four hour focus and other learning is built around the sport. The universities have set up summer schools for bright young scientists and mathematicians. One can imagine similar residential experiences being set up for musicians, writers or historians.

A significant residential experience ought not to be an option only for the wealthy or the specially talented but an experience available to all students. If we believe in community, in the school as a microcosm of society, in the process of engaging intellectually and personally with significant others — teachers and peers — then the appropriate preparation is unlikely to be achieved in a day school with restricted hours and scope. The need is for a residential community experience of significant duration creating an experiential workshop setting: in which the study of the community is possible; where the achievement of mutual respect is supported; where interpersonal skills can be fostered and where the growth in self esteem of all members is the goal.

Radical?

While many will ask whether society can afford such an expensive education, I am asking whether the community can afford not to provide such an education. As we have seen, if the community is threatened from outside, then the money is found for military training and for war equipment. When the community is threatened from within, the response is that we cannot afford to do anything more than we are now doing!

And we are threatened from within. Postman (1987) makes a frightening comparison between two great writers — Orwell and Huxley. Orwell, the author of *1984* and *Animal Farm*, described a culture that had become a prison. Huxley, author of *Brave New World,* described a culture that had become a burlesque. Orwell warns that we will be overcome by an externally imposed oppressor — whilst it was Huxley's impression that no big brother is required, we deprive ourselves of our autonomy. Orwell feared that the truth would be concealed from us. Huxley feared that the truth would be drowned in a sea of irrelevance. Orwell feared that what we hate would ruin us. Huxley feared that what we love will ruin us. What Huxley teaches us is that in a age of advanced technology, spiritual devastation is more likely to come from an enemy with a smiling face. The enemy will not have an articulated ideology, no communist manifesto. Rather the enemy comes as the unintended consequence of a dramatic change in our modes of public conversation.

What is proposed to confront such a fearful situation is radical. It is not a rearrangement of the existing deckchairs on the massive Titanic of state education but a renovated ship of society that is purpose-built for an achievable task and will not sink. What is not functional needs to be abandoned. Neither the deckchairs — teachers, curriculum — nor the Titanic — buildings, school systems — have any intrinsic value. They exist only to serve and have no independent existence. These are tough words and there will be many who will not tolerate them. A larger battle has to be fought for our young people and for our community. The education that we currently provide is inadequate as it does not properly address the intellectual, social and spiritual needs of our young people.

To change schools significantly will not be easy. The forces acting to maintain the present culture include the physical buildings. Their design, to a significant extent, determines what can happen in them. The buildings are designed for instruction rather than collaboration. Another constraining force is the entrenched rituals which are more about controlling learning: raising one's hand before answering; listening to teachers and taking notes; taking tests; writing book reports (Brooks and Brooks, 1993, p. 126). There are the myths and popular stories about key people: Kotter, Mr Chipps are mythological saviours. Then there are perceptions including student unreadiness to learn; the lack of resources even to maintain the status quo; the evaluation/reward criteria for students and staff; the mission statement for schools, espoused by the community, such as to obtain employment and to achieve the clever country. Even more fundamental is the perception that schools are about teaching, not learning and that knowledge is objective, not subjective. It is important to identify, examine and even question our mental pictures, our 'mind forged manacles', of what we see as our primary task in schools.

A new set of images, metaphors, stories and mission statements is necessary. We need to see the student as wanting to learn, thinkers making connections, students taking the initiative, learners working with others. We need to understand knowledge as 'temporary, developmental, socially and culturally mediated'. Learning is then 'a self-regulated process of resolving inner cognitive conflicts that often become apparent through concrete experience, collaborative discourse, and reflection.' (*ibid*, p. vii).

Some of what is currently happening in schools could be achieved away from schools. With teacher salaries as the major school cost, there are significant savings to be made by reducing the number of teachers provided in today's schools. For a lot of what happens in schools, the school is a community of learners joined in an enterprise, needing one another but not always in one physical place. New technology and methodologies of distance learning enable the individual to cope away from the school building and independent of teachers in ways that were not possible before.

Homes Colonized

For many people, the home of the future will play a more important role in education. Many of tomorrow's homes will be less deserted places because of the change in the nature of employment, with adults working from the home too. In these homes a fuller family life could be expected. Some homes would need to be supported but not just by teachers who, incidentally, could visit electronically as well as physically, but by social workers, youth workers, community counsellors and other newly emerging professional and non-professional people (Thwaites *et al.*, 1983, p. 25).

Unfortunately not all homes will be able to support a culture of learning. This lack of support for the enterprise called schooling is a problem in existing schools and will be also in the dispersed concept of schooling although this problem can be addressed in the dispersed school by providing for the education of the parents, a total service, as well as the children. Schooling has carried an implication that the members of the school are young, but does such a notion continue to be relevant? If the purpose of schooling is to educate for society, then the relevance of what happens in schools extends beyond the young. A unique characteristic of the school of the twenty-first century could be its provision for adults as well as for young people. Education as an experience totally concentrated in one's youth stems from the ideas and necessities of the late nineteenth century. In our rapidly changing society, people of all ages will need access to educational opportunities for personal growth, for community development, for professional training and to support the schooling of the young.

In the past the school's role has been thought of as an information giver. As a result the school has been organized in such a way as to enable the delivery of information in the most efficient and effective way. Now we are envisaging schooling as experience, interaction, challenge, enterprise, with extended social as well as with intellectual dimensions. As a result a different place is appropriate and a different role for the teachers and other professionals is needed.

Shirpas

There will always be a role for teachers. They are important 'others' in the 'I-Thou' relationships. They are role models, they have knowledge and life experiences, they are successful learners, trained professionals and caring adults but they need to reconceptualize their role and may even need to change their name. Their primary role is no longer teaching. Their primary role is to support student learning. The difference is not a matter of semantics. I like the metaphor of teachers as Shirpas. The student indicates that s/he wants to climb the mountain. The Shirpa asks if s/he has her/his oxygen, should s/he set out today or wait for better weather, attack this side of the mountain or the other. The Shirpa brings knowledge, experience and courage but the student has to have the desire and the motivation. The Shirpa analogy is not perfect. Teachers are learners too whereas Shirpas are professionals who are paid to know their job. I see schools as places where teachers and students are learners together. Schools need to be environments that accommodate and encourage both student and staff initiated learning. The teacher is the expert learner. For this reason a teacher needs to understand how s/he learns and be an expert in learning styles where as in the past the teacher was an expert in teaching styles.

Teachers need to come out of their isolation in classrooms and enter into new collegiate relationships. In the dispersed educational environment envisaged, teachers will need to work not only with other teachers but also with other professionals and non-professionals. The teacher, instead of being the controller of the learning and of the student, will offer services of which students and their families might avail themselves. The basic unit of education will no longer be the teacher's class but the student assisted by the teacher and other professionals. These changes cannot be sustained unless priority is given to the continuous learning by all members of the community.

R.S. Peters helps us understand the important role to be played by adults. In his book *Ethics and Education*, Peters devotes a chapter to 'Education as initiation'. He sees education as an initiation, whereby 'experienced people turn the eye of others outward to what is essentially independent of persons'. Initiation is an avenue of access to a body of belief, to mysteries that need to be revealed to the youth of our society. Initiation conveys the suggestion of 'being placed on the inside of a form of thought or awareness' (Peters, 1966, p. 54).

At a time when the extrinsic view of education dominates — education for employment or education for the economy to prosper — Peter's view of education reminds us of the intrinsic value of education, of the quality of life and of the unique nature that is human. Literature, music, science, history, drama, art, debating, chess, physical education are important ingredients in our culture and therefore in our education. They are areas into which students need to be initiated. In this 'liberal' view of education, the development of the mind is sought with an outcome that gives the student a cognitive perspective. An educated person needs to be able to see a social significance, to be able to appreciate an aesthetic merit and to achieve a scientific understanding. But education is more than this. It requires of students that they address the big questions. Who am I? Where is society going? How will that society find meaning?

Helping students (young and old) make the transition from an egocentric position to one that acknowledges and respects others, and values what is worthwhile, is a Herculean challenge in itself. But have we agreed on what is worthwhile? Education today is a task without a mission statement. If ever there was a time for achieving a consensus about values, identifying a society that we want to build and working out how to achieve this, then surely it is now.

Unlike many business institutions, places of learning have their primary impact in the distant future. Consequently they must operate from a long-range perspective which makes the task so much harder. A planning horizon of decades rather than years needs to be envisaged. Today is a time for imaginings, for enterprise, for variety, for daring; and from the best of these ventures future places of learning and of relationships will be developed.

Jessica and Jennifer

In year 5 we introduced some changes that placed a lot more emphasis on student responsibility for learning. Jennifer is the fictitious name that I will give to a real student who was in year 4 at MLC. Her father, at a parent teacher meeting, pounds the table and asks: 'There is no teaching in my daughter's classroom.' I enquire if he is saying that his daughter is not learning anything at school. The reply is louder and firmer: 'My daughter tells me that there is no teaching occurring in her classroom.' Again I ask: 'Is your daughter not learning anything?' Now he is annoyed. 'I changed schools so that my daughter could have teaching and it is not happening.'

Compare this story to that of Jessica, a person who may be in any school today:

From the time Jessica emerged from her mother's womb, she experienced sounds of music and . . . voices that were not her Mom, Dad, . . . These sounds were electronic . . . made by radio, television, compact discs, videocassettes and computers . . . . Her parents taught her to use the remote controls . . . She could join the songs, say the words, and play in her imagination with the characters. . . . In addition to playmates in the neighbourhood and at day-care, Jessica invited elements of the larger world into her home as intimate friends . . . (like *Big Bird* and the *Sesame Street* gang.) . . . At Christmas in 1993, Jessica got a *Speak and Spell* and a *Lego* set. Mom and Dad got a multimedia computer and placed some things on it for Jessica . . . So, with her parents' help, she began to use a mouse to point to things and touch buttons to name colours, numbers and letters, to draw, to colour images, and to manipulate geometric shapes. By clicking a mouse button, she could sometimes make pictures of animals do her bidding. . . . By the time Jessica turned 4, she'd learned many things at a practical level which she had no words for — . . . montage, hypertext, zoom, editing, animation, telepresence, musical beat, hand-eye coordination. . . . The ninth word Jessica ever spoke was 'pone', and ever since she could utter a sound into its mouthpiece, Jessica used the telephone. . . . From her five years in the presence of television, books, movies, compact discs and computing, Jessica has seen more images, heard more stories, captured more impressions about the broad world than most nineteenth century children did in a lifetime. She's somehow acquainted with Bosnia and country music, perfume and toilet paper, the White House, volcanoes, dinosaurs, literature and literacy, and candy kisses . . . . Jessica has become the master of many of her technologies. . . .

Down the street from Jessica's home is . . . The Eisenhower School . . . and in September she went there for the first time. . . . Devices she has used, like the telephone, don't exist in Miss Jefferds' kindergarten classroom. There will be new things to explore in centres for art, science, writing, reading, and housekeeping, and familiar things like clay, paints, blocks, and books, but the room has only two computers that Jessica won't get to use until December, and they're really not very good at showing pictures and they have limited sounds. Sometimes a TV and VCR come in on a cart, but only when Miss Jefferds wants to show something, and she controls what and when. . . . Helping youngsters take more and better advantage of the technology in their homes is not her mission.

Jessica won't know that the Eisenhower School, like many schools, is falling behind the times at an increasing rate.

After Jessica spends some time with Miss Jefferds, she might ask . . . Do I have to go to school every day? Couldn't Miss Jefferds come to my house on TV or on computer some days? Then maybe my Grandma and Grandpop could be part of school too? And can I do school some days with kids from other places instead of just these kids in Miss Jefferds' room? (To read more see *Jostens Learning Internet* home page http//www.jlc.com)

Returning Home

Increasingly schools are being asked to take over more and more. Perhaps it is time that more responsibility for the education of the young is handed back to the families and that these families are supported where they need it most, in the home. Consider this report which appeared under the heading, 'Homeless risk for students':

> About one in ten high school students is at risk of becoming homeless, a national study has found.
>
> The joint study by Monash University and the Royal Melbourne Institute of Technology set out to estimate the risk of homelessness by looking at 41,000 secondary students in nine communities in five states. It revealed that in a typical school with 1000 students, 100 to 140 would be at risk of homelessness and forty to sixty of these would be seriously at risk.
>
> The national census of homeless school students in May 1994 reported that 11,000 secondary students were homeless in census week, and it estimated that 25,000 to 30,000 school students experience a period of homelessness each year.
>
> ... homeless school students are usually staying temporarily with friends or relatives or moving between accommodation. Under these circumstances, it found, the young people were able to maintain relationships with friends, teachers and other important figures in their lives. 'It is only when they drop out of school that they usually become deeply involved in the homeless sub-culture,' the study says.
> (*The Age*, Friday 6 September 1996, page A3)

If the problem is in the home, why not address the source of the problem? Is this such a radical idea?

Total Service Schools

So what might a school of the future look like? What I offer are some tentative thoughts.

The goal is a learning community rather than a place. It will have many homes rather than one home. In each home there will be links to the other homes as well as to the world so that data, sound and visual images can be transmitted. It will be open twelve hours a day, 340 days a year and 'attended' physically or electronically by people of all ages. Families, friends and communities will 'own' these 'schools'. The goal will be to achieve a learning community where one can learn, where one can learn with others and where the organization also learns. The learning is not preparation for university, career, ... but lifelong learning into which one dips when ready. The units can be constructed by the learner or could be units that are free floating, not tied into some age-of-learner related sequence.

The many 'homes' will be of a 'total service' variety, one stop shopping, where one will find many professionals who can help with learning. We will find teachers of traditional academic subjects; professionals such as doctors, nurses and social workers in the health school; sports professionals including trainers, coaches, psychologists, physiotherapists, dieticians in the sports centre; crèches, kindergartens, child care in the early learning centre; carpenters, plumbers, architects in the building centre; office spaces for hire where one could work and have access to support staff such as researchers, librarians, public relations consultants, publishers. This list is not exhaustive, only illustrative of possibilities of what could be included in these 'homes' of life long learning for communities that want to stay together and not break up into discrete units according to age, status of the learning or type of certification. These homes, centres, sites, ... would be 'Total Service Schools'. They could also have auxiliary units such as shopping centres, markets, social centres and theatres. 'It isn't clear where the organization begins and ends, with customers, suppliers and allied organisations linked into a varying "network organisation"' (Handy, 1994, pp. 73–4).

Physically attending a day school will not be compulsory but achieving certain levels of knowledge and skill, participating in certain events and experiences and contributing certain services to others will be required. These requirements will have age-related components. For example a 10-year-old needs to be able to read, to be numerate, ... There will be an emphasis on individual learning outcomes rather than upon general inputs into education. It is assumed that teachers are not the only providers of education and that other individuals, groups and institutions have much to offer. Technology to facilitate learning is assumed as is the understanding that efficiencies need to be delivered.

Participating in some form of group experience will be compulsory. This community experience needs to include a significant residential component in a stimulating environment where the substance of the education is taken from the setting and the community experience. The settings could vary from country to city, work to leisure pursuits, academic to community service, research to training. The models for such settings could come from kibbutzim, monasteries, Marshmead and boarding schools. The student and the student's family would be given a variety of residential experiences from which to choose but be required to choose at least one. The cost of these residential components of schooling would be the responsibility of the government but the providers would not be government institutions.

The student learning group would not necessarily be in the one physical setting. Students would be joined together according to their task, sometimes living together, sometimes sharing the same facilities and sometimes linked electronically, being able to visit electronically in a virtual reality.

The individual student will own his/her learning and will be held responsible for its management. In this the student is supported by the family, the communities of which the student is a member and the school. In such a setting, the school would not determine the agenda. There would be room for individuals, for individual differences and for communities. The education will start where the local commnity and the individual are now. This model allows for changes in knowledge, can cope with the tension between theoretical and practical, provides for reentry, motivation and retraining and reflects the true complexity that individuals and communities experience.

In evolving from our present state of schooling to some distant, chosen destination, the progress will be through a number of steps and will involve intermediate structures for most of us. Each such structure in the evolutionary progress to our desired objective will need to be more rewarding to its stakeholders. However there will be some who are designing new schools in new communities and they may be able to leap 'frog' over us who are constrained by buildings, traditions and bureaucracy.

Four walls around a future was a good way to envisage the twentieth century school. Today those four walls can be restricting and expensive. They may even be too firmly implanted ever to change. At best the four walls are the base from which we launch the education and oversee its coherence and execution.

Notes

1   See page 39 for further discussion of this.
2   Reported at a course at Melbourne University for aspiring principals, January 1994.
3   Many other schools now do this.
4   This is described in detail in 'The Dreaming Principal'.

References

ABBOTT, J. (1996) 'The search for next-century learning', *Education 2000 News*, June.

ANDERSON AND OTHERS, (1980) *Schools to Grow in, and Evaluation of Secondary Colleges*, Canberra, ANU Press.

ARCHDALE, B. (1972) *Indiscretions of a Headmistress*, Sydney, Angus and Robertson.

BAIN, A. and LOADER, D. (1996) 'Leadership and vulnerability,' unpublished paper.

BARTH, R.S. (1991) *Improving Schools from Within*, San Francisco, CA, Jossey Bass Publishers.

BELASCO, J.A. and STAYER, R.C. (1994) *Flight of the Buffalo*, New York, Warner Books.

BENDER, S. (1991) *Plain and Simple, A Woman's Journey to the Amish*, New York, Harper Collins.

BIRKERTS, S. (1994) *The Gutenberg Elegies — The Fate of Reading in an Electronic Age*, Boston, MA, Faber and Faber.

BOISOT, M. (1995) 'Preparing for turbulence; the changing relationship between strategy and management development in the learning organisation' in GARRATT, B. (Ed) *Developing Strategic Thought — Rediscovering the Art of Direction-giving*, London, McGraw-Hill Book Company.

BROOKS, J. and BROOKS, M. (1993) *In Search of Understanding: The Case for Constructionist Classrooms*, Alexandria, VA, ASCD.

BROWN, C. (1996) *Dismantling the Walls that Divide*, Zadok Paper S78, summer 1996, Victoria, Zadok Institute.

CHAPMAN, J. (1996) 'Leadership for the learning community', an address to the Australian College of Education and Australian Council for Educational Administration, Perth.

COELHO, P. (1994) *The Alchemist*, San Francisco, CA, Harper.

DAVIS, S. and BOTKIN, J. (1994) *The Monster Under The Bed — How Business Is Mastering The Opportunity Of Knowledge For Profit*, New York, Simon and Schuster.

DE BOARD, R. (1978) *The Psychoanalysis of Organisations; A Psychoanalytic Approach to Behaviour in Groups and Organisations*, Cambridge, Tavistock Publications.

DENNETT, D. (Professor of Arts and Science, Tufts University, Massachusetts) reported in the *New Scientist*, 6 November 1993, p. 46.

DOWLING, C. (1981) *The Cinderella Complex: Womens' Hidden Fear of Independence*, NY, Summit Books.

References

DRUCKER, P.F. (1995) *Managing in a Time of Change*, Oxford, Butterworth Heinemann.

ELLMANN, R. and FEIDELSON, C. (1965) 'Yeats: The man and the masks', in *The Modern Tradition, Backgrounds of Modern Literature*, New York, Oxford University Press.

FAWNS, R.A. and TEESE, R.V. (1980) *Students' Attitude to their Schooling*, Canberra, Schools Commission.

FEYNMAN, R.P. (1986) *Surely You Are Joking Mr Feynman*, New York, Phantom Books.

FULGHUM, R. (1986) *All I Really Needed to Know I Learned in Kindergarten*, London, Grafton Books.

FULLAN, M.G. (1996) 'Turning systemic thinking on its head', *Phi Delta Kappan*, February, pp. 420–3.

FULLAN, M. and HARGREAVES, A. (1991) *Working Together For Your School*, Hawthorn, ACEA.

GILMORE, T.N. and KRANTZ, J. (1989) *The Splitting of Leadership and Management as a Social Defence,* an occasional paper read as part of AISA Conference, Lorne, July 1996.

GOODLAD, J.I. (1984) *A Place Called School*, New York, McGraw Hill.

GORDON, R. (1989) 'Problem based learning: A focus for the quiet revolution', in *Proceedings for the 4th Annual Conference of the Society for the Provision of Education in Rural Australia*, Launceston, Tasmania.

HALES, D. and HALES, R.E. (1995) *Caring for the Mind*, New York, Bantam Books.

HANDY, C. (1994) *The Empty Raincoat — Making Sense Of The Future*, London, Hutchinson.

HANDY, C. (1996) *Beyond Certainty*, London, Arrow Books.

HANH, T.N. (1994) 'The art of living', in WHITMYER, C. *Mindfulness and Meaningful Work*, California, Parallan Press.

HANSON, E.M. (1991) 'Educational restructuring in the USA: Movements of the 1980s', *Journal of Educational Administration*, **29**, 4.

HOOKER, C.A. (1988) *Brave New World or Grave New World? Education for the Future/Futures in Education*, occasional paper.

HOOKER, C.A. (1994) 'Notes on a context for educational futures', a paper delivered to a conference in Melbourne.

JOHNSON, D.W. and JOHNSON, R.T. (1995) *Reducing School Violence Through Conflict Resolution*, Alexandria, VA, ASCD.

JOSTENS LEARNING EDUCATION FORUM, 'Educating Jessica's generation: Learning, technology, and the future of K-12 education', http//www.jlc.com.

KAYE, M. (1996) *Myth-Makers and Story-tellers*, Sydney, Business and Professional Publishing.

KENNEDY, J.F. (1957) *Profiles in Courage*, New York, Harper Perennial.

KING, C.S. (1983) *The Words of Martin Luther King Jr.*, New York, Newmarket Press.

KRESS, G. (1996) 'Reimaging English: Curriculum, Identity, and Productive Futures', *Idiom*, **xxxi**, 2, October, pp. 11–19.

LACEY, P.A. (1993) *Running on Empty*, Philadelphia, PA, Friends Council on Education.

LAMBERT, R. (1975) *The Chance of a Lifetime? The Study of Boarding Education*, London, Weidenfeld & Nicholson.

LANG, T. and LANG, M. (1986) *Corrupting the Young and Other Stories of a Family Therapist*, Melbourne, René Gordon Pty Ltd.

LAPIERRE, L. (1991) *Exploring the Dynamics of Leadership in Organisations on the Couch* by Kets de Veries and Associates, Jossey-Bass.

LAWRENCE, W.G. (1986) 'The issue of psychic and political relatedness in organisations', in Chattopadhyay, G.B. *When the Twain Meet: Western Theory and Eastern Insights in Exploring Indian Organizations*, Alla Habad, A.H. Wheeler.

LAWRENCE, W.G. (1995) 'Social dreaming as a tool of action research', International Society for the Psychoanalytic Study of Organisations Symposium, 7–9 July, London.

LEITHWOOD, K., BEGLEY, P. and COUSINS, J. (1992) *Developing Expert Leadership for Future Schools*, London, Falmer Press.

LOADER, D. (1984) 'A new definition of a good school', *The Secondary Administrator*, **2**, 2, June.

MARSDEN, J. (1996) *This I Believe*, Sydney, Random House.

MECKLENBURGER, J. (1994) 'Thinking about schooling in the global village', *Inventing Tomorrow's Schools*, Alexandria, VA, The Global Village Schools Institute.

MERTON, T. (1976) *Seven Story Mountain*, San Diego, CA, Harcourt Brace Jovanovich.

MITCHELL, J. (1993) 'Report to ANZ trustees', October, unpublished document.

MITCHELL, J. and LOADER, D. (1993) *Learning in a Learning Community: Methodist Ladies' College Case Study*, Melbourne, IARTV Case Study No. 2, February.

MITCHELL, J. and LOADER, D. (1994) 'Teachers' work: Shaping the future', an unpublished paper describing the project.

MOFFETT, J. (1994) *The Universal School House — Spiritual Awakening Through Education*, San Francisco, CA, Jossey-Bass.

PAPERT, S. (1993) *The Children's Machine*, New York, Basic Books.

PATTERSON, J.L. (1993) *Leadership for Tomorrow's Schools*, Alexandria, VA, ASCD.

PERKINS, D. (Ed) (1967) *English Romantic Writers*, New York, Harcourt Brace Jovanovich.

PETERS, R.S. (1966) *Ethics in Education*, London, George Allen and Unwin.

PETERS, T. (1988) *Thriving on Chaos*, New York, Perennial.

POSTMAN, N. (1987) *Amusing Ourselves to Death*, London, Methuen.

PUSEY, M. (1976) *Dynamics of Bureaucracy — A Case Analysis in Education*, Sydney, Wiley.

RAMSLAND, J. and ST LEON, M. (1993) *Children of the Circus*, Springwood, Butterfly Books.

REPS, P. (1957) *Zen Flesh, Zen Bones*, London, Penguin Books.

RHINEGOLD, H. (1991) *Virtual Reality*, New York, Simon and Schuster.

RICH, A. (1993) *The Dream of a Common Language*, New York, W.W. Norton.

Russ, J. (1995) 'Collaborative management and school improvement: Research findings from "Improving Schools" in England', *Journal of the Commonwealth Council of Educational Administration*, **23**, 2, winter.

Schools Council (1990) *Australia's Teachers: An Agenda for the Next Decade*. Canberra, Australian Government Publishing Service.

Segal, L. (1987) *Is the Future Female?: Troubled Thoughts on Contemporary Feminism*. London, Virago Press.

Senge, P.M. (1992) *The Fifth Discipline, The Art and Practice of The Learning Organisation*. Sydney, Random House.

Shor, I. and Freire, P. (1987) *A Pedagogy for Liberation*, New York, Bergin and Garvey.

Singer, P. (1996) *This I Believe* (edited by Marsden, J.) Sydney, Random House.

Smith, W.G. (1966) 'The principal's weekly spelling test', *School Management Bulletin*, No. 9, NSW, Department of Education.

Starratt, R.J. (1986) 'Excellence in education and quality leadership', occasional paper no 1, published by *Southern Tasmanian Council for Educational Administration*.

Starratt, R.J. (1996) *Transforming Educational Administration*, USA, McGraw-Hill.

Stevens, W. (1984) *The Collected Poems of Wallace Stevens*, London, Faber and Faber Ltd.

The World Book Encyclopaedia, (1994) Vol. 4, Chicago, IL.

Thich, N.H. (1994) 'The art of living', in Whitmyer, C. (Ed) *Mindfulness and Meaningful Work*, California, Parallan Press.

Thwaites, B. and Wysock-Wright, C. (1983) *Education 2000: A Consultative Document on Hypotheses for Education in AD 2000*, Cambridge, Press Syndicate of University of Cambridge.

Tiffin, J. and Ragasingham, M. (1995) *Virtual Class*, New York, Routledge.

Toffler, A. (1970) *Future Shock*, London, Pan Books.

Vaill, P.B. (1984) 'A note on the idea of courage', *O D Practitioner*, pp. 9–11.

Vygotsky, L. (1978) *Mind in Society; Development of Higher Psychological Processes*, Cambridge, MA, Harvard University Press.

Weinstein, J. (1975) *Buber and Humanistic Education*, New York, Philosophical Library.

Zainu'ddin, A.G. (1982) *They Dreamt of a School*, Melbourne, Hyland House.

Zohar, D. and Marshall, I. (1994) *The Quantum Society*, London, Flamingo-Harper Collins Publishers.

Index